HOME-KITCHEN FOOD STORAGE

Pantry-shelf Storage, Room Temperature

food item	storage time	keep in mind
baking powder, baking soda	18 months	keep dry, tightly covered
bouillon cubes & powders	1 year	
breads & rolls	3 days	in original wrapping
cake mixes	1 year	keep dry
cakes, baked	2-3 days	refrigerate if with cream or custard filling
canned foods, all kinds	1 year or more	use oldest first
coffee, vacuum can	1 year, unopened	store in refrigerator or freezer 1 week after opening
coffee, instant	6 months, unopened	store in refrigerator or freezer 1 week after opening
coffee lightener, nondairy	6 months	keep dry
cookies, packaged	4 months, unopened	1 week after opening
crackers	3 months	keep dry, tightly closed
crumbs, cracker/bread	6 months	keep dry, tightly closed
flour, all-purpose/cake	6 months	keep dry, tightly closed
frostings, mixes & canned	6 months	
fruit, dried	6-8 months	
gelatin, unflavored/fruit	6 months	keep dry
herbs & spices, whole	1 year	keep tightly closed
herbs & spices, ground	6 months	keep tightly closed
honey	1 year	do not refrigerate
hot-roll/quick-bread mixes	1 year	keep dry
jam, jelly	1 year	refrigerate after opening
molasses	1 year	
nonfat dry milk	6 months	keep dry; refrigerate after reconstituting
oil, salad & cooking	3 months	keep tightly closed
pancake, waffle mixes	6 months	keep dry, tightly closed
pasta	6 months, unopened	keep dry
peanut butter	6 months	2 months after opening
piecrust mixes	6 months	
pies & pastries	3 days	refrigerate cream, custard
pudding mixes	1 year	
rice, brown & wild	1 year	
rice, white	2 years	
rice, flavored mixes	6 months	
salad dressings	6 months	refrigerate after opening
sauce/soup/gravy mixes	3 months	
sauces/ketchup, barbecue	2 months	keep tightly closed
shortening, hydrogenated	8 months	keep tightly closed
soft drinks	3 months	
sugar, granulated	2 years	keep dry
sugar, brown & confectioners	4 years	
syrups	1 year	close tightly after use
tea, loose or bags	6 months	
tea, instant	1 year	
vegetables: onions, potatoes, rutabagas, sweet potatoes, winter squash	1 week	keep dry; provide for air circulation, will keep 2-3 months at 55°

Refrigerator Storage, Fruits & Vegetables
(in crisper or closed plastic bags)

food item	storage time	keep in mind
apples	1 month	or store at room temperature
apricots, avocados, pears, melons, bananas, grapes, nectarines, peaches, plums	5 days	ripen before refrigerating
berries & cherries	3 days	
citrus fruits	2 weeks	or store at room temperature
pineapples	2 days	
asparagus	3 days	
beets, carrots, parsnips, radishes, turnips	5 days	remove tops before storing
cabbage, cauliflower, celery, cucumbers, green beans, eggplant, peppers	1 week	
tomatoes	1 week	ripen tomatoes before refrigerating
corn on the cob		
lettuce, spinach, all green leafy vegetables	5 days	before
lima beans, peas	5 days	leave in pods

Refrigerator Storage, Dairy Products
(tightly covered or wrapped)

food item	storage time	keep in mind
butter	2 weeks	
buttermilk	2 weeks	
cheese, spreads	2 weeks	if mold forms on hard cheese, remove before serving — it will do no harm
cheese, cottage & ricotta	5 days	
cheese, cream & neufchatel	2 weeks	
cheese, sliced	2 weeks	
cheese, in whole cuts	2 months	
cream, sweet/sour	1 week	ultrapasteurized, 1 month in original carton
eggs, whole in shell	1 month	
whites, separated	4 days	tightly covered
yolks, separated	4 days	cover with water
margarine	1 month	
milk, whole & skim	1 week	
milk, reconstituted nonfat, opened condensed & evaporated	1 week	

Refrigerator Storage, Meat, Fish & Poultry (uncooked)

food item	storage time	keep in mind
beef, pork, lamb & veal: steaks, chops, roasts	5 days	leave in store plastic wrap or rewrap loosely
ground & stew meats	2 days	
fresh sausage	2 days	
variety meats	2 days	
bacon, frankfurters	1 week	after opening
ham, canned	6 months	unopened
ham, slices	3 days	
ham, whole	1 week	
luncheon meats, cold cuts	5 days	after opening
sausage, dry & semidry	3 weeks	
fish, shellfish (all kinds)	1 day	keep closely wrapped
poultry, fresh or thawed	2 days	

Refrigerator Storage, Leftovers & Packaged Foods (after opening)

food item	storage time	keep in mind
broth, gravy, soup	2 days	tightly covered
cakes, pies: cream or custard fillings	2-3 days	
casserole dishes, stews	3 days	
coffee	1 week	after opening
coffee lighteners, frozen	3 weeks	after thawing
flour: rye, whole wheat, wheat germ	1 year	tightly covered container — not original package
fruits	3 days	
juices, beverages	6 days	
meat, fish, poultry	2 days	remove stuffing from poultry
nutmeats	6 months	tightly covered
pickles, olives	1 month	original container
refrigerated doughs: rolls, biscuits, cookies, breads	check final-use date on package; do not open until ready to use	
salad dressings	3 months	original container
salads: potato, chicken, fish, coleslaw	2 days	tightly covered
wine, white table	3 days	after opening

Continued on back Endsheet

Freezer Storage, Commercial Frozen Foods

food item	storage time	keep in mind
breads, rolls (baked)	3 months	overwrap commercial wrappings
breads, unbaked loaves	3 months	overwrap commercial wrappings
cakes: butter, pound-type	6 months	unfrosted, overwrap
cake, angel food	2 months	overwrap
cake, frosted layer	4 months	
coffee lighteners	1 year	
doughnuts, danish pastry	3 months	overwrap
fish (fat types): trout, mackerel, salmon	3 months	overwrap if package damaged
fish, (lean types): cod, flounder, sole	6 months	if thawed, do not refreeze
shellfish, breaded, cooked	3 months	
lobster, scallops	3 months	
king/queen crab	10 months	
shrimp, uncooked, unbreaded	1 year	
fruit	1 year	
ice cream, sherbet	1 month	overwrap leftovers
main-dish pies, fish or meat	3 months	
main-dish pies, poultry	6 months	
meats, beef roasts, steaks	1 year	overwrap
ground beef	4 months	overwrap
lamb, veal roasts, & steaks	9 months	overwrap
pork chops	4 months	overwrap
pork roasts	8 months	overwrap
pancake/waffle batter	3 months	
pies, unbaked	8 months	
pies, ready to thaw & eat	4 months	
poultry: chicken, turkey parts	6 months	
whole chicken, turkey	1 year	
duck, goose	6 months	
turkey rolls, roasts	6 months	
vegetables, all	8 months	

USEFUL SUBSTITUTIONS

if the recipe calls for	use instead
2 tablespoons all-purpose or whole wheat flour (for thickening)	1 tablespoon cornstarch or arrow-root or potato starch or quick-cooking tapioca
1 cup beef or chicken broth	1 bouillon cube or 1 envelope or 1 rounded teaspoon bouillon powder + 1 cup boiling water
2 egg yolks	1 whole egg
1 cup grated coconut	1⅓ cups flaked coconut
1 pound fresh mushrooms	12 ounces canned mushrooms, drained, or 3 ounces dried mushrooms, rehydrated
1 teaspoon lemon juice	½ teaspoon distilled white vinegar
1 teaspoon grated lemon peel	½ teaspoon lemon extract
1 cup homogenized milk	1 cup skim milk + 2 tablespoons butter or margarine; or ½ cup evaporated milk + ½ cup water, or ¼ cup powdered whole milk + 1 cup water
1 square (1 ounce) unsweetened chocolate	3 tablespoons cocoa + 1 tablespoon butter or margarine
½ cup butter or margarine	7 tablespoons vegetable shortening
1 cup sifted cake flour	⅞ cup sifted all-purpose flour
1 teaspoon baking powder	½ teaspoon cream of tartar + ¼ teaspoon baking soda
1 cup sour cream (for use in cooking)	1 tablespoon lemon juice + evaporated milk (undiluted) to make 1 cup, or ⅓ cup butter + ¾ cup yogurt or buttermilk

1 cup buttermilk or sour milk	1 tablespoon lemon juice or white vinegar + milk to make 1 cup (let stand 5 minutes)
1 cup honey or corn syrup	1¼ cups sugar + ¼ cup liquid
1 tablespoon snipped fresh herb	1 teaspoon dried herb, same kind
1 medium onion, chopped	1 tablespoon instant minced onion, rehydrated
1 cup light cream or half-and-half	3 tablespoons butter + ⅞ cup milk
1 cup heavy (whipping) cream	⅓ cup butter + ¾ cup milk
2 cups tomato sauce	¾ cup tomato paste + 1 cup water
1 cup tomato juice	½ cup tomato sauce + ½ cup water
1 small clove garlic	⅛ teaspoon garlic powder or ¼ teaspoon commercial garlic juice
1 tablespoon gelatin	1 envelope
1 cake compressed yeast	1 envelope active dry yeast
1 cup yogurt (in cooking)	1 cup buttermilk

FOOD-MEASURE EQUIVALENTS

start out with	to end up with
apples, 3 medium (1 pound)	3 cups sliced
bananas, 3 medium (1 pound)	1½ cups mashed
bread, 1-pound loaf	14 to 20 slices
bread, 1 slice (including crust)	½ cup crumbs
butter or margarine, ¼ pound	½ cup (1 stick or cube)
cheese, ¼ pound	1 cup shredded
cheese, cottage, 8-ounce container	1 cup
cheese, cream, 3-ounce package	6 tablespoons
chocolate, unsweetened, 1 square	1 ounce
chocolate, semisweet pieces, 6 ounces	1 cup
coconut, flaked, 3½-ounce can	1⅓ cups
coconut, shredded, 4-ounce can	1⅓ cups
cream, heavy or whipping, 1 cup	2 cups whipped
cream, sour, 8-ounce container	1 cup
egg whites, large, 8 to 10	1 cup
egg yolks, large, 12 to 14	1 cup
flour, all-purpose, 1 pound	about 3½ cups
flour, cake, 1 pound	about 4 cups
lemon, 1 medium	3 tablespoons juice, 1 tablespoon grated peel
lime, 1 medium	2 tablespoons juice, 1 teaspoon grated peel
milk, evaporated, 5⅓ or 6-ounce can	⅔ cup
12- or 14½-ounce can	1⅔ cups
sweetened condensed, 14-ounce can	1¼ cups
nuts, 1 pound almonds in shell	1 to 1¼ cups nutmeats
almonds, 1 pound shelled	3 cups
brazil nuts, in shell, 1 pound	1½ cups nutmeats
brazil nuts, shelled, 1 pound	3¼ cups
filberts, in shell, 1 pound	1½ cups nutmeats
filberts, shelled, 1 pound	3½ cups
peanuts, in shell, 1 pound	2 to 2½ cups nutmeats
peanuts, shelled, 1 pound	3 cups
pecans, in shell, 1 pound	2¼ cups nutmeats
pecans, shelled, 1 pound	4 cups
walnuts, in shell, 1 pound	2 cups nutmeats
walnuts, shelled, 1 pound	4 cups
onion, 1 large	¾ to 1 cup chopped
orange, 1 medium	¼ to ⅓ cup juice, 2 tablespoons grated peel
potatoes, 1 pound sweet, white	2¼ cups diced
raisins, 1 pound	3 cups
rice, long grain regular, 1 cup	3 cups cooked
salad oil, 16 ounces	2 cups
sugar, 1 pound granulated	2¼ to 2½ cups
brown, 1 pound	2¼ cups (packed)
confectioners, 1 pound	4 to 4½ cups
syrup, corn, 16 ounces	2 cups
maple, 12 ounces	1½ cups

Famous Brands

DESSERTS

Brand Name Publishing Corp.
Brand Name Books, Inc.

Flaming Bananas Martinique (page 100). C & H Sugar Company

Published by Brand Name Publishing Corp., 1950 Craig Road, St. Louis, Missouri 63146 and Brand Name Books, Inc., 122 East 25th Street, New York, New York 10010.

Printed in Italy by Mondadori, Verona

Acknowledgments

The editors wish to thank the following companies for permission to use their recipes, photographs, and product names in this volume:

ALCOA (Aluminum Company of America)

Amstar Corp./Domino® Sugar

Eagle® Brand Sweetened Condensed Milk, Division of Borden Inc.

ReaLemon® Lemon Juice from Concentrate, Division of Borden Inc.

California Raisin Advisory Board

C & H Sugar Company

Corning Glass Works

CPC International Inc.

Sweet'N Low® is a registered trademark of the Cumberland Packing Corporation

John DeKuyper & Son

Florida Department of Citrus

General Foods Corporation

Hamilton Beach Scovill Inc.

Knox® Unflavored Gelatine is a registered trademark of Knox Gelatine, Inc., Englewood Cliffs, NJ 07632

Libby, McNeill & Libby, Inc., The Great Pumpkin Cookbook, A Harvest of Libby's Favorite Recipe

Libby's® is a registered trademark of Libby, McNeill & Libby, Inc.

Martha White Foods

National Cherry Growers & Industries Foundation

The Nestlé Company, Inc.

Ocean Spray Cranberries, Inc.

Oregon Fruit Products Company

Oregon-Washington-California Pear Bureau

Consumer Products Division, Reynolds Metal Company

Rice Council of America

Sioux Honey Association

Solo Food Products, Division of Sokol & Company

Sunbeam Appliance Co., a member of Allegheny International, Inc.; Sunbeam® is a registered trademark of the Sunbeam Corporation

Sunkist® is a registered trademark of Sunkist Growers, Inc.

Sun-Maid Growers of California

Uncle Ben's, Inc.

Invitation

food is good

The Famous Brands Cookbook Library invites you, the modern cook, to a new experience in your own kitchen. Have you ever wished you had a larger repertoire of company's-coming menus? Ever searched for a different and exciting way to prepare favorite products? Ever felt that if you could just have a certain technique explained simply, you could master an entire new world of cooking?

The solutions to these dilemmas and others are the cornerstone of the twelve volumes that comprise *The Famous Brands Cookbook Library*. Whether you are just getting to know your kitchen—or have a long-standing relationship with it—the recipes and hints provided here offer the very best and latest information available from the test kitchens of many of America's finest food companies. Once you have had a chance to discover the treasures inside this volume, you'll want to collect each of the other volumes in this series—and an invaluable home cooking library will be yours.

Famous Brands Desserts
Famous Brands Every Oven Microwave Cookbook
Famous Brands Great Vegetable Dishes
Famous Brands Meat Cookbook
Famous Brands Chicken & Poultry
Famous Brands Breads, Quick Breads, & Coffee Cakes
Famous Brands Soups & Salads
Famous Brands Pasta Dishes
Famous Brands Fish & Seafood Cookbook
Famous Brands Cooking with Eggs & Cheese
Famous Brands Main Dishes
Famous Brands Chocolate Classics

Desserts for Every Occasion

You are a discriminating cook: you use only the finest ingredients, select nutritionally sound menus, and get value from your food dollar by buying quality products from companies whose reputations are based on satisfying the requirements of good cooks like you.

Because they know they have to meet your standards, the test kitchens of America's most respected food companies work constantly to create and perfect new and innovative ways to use the products you've come to rely on. Here, from the experienced cooks of over fifty corporate test kitchens, are the very best of the thousands of superb recipes they have to offer. Whether you're seeking an old favorite or hoping to try something new, you'll be pleased with the outstanding variety of choices presented—over 350 in each volume—in the *Famous Brands Cookbook Library*.

Famous Brands Desserts may easily become one of your favorites. Your idea of dessert may be the ultimate torte or Mom's apple pie, an elegant hot soufflé or an incredible ice cream bombe; whatever it is, you can find the delicacy that shows you care about what you serve.

As a special feature, you'll discover helpful hints on kitchen equipment, storing the foods you've carefully selected or prepared, cooking and baking times, decorating and entertaining tricks—much to make your food preparations more professional and more enjoyable.

In short, here is what every cook wants—kitchen-tested recipes; helpful information about techniques and ingredients; crowd-pleasing results—these are the treasures of *Famous Brands Desserts*.

Contents

An Infinite Variety of Cakes

A special cake, torte, or dessert roll will show family and friends just how much you care.

Black Forest Cherry Torte

Makes one 8- or 9-inch torte

- 1 12-ounce package (2 cups) Nestlé Toll House Semi-Sweet Chocolate Morsels
- ½ cup milk
- 2 tablespoons sugar
- 1¾ cups all-purpose flour
- 1 teaspoon baking soda
- 1 teaspoon salt
- ¼ cup butter, softened
- ⅔ cup sugar
- 3 eggs
- ⅔ cup milk
- 1 teaspoon vanilla extract
- ¼ cup brandy, divided
- 1 21-ounce can (2 cups) cherry pie filling, divided
  Brandied Whipped Cream (recipe follows)
  Chocolate Curls (see index)

Preheat oven to 350° F. Over hot (not boiling) water, combine Nestlé Toll House Semi-Sweet Chocolate Morsels, ½ cup milk, and 2 tablespoons sugar. Stir until morsels melt and mixture is smooth; set aside. In a small bowl, combine flour, baking soda, and salt; set aside. In a large bowl, combine butter and ⅔ cup sugar; beat until creamy. Add eggs, 1 at a time, beating well after each addition. Blend in flour mixture alternately with ⅔ cup milk. Stir in chocolate mixture and vanilla extract. Pour evenly into two well-greased and floured 8- or 9-inch cake pans. Bake 25 to 30 minutes. Cool 10 minutes. Remove from pans; cool completely. Using a long, thin serrated knife, slice each layer in half crosswise and sprinkle each with 1 tablespoon brandy. Spread 1 cup Brandied Whipped Cream on one layer. Spread about ⅔ cup cherry pie filling over whipped cream ½ inch from edge. Repeat with next two layers. Place last layer on top; spread with remaining whipped cream. Garnish with Chocolate Curls, if desired.

Brandied Whipped Cream

- 2 cups heavy cream, whipped
- 3 tablespoons brandy
- ⅓ cup sifted confectioners sugar

In a large bowl, beat heavy cream. Gradually add brandy and confectioners sugar, beating until soft peaks form.

Sachertorte

Makes one 9-inch layer cake

- 1 6-ounce package (1 cup) Nestlé Toll House Semi-Sweet Chocolate Morsels
- 1¼ cups water
- 1¾ cups all-purpose flour
- 1½ teaspoons baking soda
- 1 teaspoon salt
- 6 eggs
- 1 teaspoon vanilla extract
- 1½ cups sugar
- 1 12-ounce jar apricot preserves, divided
  Chocolate Glaze (recipe follows)

Preheat oven to 350°F. Over hot (not boiling) water, combine Nestlé Toll House Semi-Sweet Chocolate Morsels and the water; heat until morsels melt and mixture is smooth. Remove from heat; set aside. In a small bowl, combine flour, baking soda, and salt; set aside. In a large bowl, beat eggs and vanilla until foamy. Gradually add sugar, beating until thick and lemon colored, about 5 minutes. Gradually add flour mixture alternately with chocolate mixture. Pour batter into three well-greased and floured 9-inch round pans. Bake 25 minutes. Loosen edges of cakes from pans. Remove from pans; cool completely. Spread ½ jar preserves over one cake layer. Place second layer on top; spread with remaining ½ jar preserves. Top with plain layer. Spread top and sides of cake with Chocolate Glaze.

Chocolate Glaze

Makes 1 cup

½ cup evaporated milk
   Dash salt
1 6-ounce package (1 cup) Nestlé Toll House Semi-Sweet Chocolate Morsels

In a small saucepan, combine evaporated milk and salt. Bring *just to a boil* over moderate heat. Remove from heat. Add Nestlé Toll House Semi-Sweet Chocolate Morsels; stir until morsels melt and mixture is smooth.

Angel Food Cake

Makes one 10x4-inch tube cake

1¼ cups sifted cake flour
1¾ cups sugar
½ teaspoon salt
1½ cups egg whites (12 to 13 eggs)
1 teaspoon cream of tartar
1 teaspoon vanilla extract
½ teaspoon almond extract

Sift flour, sugar, and salt together 9 times; set aside. Beat egg whites until frothy. Add cream of tartar; continue beating until whites are stiff but not dry. Beat in vanilla and almond extract. Fold in flour mixture, about 2 tablespoons at a time; scrape down sides of bowl several times; continue folding until all of mixture has been added and batter is smooth. Pour into ungreased pan; spread evenly. Bake 65 to 70 minutes at 325°F. When done, remove from oven; invert at once; let cake hang in pan until cold, at least 1 hour. Ice or not as desired.

Yellow Layer Cake

Makes 1 cake

2 cups sifted Martha White Self-Rising Flour
1½ cups sugar
1 cup buttermilk★
3 eggs
⅓ cup vegetable shortening
⅓ cup butter or margarine
1 teaspoon vanilla extract
   Real Fudge Frosting (recipe follows)

Preheat oven to 350°F. Grease and flour two 9-inch or 8-inch square baking pans; set aside. Combine all ingredients, except frosting, in large mixing bowl. Beat at low speed of electric mixer 30 seconds, or just until blended, scraping bowl constantly. Beat at high speed 3 minutes, scraping bowl occasionally. Pour into prepared pans. Bake 30 minutes, or until toothpick inserted in centers comes out clean. Cool in pans completely. Frost with Real Fudge Frosting.

★For a more open-textured cake, substitute ⅞ cup whole milk for 1 cup buttermilk.

Real Fudge Frosting

Makes about 3 cups

2 squares (1 ounce each) unsweetened chocolate
½ cup heavy cream
¼ cup milk
2 cups sugar
   Pinch salt
1 tablespoon corn syrup
1 tablespoon butter or margarine
1 teaspoon vanilla extract

Combine chocolate, cream, and milk in saucepan. Cook over low heat, stirring constantly, until chocolate melts. Add sugar, salt, and corn syrup. Bring to a boil over moderate heat, stirring constantly, until soft-ball stage (232°F. on candy thermometer; drop of mixture forms a soft ball when dropped in cold water). Remove from heat. Add butter and vanilla. Let stand 15 minutes. Beat with electric mixer until spreading consistency. If frosting becomes too thick, beat in small amount additional heavy cream.

First Prize Chocolate Cake

Makes 1 cake

½ cup butter or margarine
4 squares (1 ounce each) unsweetened chocolate
2 eggs
2 cups buttermilk
2 teaspoons vanilla extract
2½ cups sifted Martha White Self-Rising Flour
2 cups sugar
1 teaspoon baking soda
   Dark Chocolate Frosting (recipe follows)

Preheat oven to 350°F. Grease and flour two 9-inch round or 8-inch square baking pans; set aside. Combine butter and chocolate in top of double boiler or saucepan. Place over low heat until chocolate melts, stirring constantly. Break eggs into large mixing bowl; beat with electric mixer 2 minutes, or until frothy. Add buttermilk and vanilla; blend well. Sift flour, sugar, and baking soda into separate bowl. Stir flour mixture into buttermilk mixture. Add melted butter and chocolate; blend well. Pour into prepared pans. Bake 30 minutes, or until toothpick inserted in centers comes out clean. Cool in pans 10 minutes. Turn out onto wire racks to cool completely. Frost with Dark Chocolate Frosting.

Dark Chocolate Frosting

Makes about 3 cups

½ cup butter or margarine
4 squares (1 ounce each) unsweetened chocolate
4½ cups (16 ounces) sifted confectioners sugar

Combine butter and chocolate in top of double boiler or saucepan. Place over low heat until chocolate melts, stirring constantly. Gradually stir in confectioners sugar. Add salt, milk, and vanilla; beat with electric mixer until smooth.

Double Boiler Frosting

    2 egg whites
1½ cups sugar
    5 tablespoons cold water
1½ teaspoons white corn syrup
    1 teaspoon vanilla extract

Place egg whites, sugar, water, and corn syrup in top of double boiler; beat until thoroughly blended. Place over rapidly boiling water. Beat constantly with hand or electric beater until frosting will stand in peaks on beater. Remove from heat; add vanilla; blend.

Marshmallow Frosting
Make Double Boiler Frosting. After removing from heat, fold in 6 to 8 quartered marshmallows or 4 tablespoons marshmallow creme.

Chocolate Frosting
Make Double Boiler Frosting. Melt 3 squares unsweetened chocolate; cool slightly. Gently fold chocolate into frosting after removing from heat.

Sea Foam Frosting
Make Double Boiler Frosting. Substitute 1½ cups firmly packed brown sugar for granulated sugar; omit corn syrup; add speck of salt.

Orange Mist Frosting
Make Double Boiler Frosting. Substitute orange juice for water, add 1 tablespoon grated orange rind; omit vanilla.

Peppermint Frosting
Make Double Boiler Frosting. Substitute a few drops peppermint for vanilla. Tint pale green or pink, or fold in ½ cup crushed peppermint stick candy.

Vanilla Butter Cream Icing

    5 tablespoons butter or margarine, melted
    3 tablespoons cream or undiluted evaporated milk
1½ teaspoons vanilla extract
    3 cups sifted confectioners sugar

Combine butter, cream, and vanilla. Add sugar gradually; beat until smooth.

Chocolate Butter Cream Icing
Make Vanilla Butter Cream Icing; add 3 squares unsweetened chocolate, melted, before adding sugar.

Mocha Icing
Make Chocolate Butter Cream Icing; substitute strong black coffee for cream; omit vanilla.

Orange Butter Cream Icing
Make Vanilla Butter Cream Icing; omit vanilla; substitute orange juice for part of cream; add 1 tablespoon grated orange rind.

Tutti Fruitti Icing
Make Vanilla Butter Cream Icing; substitute 1 tablespoon maraschino cherry juice for 1 tablespoon cream. Add ½ cup chopped maraschino cherries and ½ cup chopped nuts.

Cream Cheese Icing

Makes 3 cups
    1 package (8 ounces) cream cheese, at room temperature
½ cup butter or margarine, softened
4½ cups (16 ounces) sifted confectioners sugar
    2 teaspoons vanilla extract

Combine all ingredients in mixing bowl. Beat with electric mixer until smooth and creamy.

Note: This recipe frosts 8- or 9-inch layer cake or 13x9x2-inch sheet cake. For smaller cake, cut recipe in half.

Frosting Know-how

Cakes to be iced with cooked frosting must be thoroughly cooled before the frosting is applied; those using uncooked frosting may be cold or very slightly warm.

Brush cake gently to remove loose crumbs. If it is a layer cake, place the bottom layer topside down on the serving plate; the second layer, after frosting or filling is spread over the first, should go in place with its topside down as well.

If possible, frost the cake on its serving plate; protect the plate from dribbles of frosting by placing strips of foil or wax paper on the plate and positioning the cake on them. Later, they can be tugged out gently, leaving the plate clean. If you must frost the cake on a different plate or on a revolving stand, place several strips of heavy paper under it, long enough to protrude on each side and be used as handles. Even with this precaution, moving a large frosted cake from one plate to another is a chancy business.

Use between one-fourth and one-third of the frosting between the layers; put the second layer (and the third, if there is one) in place on the frosting or filling, and then let the cake stand for about 15 minutes before proceeding; this gives the frosting time to set. Then cover the entire outside of the cake, top and sides, with a very thin layer of frosting. Again, give this time to set—it captures the crumbs and gives you an excellent working surface. Add the remaining frosting, swirling it on as fancy dictates. Let it set somewhat before you cover the cake. A cake keeper with a high domed cover is ideal. If you don't have one, invert a large mixing bowl over the cake, making sure it doesn't touch the frosting.

Quick Party Log

Makes 16 servings

>   1 12-ounce package (2 cups) Nestlé Toll House Semi-
>   Sweet Chocolate Morsels
>   1 cup sour cream
>   1 teaspoon vanilla extract
>   ¼ teaspoon salt
>   3 cups sifted confectioners sugar
>   2 frozen pound cakes (11½-ounces each), thawed
>   Chocolate Curls (recipe follows) and/or chocolate
>   shavings (optional)
>   Meringue Mushrooms (see index) (optional)

Melt Nestlé Toll House Semi-Sweet Chocolate Morsels over hot (not boiling) water. Transfer to a small bowl; cool 5 minutes. Blend in sour cream, vanilla, and salt. Gradually add confectioners sugar; beat until smooth. Set frosting aside.

Place pound cakes end to end to form one long cake. To form a log-shaped cake, round off edges by running a sharp knife down length of cake, slicing off all four corner edges (cake should resemble a cylinder). Cut cake crosswise into three layers. Fill and frost cake with prepared frosting. Run tines of fork lengthwise through frosting to simulate bark. Garnish with Chocolate Curls, chocolate shavings, and Meringue Mushrooms, if desired.

Chocolate Curls

Makes 1¼ cups melted chocolate

>   1 12-ounce package (2 cups) Nestlé Toll House Semi-
>   Sweet Chocolate Morsels
>   ¼ cup vegetable shortening

Over hot (not boiling) water, combine Nestlé Toll House Semi-Sweet Chocolate Morsels and vegetable shortening; stir until morsels melt and mixture is smooth. Pour into foil-lined 9x5x3-inch loaf pan. Chill until firm (about 2 hours). Remove foil from chocolate block. Make chocolate curls using one of the following: vegetable peeler, cheese slicer, cheese plane, lemon zester, or butter curler.   Place curls on cookie sheet; chill until ready to use.

Lemon Sponge

Makes 4 to 6 servings

>   ¾ cup sugar
>   1½ tablespoons butter or margarine
>   2 teaspoons grated lemon peel
>   3 eggs, separated
>   3 tablespoons all-purpose flour
>   ¼ cup lemon juice
>   1 cup milk

Lemon Chiffon Cake (page 16). Mazola

Quick Party Log with Chocolate Curls; Meringue Mushrooms (page 57). The Nestlé Company, Inc.

You will need: Pyrex 1½-quart 8-inch round cake dish, buttered; Corning Ware glass-ceramic rack; Corning Ware 12¼x10¼x2¼-inch open roaster

Cream together sugar, butter, and lemon peel. Add egg yolks; beat well to blend. Stir in flour alternately with the lemon juice. Gently stir in milk. Beat egg whites until stiff but not dry. Gently fold into the butter mixture until no streaks of white remain. Spoon into prepared cake dish. Set rack in roaster; pour 1 inch of hot water into roaster. Set cake dish on rack. Bake in preheated 350°F. oven about 1 hour, until set.

Orange Sponge

Substitute 1 tablespoon grated orange peel for the lemon peel and ⅓ cup orange juice for the lemon juice.

Scratch or Mix?

If you are a timid baker, by all means use a mix. Choose a brand you know from experience to be reliable. Follow the directions concerning measuring, beating, pan size, oven temperature, and times. If you wish, reinforce the flavor with a teaspoon of good "real" flavoring extract, added with the liquid. With these simple instructions, you will have a cake everyone will enjoy.

Hot Milk Sponge Cake

Makes 8 to 10 servings

2   cups C & H Granulated Sugar
4   eggs
2   cups cake flour (or 1¾ cups all-purpose flour)
2   teaspoons baking powder
¼   teaspoon salt
2   teaspoons vanilla extract
1   cup milk
2   tablespoons butter
    Mocha Frosting (recipe follows)

Preheat oven to 350°F. Cream sugar and eggs, beating until light and fluffy. Combine flour, baking powder, and salt. Stir into creamed mixture, then beat well. Stir in vanilla. Heat milk and butter almost to boiling; quickly stir into flour mixture. Beat slightly. Pour immediately into ungreased 10-inch tube pan. Bake 40 to 45 minutes, or until cake tester inserted in center comes out clean. Invert pan over bottle to cool. With long spatula, gently loosen cake from pan and turn out onto serving plate. Frost with Mocha Frosting.

Mocha Frosting

4   cups C & H Powdered Sugar
1   teaspoon instant coffee powder
3   tablespoons cocoa powder
⅓   cup butter, melted
1   teaspoon vanilla extract
4   to 5 tablespoons water

Sift sugar, coffee, and cocoa in a bowl. Cream half the sugar mixture with butter. Stir in remaining sugar mixture, the vanilla, and enough water to make a spreading consistency. Beat until smooth. Frosts two 8- or 9-inch layers.

Applesauce Cake with Hot Milk Icing

Makes 1 cake

1¾   cups sugar
¼   cup firmly packed light brown sugar
½   cup butter or margarine
2   eggs
2½   cups sifted Martha White Self-Rising Flour
1   teaspoon ground cinnamon
½   teaspoon ground nutmeg
¼   teaspoon allspice
¼   teaspoon baking soda
1⅔   cups (16½ ounces) applesauce
⅔   cup raisins (optional)
¼   cup chopped walnuts
    Hot Milk Icing (recipe follows)

Preheat oven to 350°F. Grease and flour 13x9x2-inch baking pan; set aside. Cream sugars and butter with electric mixer in mixing bowl until light and fluffy. Add eggs, 1 at a time, beating well after each addition. Sift flour, cinnamon, nutmeg, allspice, and baking soda into separate bowl. Alternately add flour mixture and applesauce to creamed mixture; blend well. Stir in raisins and nuts. Pour into prepared pan. Bake 50 minutes, or until toothpick inserted in center comes out clean. Spread Hot Milk Icing over warm cake. Cool completely in pan.

Hot Milk Icing

2   cups sifted confectioners sugar
¼   cup hot milk
2   tablespoons butter, melted
½   teaspoon vanilla extract or rum flavoring

Combine all ingredients in small mixing bowl; beat with electric mixer until smooth.

Clever Cake Cutting

To cut a butter cake: Use a thin-pointed, sharp knife, cutting with a sawing motion. Wipe off the blade after each cut.

To cut a foam cake (chiffon, angel food, sponge): Use a cake breaker—a special tool with a series of long teeth—or pull pieces apart gently with two forks, holding one in each hand.

To cut a rolled cake (jelly roll, chocolate cream roll): Use a piece of heavy white sewing thread about 15 inches long; slip it under the roll at the point where you want to cut, bring up the ends and cross them over the top, one in each hand; pull the ends down, in opposite directions, to cut a slice.

Jelly Roll

A dessert favorite for generations, jelly roll is made of sponge cake baked as a flat sheet, then spread with jelly and rolled. Traditionally it is not frosted, but instead sprinkled liberally with confectioners sugar. Although jelly is the usual filling, no law says that a custard—vanilla, chocolate, or butterscotch flavored—cannot be used instead, or a sweetened and flavored whipped cream, if that is your pleasure.

The cake is simple to make. The only trick lies in turning it out of the pan immediately after it is done, onto a towel sprinkled with confectioners sugar. Roll up at once, using the towel to help you—easy does it—and allow it to cool. Then unroll and spread with jelly of any flavor, and reroll.

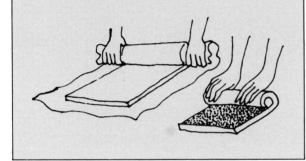

Jelly Roll

Makes 10 servings

    3 large eggs
    1 cup sugar
    ¼ cup water
    1 teaspoon vanilla extract
    1 cup sifted Martha White Self-Rising Flour
       Confectioners sugar
    1 cup red jelly or jam, such as strawberry,
          raspberry, or cherry

Preheat oven to 375°F. Grease and flour 15x10x1-inch jelly roll pan; set aside. Break eggs into small mixing bowl; beat with electric mixer until thick and lemon colored. Gradually beat in sugar. Add water and vanilla; blend well. Gradually beat in flour until smooth. Pour into prepared pan. Bake 12 minutes, or until golden brown. Remove from oven; loosen edges with sharp knife. Immediately turn out onto tea towel sprinkled with confectioners sugar. Trim any stiff edges. Spread jelly over cake. Carefully roll up, jelly roll fashion, from narrow end, using towel to ease cake over. Cool, wrapped in towel, on wire rack about ½ hour. Carefully remove towel. Sprinkle confectioners sugar over top, if desired. Slice to serve.

Poppy Seed Dessert Roll

Makes 1 cake

This rich yeast-raised cake is a special holiday treat in central Europe, where it is served as a dessert. It is also a wonderful coffee cake.

Dough

    ⅓ cup plus 1 tablespoon milk, divided
    1 package active dry yeast
    2¼ to 2½ cups all-purpose flour, divided
    ⅓ cup sugar
    2 eggs
    ¼ cup butter or margarine, softened

Heat ⅓ cup of the milk until lukewarm (110° to 115°F.). Pour warmed milk into a large electric mixer bowl. Add yeast and stir until dissolved. Add ½ cup of the flour and the sugar. Beat at medium speed for 5 minutes. Beat in the eggs and ¾ cup of the remaining flour. Beat at high speed for 5 minutes, or until the batter is shiny and sheets off a spoon. Beat in the softened butter until the batter is smooth. Stir in 1 cup of the remaining flour, or enough to make a soft, sticky dough. Turn out on a well-floured surface and knead until silky smooth; the dough should be soft. Place in a greased bowl and turn once to grease the surface. Cover and let rise in a warm place, free from draft, until double in bulk, about 45 minutes.

Filling

    ¾ cup poppy seed
    1 egg
    ¼ cup sugar
    ½ cup milk
    ½ cup Sun-Maid® Seedless Golden Raisins
    ½ cup ground almonds
    ½ teaspoon grated lemon peel
    2 tablespoons butter or margarine

Process the poppy seed in a blender container at high speed for 2 to 3 minutes, or until the seed is pulverized. (Or mash in a mortar with pestle until pulverized.) Beat the egg and sugar until light and fluffy. Add the poppy seed, milk, raisins, almonds, and lemon peel, stirring until well mixed. Turn into a small saucepan, add the butter, and cook, stirring, until the mixture is thick. Cool to room temperature.

To assemble and bake: Grease a 10x6x1½-inch baking dish. Punch the dough down and knead on a lightly floured surface until smooth. Cover with a bowl and let stand for 10 minutes. Preheat the oven to 375°F. Roll out the dough into a 20x10-inch rectangle. Spoon the filling over the dough and spread it evenly to within ¼ inch of the edges. Starting at both narrow ends of the rectangle, roll the dough up until it meets in the center. Place the loaf seam-side down in the prepared dish. Brush the remaining 1 tablespoon milk and bake (do not set out to rise) for 35 to 40 minutes, or until golden brown. Remove from the dish and cool on a wire rack.

Double Caramel Cake

Makes 6 to 8 servings

  1 **cup firmly packed C & H Brown Sugar**
  ½ **cup shortening**
  2 **eggs, separated**
1½ **cups cake flour (or 1¼ cups plus 1 tablespoon all-purpose flour)**
1¾ **teaspoons baking powder**
  ¼ **teaspoon baking soda**
  ½ **cup milk**
  1 **teaspoon vanilla extract**
      Pinch *each* **salt and cream of tartar**
      Caramel Frosting (recipe follows)
      Chocolate Curls (see index)

Preheat oven to 350°F. Grease and flour two 8-inch cake pans. Cream sugar and shortening until light and fluffy. Stir in egg yolks, 1 at a time, beating well after each addition. Combine flour, baking powder, and soda. Mix milk and vanilla. Add dry ingredients and milk alternately to creamed mixture, beating gently after each addition. Beat egg whites with salt and cream of tartar until stiff but not dry. Fold into flour mixture. Spread batter in pans. Bake 25 minutes, or until cake tester inserted in centers comes out clean. Frost with Caramel Frosting and garnish with Chocolate Curls.

Caramel Frosting
  ½ **cup butter or margarine**
  1 **cup firmly packed C & H Dark Brown Sugar**
  ¼ **teaspoon salt**
  6 **tablespoons milk**
  3 **cups C & H Powdered Sugar**

Melt butter in 2-quart saucepan; stir in brown sugar and salt. Bring to rolling boil and boil rapidly 2 minutes, stirring constantly. Remove from heat, stir in milk, then return to rolling boil. Cool 20 minutes or until lukewarm. Add powdered sugar and beat until smooth and cool enough to spread. If frosting stiffens too quickly while spreading, beat in several drops of milk. Frosts two 8- or 9-inch layers.

Elegant Layer Cake

Makes 16 servings
- 1 cup butter or margarine
- 2 cups sugar
- 5 eggs
- 1 teaspoon vanilla extract
- 2½ cups all-purpose flour
- 1 teaspoon baking soda
- 1 teaspoon baking powder
- ⅛ teaspoon salt
- 1 cup milk, soured★
- 1 can (22 ounces) lemon pie filling
- 1 box (7.2 ounces) fluffy white frosting mix
- 2 cups flaked coconut
- Crystallized Flowers (recipe follows)

Preheat oven to 350°F. Grease 4 Reynolds Redi-Pan cake pans. Cream together butter and sugar 5 minutes, or until fluffy. Add eggs, 1 at a time, beating well after each addition. Mix in vanilla. Combine flour, baking soda, baking powder, and salt. Add to creamed mixture alternately with milk, starting and ending with flour mixture. Spoon batter into pans. Bake 20 to 25 minutes, or until toothpick inserted in center comes out clean. Cool 10 minutes. Remove from pans; cool.

To assemble cake, place first layer on platter; top with ⅔ cup lemon pie filling and spread ¾ inch from edge. Repeat with remaining layers except top layer. Prepare frosting according to package directions. Frost top and sides of cake. Pat coconut on sides and make a 1-inch border of coconut on top. Freeze 30 minutes, or until frosting is set. Place cake on a sheet of Heavy Duty Reynolds Wrap aluminum foil large enough for adequate wrapping. Bring longer sides of foil together over food. Fold down in locked folds, pressing air out until foil is tight against food. Fold up short ends; crimp to seal. Label, date, and freeze. To serve, unwrap and thaw completely. Place Crystallized Flowers in center.

★Add 1 tablespoon lemon juice or vinegar to milk; let stand 10 minutes.

Crystallized Flowers
- White or brightly colored flowers, with simple petal arrangements (such as small orchids or roses, sweet peas or violets)
- 1 egg white
- Superfine sugar

Place egg white in a small bowl. Stir lightly. Dip flower in egg white or brush with small artist's brush to cover all parts of petals. Remove excess egg white that could cause petals to stick together. Sprinkle or sift superfine sugar over petals. Cover all egg white, shaking to avoid clumping. Blow softly on flower to remove excess sugar. Place flower on foil-lined baking sheet. Let dry in cool area 2 to 3 days.

Elegant Layer Cake. The Reynolds Wrap Kitchen

Q. *Why do my cakes, whether made from scratch or a mix, develop a mound like a young mountain in the middle as they bake?*
A. It's possible that the from-scratch cakes have too much flour. This is not possible with mixes, however, so the second diagnosis must be the right one: your oven is too hot. If you are baking the cakes at the temperature the recipe directs, your oven thermostat may be out of kilter. Check it with a separate oven thermometer, or call the electric or gas company or the dealer from whom you bought the stove to send someone to check it.

Aunt E. C.'s Pound Cake

Makes 1 cake
- 3½ cups sugar
- 2 cups butter
- 10 large or 12 small eggs
- 4 cups sifted Martha White All-Purpose Flour

Generously grease 10-inch tube pan; set aside. Preheat oven to 300°F. Cream sugar and butter with electric mixer in mixing bowl until light and fluffy. Add eggs, 1 at a time, beating well after each addition. Gradually beat in flour; blend well. Pour into prepared pan. Bake 2 hours, or until toothpick inserted in center comes out clean. Cool in pans 10 minutes. Turn out onto wire rack to cool completely.
Idea: For an extra special serving touch, top with sweetened whipped cream and sliced bananas.

Lemon Chiffon Cake

Makes 14 to 16 servings

  2¼ cups sifted cake flour
  1½ cups sugar
   1 tablespoon baking powder
  ½ teaspoon salt
   6 egg yolks
  ½ cup Mazola Corn Oil
  ½ cup water
   1 tablespoon grated lemon rind
  ¼ cup lemon juice
   6 egg whites, at room temperature
  ½ teaspoon cream of tartar
     Lemon Glaze (recipe follows) (optional)
     Lemon and/or orange rind, cut in strips
        (optional)

Into large mixer bowl, sift flour, sugar, baking powder, and salt. Make well in center; add egg yolks, corn oil, water, lemon rind, and juice. With mixer at medium speed, beat until smooth. In large bowl, with mixer at high speed, beat egg whites and cream of tartar until very stiff peaks form. Gently fold flour mixture into egg whites until well blended. Pour into ungreased 10x4-inch tube pan. Bake in 325°F. oven 65 to 70 minutes, or until cake springs back when lightly touched. Immediately invert pan over funnel or bottle. Cool completely. Loosen edges of cake with spatula. Remove from pan. If desired, glaze with Lemon Glaze and garnish with very thin strips of lemon and/or orange rind.

Orange Chiffon Cake

Follow recipe for Lemon Chiffon Cake. Omit lemon rind, juice, and water. Use 2 teaspoons grated orange rind and ¾ cup orange juice. If desired, glaze with Orange Glaze (recipe follows).

Banana-Orange Chiffon Cake

Follow recipe for Lemon Chiffon Cake. Omit lemon rind, juice, and water. Use 1 cup mashed bananas (about 2), 2 teaspoons grated orange rind, and ⅓ cup orange juice. If desired, glaze with Orange Glaze (recipe follows).

Wine Chiffon Cake

Follow recipe for Lemon Chiffon Cake. Omit water and lemon juice. Use ¾ cup sauterne or sweet white wine. Glaze as desired.

Apple-Cinnamon Chiffon Cake

Follow recipe for Lemon Chiffon Cake. Add 1 teaspoon ground cinnamon to flour mixture. Omit water, lemon rind, and juice. Use ¾ cup apple juice. If desired, glaze with Apple Glaze (recipe follows).

Lemon or Orange Glaze

Makes about ½ cup

   1 cup sifted confectioners sugar
  ½ teaspoon grated lemon or orange rind
   1 to 2 tablespoons lemon or orange juice

In small bowl, stir together confectioners sugar, lemon or orange rind, and lemon or orange juice until sugar dissolves completely and mixture is smooth.

Apple Glaze

Follow recipe for Lemon or Orange Glaze. Substitute 1 to 2 tablespoons apple juice for lemon or orange juice; omit lemon or orange rind.

Tips for Perfect Cakes

To make a moist, velvety shortening-type cake, follow the recipe carefully. And, for best results, do the following:

● Sift flour before measuring.
● Cream shortening and sugar until light and fluffy, or until sugar is dissolved.
● Always use fresh eggs. Eggs separate easily when cold, but should be at room temperature for beating the whites.
● Preheat oven to correct temperature. If using glass pans, reduce oven temperature by 25°F.
● If using melted chocolate, cool slightly before stirring it into batter.
● Scrape sides of bowl frequently with a rubber spatula during mixing.
● Use baking pans with a shiny surface. Grease and lightly flour the pan or grease the bottom and cover it with greased waxed paper.
● Spread batter evenly in pans.
● Position pans as near to center of oven as possible. Pans should not touch sides of oven or each other.
● Cool cake in a layer pan 10 minutes and in a loaf pan 15 minutes before loosening the edge and turning it out onto a wire rack to cool.
● Use vegetable shortening if the recipe calls for it. Do not use a substitute.
● Cool cake completely before frosting, unless the recipe instructs otherwise.
● Cake is done when the sides shrink slightly away from the pan and a cake tester or toothpick inserted in the center comes out clean.

Strawberry Shortcake

Makes 8 to 10 servings

   2 cups sifted Martha White Self-Rising Flour
   3 tablespoons sugar
  ⅓ cup butter or margarine
   1 egg
     About ½ cup milk
   3 to 4 cups sliced strawberries, sweetened with
        sugar to taste
  ½ pint heavy cream, whipped

Preheat oven to 450°F. Grease large baking sheet; set aside. Combine flour and sugar in mixing bowl. Cut in butter with pastry blender or 2 knives until mixture is consistency of coarse crumbs. Beat egg with fork in measuring cup. Add enough milk to measure ⅔ cup. Add to flour mixture; stir with fork until dough leaves sides of bowl. Turn out onto lightly floured board or pastry cloth. Knead 3 or 4 times, or until smooth. Roll dough out to ½-inch thickness. Cut into rounds with floured 2½-inch biscuit cutter. Place on prepared baking sheet. Bake 10 to 12 minutes, or until golden brown. Transfer to wire rack to cool 5 minutes. Split shortcake in half crosswise. Spoon sweetened strawberries and whipped cream onto bottom halves. Replace tops. Top with remaining strawberries and whipped cream.

Sometimes you may wish to cut a tall cake that has been baked in a springform or tube pan into layers or to split a cake layer into two equal layers. There's a neat and easy way. Mark the cake all the way around or on all sides with food picks. (If your eye is good, fine; if you're not sure of yourself, use a ruler to measure. Little mistakes made along the way have a nasty habit of magnifying themselves in the finished product.) Using a sawtooth knife, cut through the cake, using the picks as a guide. Or, with the picks to guide you, pull heavy sewing thread back and forth through the cake with a gentle sawing motion.

Peaches-and-Cream Cake

Makes 8 to 10 servings

  1 **cup C & H Granulated Sugar**
  ½ **cup butter or margarine, softened**
  3 **eggs**
  1 **cup all-purpose flour**
  1 **teaspoon baking powder**
  ¾ **teaspoon salt**
  1 **teaspoon vanilla extract**
  1 **tablespoon peach syrup**
  1 **package (3 ounces) cream cheese, softened**
  ¼ **cup sour cream**
     Topping (recipe follows)

Preheat oven to 325°F. Cream ⅔ cup sugar and the butter. Beat in 2 eggs. Combine flour, baking powder, and ½ teaspoon salt. Add to creamed mixture and beat until well mixed. Stir in vanilla and peach syrup. Spread evenly on bottom and sides of ungreased 10-inch pie pan.

Cream remaining ⅓ cup sugar with the cream cheese. Beat in sour cream. Add remaining egg and ¼ teaspoon salt; mix well. Spoon over batter in pie pan. Bake 30 to 35 minutes. Remove from oven and add topping.

Topping

  1 **can (29 ounces) cling peach slices**
  1 **cup sour cream**
  2 **tablespoons C & H Golden Brown Sugar**

Drain peaches (reserve 1 tablespoon syrup for cake batter). Arrange slices on top of cake. Blend sour cream with brown sugar. Spoon over peaches and return cake to oven for 5 minutes. Chill before serving.

Note: To substitute fresh peaches for canned, poach as follows: Combine 1 cup C & H Granulated Sugar, ½ cup water, and 1 tablespoon lemon juice in heavy saucepan. Cook over low heat until sugar dissolves, swirling pan occasionally. Cover pan and cook 5 minutes. Peel 3 large peaches and slice ¼-inch thick. Add to sugar mixture, cover, and simmer gently, 3 to 4 minutes. Peaches should be tender when pierced with a knife. Cool in syrup. Proceed with topping recipe. Leftover syrup (canned or poaching) can be saved to top ice cream or other desserts.

Solo Poppy Cake

Makes one 10-inch tube cake

  1   **cup butter or margarine, softened**
  1½ **cups sugar**
  1   **can (12½ ounces) Solo Poppy Filling**
  4   **eggs, separated**
  1   **teaspoon vanilla extract**
  1   **cup sour cream**
  2½ **cups all-purpose flour**
  1   **teaspoon baking soda**
  1   **teaspoon salt**
       Confectioners sugar

Preheat oven to 350°F. Grease and lightly flour a 9- or 10-inch tube pan. Cream butter and sugar together until light and fluffy. Add poppy filling. Add egg yolks, 1 at a time, beating well after each addition. Add vanilla and sour cream. Sift together flour, baking soda, and salt; add to mixture gradually, beating well after each addition. Beat egg whites until stiff but not dry; fold into batter. Turn batter into prepared pan. Bake about 1 hour and 10 to 15 minutes, or until a cake tester inserted in center comes out clean. Allow cake to cool about 5 minutes. Remove from pan. To decorate, sift confectioners sugar through a paper doily or a cut-out on the top of the cake.

Good idea: If you prefer, bake two 9-inch round layers and reduce baking time to 45 minutes, or until done. Cool layers and put together with a cream filling.

Carrot Layer Cake

Makes 8 to 10 servings

> 2 **cups firmly packed C & H Dark Brown Sugar**
> 4 **eggs**
> 2 **cups all-purpose flour**
> 2 **teaspoons** *each* **baking soda and ground cinnamon**
> ¾ **teaspoon salt**
> 1½ **cups vegetable oil**
> 2 **cups coarsely grated carrots**
> 1 **cup coarsely chopped walnuts**
> **Orange Butter Cream Frosting (recipe follows)**

Preheat oven to 350°F. Grease and flour two 9-inch cake pans. Gradually beat sugar into eggs. Combine flour, soda, cinnamon, and salt; add to egg mixture alternately with oil, beginning and ending with flour. Fold in carrots and walnuts. Pour batter into pans, dividing evenly. Bake 35 to 40 minutes. Cool 10 minutes in pans, then turn out onto rack to finish cooling. Frost with Orange Butter Cream Frosting.

Orange Butter Cream Frosting

> 4 **cups C & H Powdered Sugar**
> ½ **cup butter or margarine, softened**
> **Pinch of salt**
> ¼ **cup orange juice**
> 1 **teaspoon grated orange rind**

Combine all ingredients in bowl and beat about 3 minutes, until smooth and creamy. Frosts tops and sides of two 8-inch or 9-inch layers.

Raspberry Sour Cream Torte

Makes 8 to 10 servings

> ½ **cup butter**
> 3 **tablespoons sugar**
> 1 **egg**
> 1½ **cups all-purpose flour**
> ¾ **teaspoon baking powder**
> ¼ **teaspoon salt**
> 1 **can (16 ounces) Oregon raspberries, drained, reserving syrup**
> 1½ **tablespoons cornstarch**
> ¼ **teaspoon ground cinnamon**
> 1 **egg, lightly beaten**
> 1½ **cups sour cream**
> ⅓ **cup sugar**
> 1 **teaspoon vanilla extract**

Cream butter and sugar. Add egg; beat until fluffy. Blend in flour, baking powder, and salt. Press two-thirds of mixture on bottom of 7½- or 8-inch springform pan. Bake at 400°F. 10 minutes, or until lightly browned. Cool. Reduce oven temperature to 350°F. Press remaining crust mixture up sides of pan.

Combine cornstarch and cinnamon in small saucepan; gradually blend in reserved syrup. Cook and stir over medium heat until thickened and clear. Stir in

Raspberry Sour Cream Torte. Oregon Fruit Products Company

berries; pour into prepared crust.

Blend together egg, sour cream, sugar, and vanilla; spoon gently over fruit filling. Bake at 350°F. 65 minutes, or until edges are lightly brown and surface has a 1½-inch dull opaque edge along crust. Cool, then chill thoroughly. Remove ring from springform just before serving.

Linzer Torte

Makes one 9-inch torte

> 1¾ **cups plus 2 tablespoons all-purpose flour**
> ½ **cup firmly packed light brown sugar**
> ½ **teaspoon baking powder**
> ½ **teaspoon ground cinnamon**
> ⅛ **teaspoon salt**
> ½ **cup Mazola Margarine**
> ¼ **cup Karo Light Corn Syrup**
> 1 **egg, lightly beaten**
> ½ **cup raspberry jam or preserves**

Line bottom of 9x3-inch springform pan with 8½-inch round of waxed paper. In large bowl, stir together 1¾ cups flour, brown sugar, baking powder, cinnamon, and salt. With pastry blender or 2 knives, cut in margarine until coarse crumbs form. With fork, stir in corn syrup and egg just until well mixed. Reserve ½ cup dough. Press remaining dough evenly into bottom of prepared pan. Spread with jam to within ½ inch of edges. Stir 2 tablespoons flour into reserved dough. On lightly floured surface, roll out to ⅛-inch thickness. Cut into ¼-inch wide strips. Lattice strips over jam. Place strips around edge to cover ends of lattice strips and form a border. Bake in 375°F. oven 25 to 30 minutes, or until set and lightly browned. Cool completely in pan on wire rack. Remove from pan. Carefully remove waxed paper. Cut in wedges to serve.

German Chocolate Cake

Makes 1 cake

- 1 **bar (4 ounces) German sweet chocolate**
- ½ **cup hot water**
- 2 **cups sugar**
- 1 **cup butter or margarine**
- 4 **eggs**
- 2½ **cups sifted Martha White Self-Rising Flour**
- 1 **cup milk**
- 1 **teaspoon vanilla extract**
  German Coconut Topping (recipe follows)

Preheat oven to 350°F. Grease and flour bottom of one 15x10x2-inch or three 9-inch round baking pans; set aside. Combine chocolate and water in small bowl; stir to melt chocolate; set aside to cool. Cream sugar and butter with electric mixer in mixing bowl until light and fluffy. Add eggs, 1 at a time, beating well after each addition. Alternately beat in flour and milk, beginning and ending with flour. Add chocolate mixture and vanilla; blend well. Pour into prepared pans. Bake 45 minutes, or until toothpick inserted in centers comes out clean. Cool in pans 10 minutes. Turn onto serving plate. Frost with German Coconut Topping. (Frost middle and top layer, if making layer cake.)

German Coconut Topping

Makes about 5 cups

- 1 **cup sugar**
- 1 **cup undiluted evaporated milk**
- ½ **cup butter or margarine**
- 3 **egg yolks**
- 1⅓ **cups flaked coconut**
- 1 **cup chopped pecans**
- 1 **teaspoon vanilla extract**

Combine sugar, milk, butter, and egg yolks in saucepan. Cook over moderate heat, stirring constantly, 12 minutes, or until thickened. Stir in coconut, pecans, and vanilla. Beat with electric mixer until thick enough to spread.

Very Berry Chocolate Cake

Makes 1 cake

- 2 **baked 9-inch Mahogany Sour Cream Cake layers, cooled (recipe follows)**
- 1 **quart fresh strawberries**
  Chocolate Glaze (recipe follows)
- 2 **tablespoons sugar**
- 1 **teaspoon vanilla extract**
- 1¾ **cups heavy cream★**
- 3 **tablespoons sugar★**
- ¾ **teaspoon vanilla extract★**

Prepare chocolate layers as directed. Cool. Select 5 large strawberries for garnish. Partially dip into glaze and set aside. Hull and halve remaining strawberries. Add 2 tablespoons sugar and 1 teaspoon vanilla; mix gently. Whip cream with 3 tablespoons sugar and ¾ teaspoon vanilla until soft peaks form. Place one cake layer on serving plate; spoon on half of the strawberries. Drizzle with half of the glaze; top with half of the sweetened whipped cream. Repeat layers with remaining ingredients. Garnish with chocolate-dipped strawberries.

★Or use 3½ cups thawed Cool Whip Non-Dairy Topping.

Mahogany Sour Cream Cake

Makes one 9-inch cake

- 3 **squares Baker's Unsweetened Chocolate**
- ½ **cup water**
- 1 **cup sour cream**
- 1⅔ **cups all-purpose flour**
- 1½ **teaspoons Calumet Baking Powder**
- 1 **teaspoon baking soda**
- 1 **teaspoon salt**
- ⅔ **cup butter or margarine**
- ⅔ **cup firmly packed light brown sugar**
- 1 **cup granulated sugar**
- 3 **eggs**
- 2 **teaspoons vanilla extract**

Melt chocolate in water in saucepan over very low heat, stirring constantly until smooth. Cool; then stir in sour cream. Mix flour, baking powder, soda, and salt. Cream butter. Gradually beat in sugars; beat until light and fluffy. Add eggs, 1 at a time, beating thoroughly after each. Alternately add flour and chocolate mixtures, beating after each addition until smooth. Stir in vanilla.

Pour into 2 well-greased and floured 9-inch layer pans. Bake at 350°F. for 35 to 40 minutes, or until cake tester inserted in centers comes out clean. Cool in pans 10 minutes. Remove from pans and finish cooling on racks.

Chocolate Glaze

Makes about ¾ cup glaze

- 3 **squares Baker's Semi-Sweet Chocolate★**
- 3 **tablespoons water**
- 1 **tablespoon butter or margarine**
- 1 **cup sifted confectioners sugar**
  Dash salt
- ½ **teaspoon vanilla extract**

Place chocolate, water, and butter in saucepan. Stir constantly over very low heat until mixture is smooth. Remove from heat. Combine sugar and salt in bowl. Gradually blend in chocolate mixture and vanilla. For thinner glaze, add a small amount of hot water. For thicker glaze, cool until of desired consistency.

★Or use 1 package (4 ounces) Baker's German's Sweet Chocolate.

A Word or Two About Ingredients

Leaving aside the skill you bring to the making of a cake, its goodness—or lack of same—depends on the quality of the ingredients you use. Freshness is the most important. The good flavor of fresh ingredients imparts good, fresh flavor to the cake. Unless you are a constant baker, the large, economy size of anything—flour, baking powder, and all the rest—is false economy. Past-their-prime flour, eggs, butter, and some other cake ingredients will impair the flavor of the cake, which is bad enough; leavening that has lost its youthful zest can cause a complete failure.

Butter: To cream well, butter should be neither too soft nor too hard. If too hard, it flakes and chips and will not combine smoothly with the remaining ingredients; if too soft, it will not turn into the light, fluffy mass that is the desideratum of the creaming process. Take it from the refrigerator about 20 minutes before you'll be ready to use it.

Eggs: Most modern recipes are developed to use large eggs. Eggs separate best when cold, but beat up to their maximum volume at about 70°F. If your recipe calls for separated eggs, separate them immediately after you take them from the refrigerator, then allow both whites and yolks to stand until they reach room temperature before beating. To separate, crack an egg gently but firmly on the edge of a bowl or other hard surface. Using both hands (one-handed egg separators are show-offs and disaster-courters), gently pull the two halves of the shell apart, retaining the yolk in one half and letting the white drip out into a bowl beneath. Carefully slide the yolk into the other half of the shell, letting the remaining white drip down. If you are a kitchen klutz, a gadget called an egg separator was invented just for you; lacking one, pour the whole egg into a small funnel—the white will run through, the yolk remains safe and secure in the top.

Bits of egg yolk in the whites will keep them from beating up to full volume. If you were unlucky enough to break the yolk and much of it runs into the white, use that egg for another purpose. But if only a small bit of yolk drops into the white, fish it out, using a piece of eggshell as a scoop.

Sugar: Lumps in the sugar may or may not come out when you beat the batter. Make sure ahead of time by pressing lumps out or sifting the sugar before measuring. Confectioners and brown sugar both tend to be lumpy. Sift the former, remove and discard lumps from the latter. Measure granulated and confectioners sugar by spooning lightly into a measuring cup. Most brown sugar measurements call for packed sugar; spoon into the cup, pack down with the back of the spoon, and repeat until the proper packed amount is achieved.

Flour: All-purpose flour labeled presifted does not need to be sifted before measuring unless the recipe specifies that it must. (Those not so labeled must be sifted before measuring.) However, presifted flour should be aerated before measuring; stir the flour with a spoon until it is no longer compacted, then spoon lightly—do not pack—into a measuring cup. Level off with a spatula or the back of a knife. Some flours—as whole wheat, graham—should not be sifted. Be guided by the recipe. At any rate, such flours are seldom used in cakes. However, many recipes do call for cake flour—a lighter, finer type

Liquids: Measure in a see-through—glass or plastic—measuring cup designed specifically for liquids; do not use a cup designed to measure dry ingredients. Pour the liquid to the specified amount at eye level (set the cup on a flat, level surface, bend down to peer at it—a little mild exercise never hurt anyone). Milk should be whole (homogenized) unless the recipe calls for something else. Evaporated milk, mixed half and half with water, may be used in place of fresh whole milk. Do not use condensed milk unless the recipe specifies it. Dry whole milk, reconstituted as the package directs, may be substituted, but do not use reconstituted nonfat dry milk unless the directions say you can.

Molasses, oil, honey, and corn syrup are a bit easier to get out of the cup if you've first rinsed it in cold water—shake out all the water, but don't dry it. Again, check measurements at eye level. For small amounts of these ingredients, measure by the tablespoonful rather than fractions of a cup, bearing in mind that ¼ cup equals 4 tablespoons.

Flavorings, spices: Use the amount the recipe directs unless you know, from previous experience with the same recipe, that the called-for amount wasn't quite enough for your taste. Measure flavorings and spices with standard measuring spoons. Pour extracts into a proper-size spoon until it is full; measure rounded spoonfuls of spices, then level off with a spatula or the dull side of a knife.

Harvest Spice Cake

Makes 1 cake

  1 cup butter or margarine, softened
  1¼ cups sugar
  1 tablespoon grated orange peel
  3 eggs
  2½ cups all-purpose flour
  1 teaspoon baking powder
  1 teaspoon baking soda
  1 teaspoon salt
  1 teaspoon ground cinnamon
  ¼ teaspoon allspice
  1 cup sour cream
  1 cup chopped cooking apples
  1 cup Sun-Maid® Seedless Raisins
  1 cup chopped walnuts

Grease a 10-inch tube pan. Cream the butter, sugar, and orange peel until fluffy. Beat in the eggs, 1 at a time. Preheat the oven to 350°F. Combine the dry ingredients in one bowl and the sour cream and chopped apples in a second one. Add the dry ingredients to the creamed mixture alternately with the sour cream and apple mixture. Stir in the raisins and nuts. Turn the batter into the prepared pan and bake for 55 minutes to 1 hour, or until a toothpick inserted in the center comes out clean. Let stand for 10 minutes on a wire rack before turning out of the pan to cool on the rack. The cake may be served with whipped cream and a garnish of sliced oranges.

Pumpkin Cake with Coffee Frosting

Makes one 10-inch cake

  1 package (18¼ ounces) spice cake mix
  1½ cups Libby's Pumpkin Pie Mix
  4 eggs
  1 envelope (1¼ ounces) whipped topping mix
     Coffee Frosting (recipe follows)

Preheat oven to 350°F. In large mixing bowl, combine cake mix, pumpkin pie mix, and 2 eggs. Mix at low speed until moistened. Mix at medium speed 2 minutes. Add remaining eggs and topping mix. Mix at low speed until moistened, then at medium speed 3 minutes. Pour into greased and floured 12-cup fluted tube pan. Bake 45 to 55 minutes, or until toothpick inserted in center comes out clean. Cool 15 minutes; remove from pan. Cool completely.

Coffee Frosting

  ¼ cup butter
  1 cup sifted confectioners sugar
  1 tablespoon coffee-flavored liqueur
     Milk

Melt butter in saucepan. Add sugar and liqueur; mix well. Add small amount of milk, if necessary, for drizzling consistency. Drizzle over cooled cake.

How Much Frosting?

Here are some frosting amounts to guide you. In all cases, we presuppose that you wish to frost both the top and the sides of the cake, and to use the frosting for filling as well if it is a layer cake that you are working with.

cake size	frosting amount
8- or 9-inch square	¾ to 1¼ cups
8- or 9-inch 2-layer	1¾ to 2⅔ cups
8- or 9-inch 3-layer	2¼ to 3 cups
9½ x 5½ x 3-inch loaf	1 to 1½ cups
13- x 9- x 2-inch sheet	1½ to 2 cups
11- x 7-x 1½-inch sheet	1 to 1¾ cups
9- or 10-inch tube	3 cups
16 large or 24 small cupcakes	1½ to 2¼ cups

Yogurt Pound Cake

Makes 12 servings

  3 cups firmly packed C & H Golden Brown Sugar
  1 cup butter or margarine, softened
  6 eggs
  3 cups all-purpose flour
  ¼ teaspoon baking soda
  ½ teaspoon salt
  ½ pint (1 cup) plain yogurt
  2 teaspoons vanilla extract
  ⅓ cup poppy seeds
     Apricot Yogurt Frosting (recipe follows)

Preheat oven to 325°F. Grease and flour 10-inch tube pan. Cream sugar and butter until light and fluffy. Add eggs, 1 at a time, beating well after each addition. Combine flour, soda, and salt. Add alternately with yogurt to creamed mixture, beginning and ending with dry ingredients. Stir in vanilla and poppy seeds. Pour into pan. Bake 90 minutes, or until cake tester inserted in center comes out clean. Cool 10 minutes in pan, then turn out onto rack to finish cooling. Frost with Apricot Yogurt Frosting.

Apricot Yogurt Frosting

  4 cups C & H Powdered Sugar
  ¼ cup apricot preserves
  ¼ cup plain yogurt
  ¼ cup butter or margarine, softened
     Pinch of salt

Combine all ingredients in bowl. Beat until smooth and creamy. Enough to frost two 8- or 9-inch layers.

Yogurt Pound Cake with Apricot Yogurt Frosting.
C&H Sugar Company

California Christmas Cake

Makes two 9-inch loaf cakes

Splurge during the holidays with this magnificent fruit-rich cake. It has the traditional spirited fruitcake flavor.

- 3½ **cups cut-up dried figs**
- 3½ **cups sliced dried apricots**
- 3½ **cups Sun-Maid® Seedless Golden Raisins**
- 3½ **cups coarsely chopped walnuts**
- ⅓ **cup brandy**
- 1 **cup butter or margarine, softened**
- 1 **cup honey**
- 1 **tablespoon grated orange peel**
- 6 **eggs**
- 2½ **cups all-purpose flour**
- 1 **teaspoon baking powder**
- 1 **teaspoon salt**

In a large bowl, combine the fruit and walnuts with the brandy; let stand for several hours until the liquid is absorbed. Grease two 9x5x3-inch loaf pans. Preheat the oven to 275°F. In a very large bowl, cream the butter, honey, and orange peel until fluffy. Beat in the eggs, 1 at a time, beating well after each addition. (The batter may look slightly curdled.) Combine the flour, baking powder, and salt and add to the butter mixture, beating until smooth. Stir the fruit mixture into the batter. Divide the batter between the 2 prepared pans and spread evenly. Bake for 1½ hours; then increase the oven temperature to 300°F. and bake 1 hour longer, or until the cakes are golden and a toothpick inserted in the center comes out clean. Let stand on wire racks for 20 minutes before turning out of the pans to cool completely on the racks. Store well wrapped in plastic wrap or aluminum foil.

Brandied Fruit Cake

Makes one 6-pound cake

- 2 **pounds mixed candied fruit**
- 1 **pound raisins**
- 1 **cup chopped dates**
- 1½ **cups chopped nuts**
- 4¼ **cups all-purpose flour, divided**
- ½ **teaspoon baking soda**
- ½ **teaspoon ground cinnamon**
- ½ **teaspoon ground allspice**
- ½ **teaspoon ground cloves**
- ½ **teaspoon ground nutmeg**
- ½ **cup Mazola Margarine**
- 1 **cup sugar**
- 1 **cup Karo Dark Corn Syrup**
- 3 **eggs**
- ½ **cup brandy**
- ½ **teaspoon vanilla extract**
- ½ **cup Karo Light Corn Syrup**

Grease 10x4-inch tube pan. Line bottom with brown paper. In large bowl, stir together candied fruit, raisins, dates, and nuts. Stir in ¼ cup of the flour; set aside. Im medium bowl, stir together remaining 4 cups flour, baking soda, cinnamon, allspice, cloves, and nutmeg; set aside. In large bowl, stir margarine to soften. Add sugar and dark corn syrup; mix well. Beat in eggs, 1 at a time. Stir in brandy and vanilla. Gradually stir in flour mixture until well blended. Stir in fruit mixture. Turn into prepared pan; cover tightly with foil. Bake in 300°F. oven 3 hours, or until cake tester inserted in center comes out clean. Cool completely. Remove from pan. Peel off paper. Wrap in plastic wrap, then foil. Store in tightly covered container at least 1 month. Glaze a day of two before serving. To glaze, bring light corn syrup to boil. Brush over top and sides of cake. Decorate as desired with candied fruit.

Note: If desired, occasionally sprinkle cake during storage with brandy.

Sherry Fruitcake

Makes one 9-inch cake

- 2 **cups chopped dates**
- 2 **cups chopped pecans**
- 2 **cups whole candied cherries**
- 1 **cup mixed candied fruit**
- 1 **12-ounce package (2 cups) Nestlé Toll House Semi-Sweet Chocolate Morsels**
- ½ **cup cream sherry**
- 6 **eggs**
- 1 **cup sugar**
- 2 **teaspoons vanilla extract**
- 3 **cups all-purpose flour**
- 2 **teaspoons salt**

In a large bowl, combine dates, pecans, candied cherries, candied fruit, and Nestlé Toll House Semi-Sweet Chocolate Morsels; add sherry and let stand 1 hour, stirring occasionally. Preheat oven to 325°F. In a large bowl, beat eggs until thick and lemon colored (about 5 minutes). Gradually beat in sugar and vanilla. Combine flour and salt; mix with fruit mixture. Fold in egg mixture. Spread into greased and floured 9-inch tube pan. Bake 1 hour. Cool in pan 15 minutes. Remove cake from pan; cool completely on wire rack.

Cheesecake

Makes one 8-inch cake

- **Graham Cracker Crust (see index)**
- 3 **eggs**
- ½ **cup sugar**
- 1 **teaspoon vanilla extract**
- 1 **thin strip lemon rind**
- 1 **cup sour cream**
- 1 **package (8 ounces) cream cheese, cubed and softened**

Reserve 2 tablespoons Graham Cracker Crust mixture for topping. Press remaining mixture into bottom and about 2 inches up sides of greased 8-inch spring-form or round layer-cake pan at least 2½ inches deep. Chill thoroughly. Heat oven to 325°F. Put eggs, sugar, vanilla, lemon rind, and sour cream into blender container. Cover; blend at high speed about 10 seconds. While blender is running, tip center cap and add cream cheese gradually; blend until smooth. If necessary, stop blender during processing and push ingredients toward blades with rubber spatula. Pour into crumb-lined pan. Sprinkle reserved 2 tablespoons crumb mixture over top. Bake about 55 minutes, or until set in center. Filling will be soft but will firm as cake cools. Store in refrigerator.

Cakes freeze well. If frosted, freeze them uncovered for a few hours before wrapping for longer storage. Some cooks prefer cutting a cake into individual servings before freezing. Cakes made with whipped cream should be thawed in the refrigerator 3 to 4 hours. All others should be thawed in their wrappings at room temperature. Allow 30 minutes for cupcakes, 1 hour for unfrosted cakes and 2 hours for frosted cakes.

Strawberry Cheesecake

Makes 12 servings

- 32 slices zwieback (approximately)
- 1¼ cups sugar, divided
- ¾ teaspoon ground cinnamon
- ⅓ cup butter or margarine, melted
- 4 eggs
- 1 pound cottage cheese
- ¾ pound (1½ 8-ounce packages or 4 3-ounce packages) cream cheese
- 4 tablespoons all-purpose flour
- 1 cup light cream
- 1½ teaspoons grated lemon rind
- 1½ teaspoons lemon juice
- ⅛ teaspoon salt
- Strawberry Glaze (recipe follows)

Preheat oven to 350°F. Process zwieback in blender at Grate to produce 1½ cups fine crumbs. Mix crumbs, ¼ cup sugar, cinnamon, and melted butter. Line sides and bottom of a 10-inch springform pan with this mixture. Place eggs in large bowl of Sunbeam Mixmaster Mixer. Set Dial at medium and beat well. Beat in remaining sugar, cottage cheese, cream cheese, flour, cream, rind, juice, and salt. Pour mixture into crumb-lined pan and bake 1 hour, or until center is set. Turn off oven; open door and let cake cool in oven 1 hour. While it cools, prepare Strawberry Glaze.

Strawberry Glaze

- 1 quart strawberries
- 4 teaspoons cornstarch
- ½ cup sugar
- 1 teaspoon butter or margarine
- Few drops red food coloring

Wash and hull the strawberries. In blender set at Puree, process enough of the smaller berries to make 1 cup. Reserve larger berries, leaving them whole. In a saucepan, dissolve cornstarch in ½ cup cold water. Add pureed strawberries and sugar. Bring to a boil; boil 2 minutes. Stir in butter and enough food coloring to tint to desired shade. Arrange whole strawberries on top of cheesecake. Spoon Glaze over berries. Refrigerate.

Hazelnut Eggnog Cheesecake

Makes 10 to 12 servings

- 1½ cups packaged graham cracker crumbs
- 4 tablespoons butter or margarine, melted
- ⅔ cup plus 2 tablespoons sugar
- 2 packages (8 ounces each) plus 1 package (3 ounces) cream cheese, softened
- 1 cup heavy cream, divided
- 3 large eggs
- 2 egg yolks
- ¼ cup DeKuyper Hazelnut Liqueur
- Grated nutmeg
- Whipped cream (optional)
- Chopped hazelnuts (optional)

Butter a 9-inch springform pan. In a small bowl, combine crumbs, butter, and 2 tablespoons sugar; mix well. Pat mixture over bottom and 2 inches up sides of prepared pan. Chill. In the large bowl of an electric mixer, beat cream cheese until smooth. Gradually add ½ cup heavy cream, beating constantly. Beat in remaining ⅔ cup sugar. Add eggs and egg yolks 1 at a time, blending well after each addition (do not overbeat). Stir in liqueur. Pour batter into prepared pan. Sprinkle with nutmeg. Bake in a 350°F. oven 45 to 50 minutes until top of cake is dry. Cool at room temperature 1 hour. Loosen sides of pan with a spatula and remove. Chill several hours before serving. Whip remaining ½ cup cream. Garnish cake with whipped cream and hazelnuts, if desired.

Unless your oven is brand new, always preheat for about 10 minutes before baking. If you have any doubts about your oven's accuracy, test the temperature with an oven thermometer and adjust the oven controls accordingly.

Strawberry-Topped Cupcakes

Makes 8 servings

     2   cups all-purpose flour
     1   tablespoon baking powder
    ¼   teaspoon salt
    ½   cup butter or margarine
    ½   cup sugar
     1   egg
    ¾   cup milk
     1   teaspoon vanilla extract
     1   cup strawberry preserves

You will need: eight Pyrex 6-ounce custard cups, buttered

Sift flour with baking powder and salt; reserve. Cream butter and sugar until light. Add egg; beat well. Combine milk and vanilla. Add to butter mixture alternately with reserved dry ingredients, beginning and ending with the flour mixture. Beat well after each addition. Place 2 tablespoons jam in each prepared custard cup. Spoon in batter carefully, filling cups about two-thirds full. Bake in preheated 350°F. oven 25 minutes, until toothpick inserted in center comes out clean. Run a sharp knife around edges of cups; invert and unmold on serving plates.

Butterscotch Spice Cupcakes

Makes about 30 cupcakes

     1   6-ounce package (1 cup) Nestlé Butterscotch
           Flavored Morsels
     2   cups all-purpose flour
     1   tablespoon baking powder
     1   teaspoon salt
     1   teaspoon ground cinnamon
    ½   teaspoon ground nutmeg
    ½   teaspoon baking soda
    ⅛   teaspoon ground cloves
     1   cup sugar
    ¾   cup butter, melted
     1   teaspoon vanilla extract
     3   eggs
     1   cup buttermilk
          Creamy Butterscotch Frosting (recipe follows)

Preheat oven to 350°F. Over hot (not boiling) water, melt Nestlé Butterscotch Flavored Morsels; stir until smooth. Remove from heat; set aside. In a small bowl, combine flour, baking powder, salt, cinnamon, nutmeg, baking soda, and cloves; set aside. In a large bowl, combine sugar, butter, melted morsels, and vanilla. Add eggs, 1 at a time, beating well after each addition. Blend in flour mixture alternately with buttermilk. Spoon mixture into paper-lined muffin tins, filling each half-full. Bake 20 minutes. Cool completely. Frost with Creamy Butterscotch Frosting.

Creamy Butterscotch Frosting

Makes 2½ cups

     1   6-ounce package (1 cup) Nestlé Butterscotch
           Flavored Morsels
     1   teaspoon water
     1   package (8 ounces) cream cheese, softened
    ⅛   teaspoon salt
     3   cups sifted confectioners sugar

Over hot (not boiling) water, combine Nestlé Butterscotch Flavored Morsels and water; stir until morsels melt and mixture is smooth. Remove from heat. In a small bowl, combine cream cheese and salt; beat until creamy. Blend in melted butterscotch. Gradually add confectioners sugar. Beat until smooth.

Country Kitchen Gingerbread

Makes 12 to 16 servings

     2   cups sifted Martha White Self-Rising Flour
    ¼   teaspoon baking soda
     1   teaspoon ground cinnamon
     1   teaspoon ground ginger
    ½   teaspoon ground cloves
    ½   cup firmly packed brown sugar
    ½   cup vegetable shortening
     2   eggs
    ¾   cup molasses
     1   cup hot water
          Nut Topping (recipe follows)

Preheat oven to 350°F. Grease 13x9x2-inch baking pan; set aside. Combine flour, baking soda, and spices in small bowl; set aside. Cream brown sugar and shortening with electric mixer in mixing bowl until light and fluffy. Add eggs and molasses; blend well. Alternately beat in flour mixture and hot water, beginning and ending with flour mixture. Pour into prepared pan. Sprinkle Nut Topping over cake. Bake 35 minutes, or until toothpick inserted in center comes out clean.

Nut Topping

    ½   cup firmly packed brown sugar
    ½   cup chopped nuts
    ¼   cup Martha White All-Purpose Flour
   1½   teaspoons ground cinnamon
    ¼   cup butter or margarine, softened

Combine all ingredients in small bowl; blend well.

Strawberry-Topped Cupcakes. Corning Glass Works

CAKE DECORATING—A SHORT COURSE
PASTRY BAGS AND TUBES

To Make Decorating Bags: You need at least one bag for each color icing you use; and if more than one tip is used for a particular color, you'll need a bag for each tip.

Cut 12-inch square of waxed paper. Fold into triangle.

Holding thumb at A, fold a cone making sure points at top overlap.

Fasten at top by folding over several times or taping.

Cut off 1 inch at point. Drop tube into bag so that it protrudes at opening at bottom of bag.

Fill with frosting, not over ⅔ full.

Close top by folding over 2 or 3 times and tucking in ends.

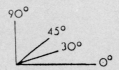

Squeeze frosting down to fill tube. Continue folding top down as tube empties.

To Make Star Border: Use tip No. 21 and hold the bag at 90° angle to cake. Pipe out individual stars.

To Make Zigzag Border: Use tip No. 21 and hold bag at 30° angle to cake. Pipe out a continuous border.

To Make Leaves: Use tip No. 67 and hold bag at 45° angle to cake.

To Write: Use tip No. 3 and hold bag at 45° angle to cake. The icing may need to be thinned down a little with a few drops of milk or water. If icing sticks in tube, use a pin to unclog it.

Greek Nut Cake

Makes one 10-inch round or tube cake

- 2 cups walnuts
- 2¼ cups sifted all-purpose flour
- 2½ teaspoons baking powder
- ½ cup butter or margarine, softened
- 1 cup sugar
- 3 eggs
- ⅓ cup milk
- ¼ teaspoon ground cloves
- ¼ teaspoon salt
- 1 teaspoon ground cinnamon
  Honey Syrup (recipe follows)

Heat oven to 350°F. Grease and flour 10-inch round or fluted tube pan. Put ½ cup walnuts into blender container. Cover; blend at medium speed until ground. Empty into large mixing bowl. Repeat process with remaining walnuts, ½ cup at a time. Sift flour and baking powder into bowl with nuts. Put butter, sugar, eggs, milk, cinnamon, cloves, and salt into blender container. Cover; blend at high speed until smooth. Add to flour-nut mixture; combine thoroughly. Pour into prepared pan. Bake 40 minutes, or until cake tests done.

When cake is done, cool 10 minutes; remove from pan. Prick surface deeply in several places with tines of fork. Baste several times with Honey Syrup until cake is soaked and all syrup is used.

Honey Syrup

- ¾ cup sugar
- ¼ cup honey
- 1 tablespoon lemon juice
- 1 cup boiling water

Put sugar, honey, lemon juice, and water into blender container. Cover; blend at high speed until smooth.

Almond Cake

Makes one 10-inch tube cake

- 1 cup butter or margarine
- 1 cup sugar
- 3 eggs
- 1 can (12½ ounces) Solo Almond Filling
- 2¼ cups all-purpose flour
- 2 teaspoons baking powder
- ½ teaspoon salt
- ¼ cup milk
  Almond Glaze (recipe follows)

Preheat oven to 350°F. Grease and lightly flour a 10-inch tube or Bundt pan. Cream butter or margarine and sugar together until light and fluffy. Add eggs, one at a time, mixing thoroughly after each addition. Beat in almond filling. Sift together flour, baking powder, and salt. Add to creamed mixture alternately with the milk, beginning and ending with dry ingredients. Blend thoroughly. Turn batter into prepared pan. Bake 50 minutes, or until a cake tester inserted in center comes out clean. Cool about 10 minutes. Remove from pan and cool thoroughly. Serve plain or frost with Almond Glaze.

Almond Glaze

- 1 cup confectioners sugar
- 2 tablespoons light cream
- ¼ teaspoon almond extract

Combine all ingredients and stir until well blended and smooth. Drizzle over top of Almond Cake.

Topsy-Turvy Mincemeat Cake

Makes 6 servings

- 4 tablespoons butter or margarine
- 1 cup prepared mincemeat
- 2 tablespoons strong brewed coffee
- ½ cup firmly packed brown sugar
- ½ cup sugar
- 1 egg, well beaten
- 1 cup all-purpose flour
- 1½ teaspoons baking powder
- 2 tablespoons instant coffee
- ⅛ teaspoon salt
- ⅓ cup milk
- 1 teaspoon vanilla extract

You will need: Pyrex 8x8x2-inch square utility dish

Preheat oven to 375°F. Place half the butter in dish; place dish in oven until butter melts. Combine mincemeat, brewed coffee, and brown sugar; spread evenly over melted butter. Cream together remaining butter and the sugar. Beat in egg. Sift together flour, baking powder, coffee, and salt. Add to butter mixture alternately with milk. Stir in vanilla. Spoon batter over mincemeat mixture. Bake 30 minutes, or until cake springs back when lightly touched with finger. Immediately invert onto serving plate, scraping out any topping that remains in dish. Serve warm.

Idea: Although this cake is delicious plain, you might like to serve it with a brandy- or vanilla-flavored hard sauce.

A Spectacular World of Pies

A true dessert lover will delight in these ideas for delicious fruits, heavenly chiffons, rich custards, and velvety cream pies.

Flaky Pastry

Makes one 8- or 9-inch double-crust pie, two 8- or 9-inch shells or 1-crust pies, 8 to 10 medium tarts

- 2¼ **cups sifted all-purpose flour**
- 1 **teaspoon salt**
- ¾ **cup shortening, lard or vegetable**
- 3 **to 4 tablespoons cold water**

Sift flour, and salt together into bowl. Cut in shortening with pastry blender or 2 knives until mixture resembles coarse meal; continue cutting until particles start to cling together in little balls about the size of peas. Mark mixture off into thirds with fork. Sprinkle about 1 tablespoon water on one part; quickly work it in with fork. Repeat operation on each part until particles will cling together when pressed between fingers. Dough should not be wet or sticky. The amount of water may vary with flour, but always use as little as possible. Empty contents of bowl onto Alcoa Wrap. Place hands under foil, cup fashion; press dough into ball; wrap; chill 10 to 15 minutes before rolling.

Butter Pie Crust

Makes one 8- or 9-inch crust

- ¼ **cup C & H Powdered Sugar**
- 1 **cup all-purpose flour**
- ⅛ **teaspoon salt**
- 6 **tablespoons cold butter or margarine, cut in pieces**
- 3 **tablespoons ice water**
- 2 **to 3 cups dried beans (for weight)**

Combine sugar, flour, and salt in bowl. Add butter and mix with pastry blender or fingertips until mixture resembles coarse meal. Add water. Gather pastry into a ball and pat into flat round. Wrap in plastic wrap and chill 1 hour.

On a lightly floured surface, roll pastry into a circle ⅛-inch thick and fit into a lightly greased 9-inch pie pan. Trim edge evenly, then flute or crimp decoratively. Place in freezer at least 15 minutes while preheating oven to 425°F.

Line pie crust with greased waxed paper or parchment and fill with dried beans (to weigh down crust). Bake 15 minutes, until edges brown and crust is firm enough to support itself. Remove paper and beans. Prick bottom of crust with a fork. For a partially baked crust, bake 5 minutes longer, until lightly browned. For a fully baked crust, bake 10 minutes longer, until completely browned.

Easy No-Fail Pie Crust

Makes 2 double-crust 9-inch pies and 1 single crust

- 4 **cups all-purpose flour**
- 1¾ **cups vegetable shortening**
- 1 **tablespoon C & H Granulated Sugar**
- 2 **teaspoons salt**
- ½ **cup water**
- 1 **egg**
- 1 **tablespoon white vinegar**

Combine flour, shortening, sugar, and salt. Mix well with fork or pastry blender. Set aside. Beat together water, egg, and vinegar. Add to flour mixture; mix until all ingredients are moistened. Form into ball and chill at least 15 minutes before shaping in desired shape. May be stored in refrigerator one week or frozen. Bake in 425°F. oven for 12 minutes for single crust. Bake following recipe instructions for double-crust pies.

To help prevent soggy bottom crusts in pumpkin and custard pies, reserve 1 teaspoonful of beaten egg and brush over pastry crust; chill, then add filling.

Cook fillings for cream pies in a heavy saucepan and stir constantly to prevent scorching.

Avoid overcooking filling that has a cornstarch base to prevent thinning the filling.

Refrigerate chiffon, custard, and cream pies and those with whipped cream toppings.

Grasshopper Pie; Grasshopper Tarts filled with orange liqueur and coffee liqueur flavor variations (page 42). The Nestlé Company, Inc.

Crumb Crusts

Makes one 9-inch pie shell

Seven outstanding crumb crusts! Mix 'n' match with your favorite pie fillings.

Chocolate Wafer Crust

- 1½ cups chocolate wafer crumbs (37 to 39 cookies)
- 1 to 2 tablespoons sugar
- ¼ cup butter or margarine, at room temperature

Vanilla Wafer Crust

- 1½ cups vanilla wafer crumbs (37 to 39 cookies)
- 1 to 2 tablespoons sugar
- ¼ cup butter or margarine, at room temperature

Gingersnap Crust

- 1¼ cups gingersnap crumbs
- ⅓ cup butter or margarine, at room temperature

Graham Cracker Crust

- 1¼ cups graham cracker crumbs (about 20 square crackers)
- ¼ cup sugar
- ⅓ cup butter or margarine, at room temperature

Chocolate Graham Crust

- 1½ cups graham cracker crumbs
- 2 squares (2 ounces) semisweet chocolate, finely grated
- ¼ cup sugar
- ⅓ cup butter or margarine, at room temperature

Toasted Coconut Crust

- 1 cup flaked or shredded coconut, toasted
- 1 cup vanilla wafer crumbs
- 2 tablespoons sugar
- ⅓ cup butter or margarine, at room temperature

Crunchy Nut Crust

- 1½ cups ground walnuts, pecans, filberts, or blanched almonds
- ¼ cup sugar
- 2 tablespoons butter or margarine, at room temperature

Note: Butter pie plate generously. Bake at 400°F. 6 to 8 minutes.

You will need: Pyrex 9-inch pie plate

Combine dry ingredients in a bowl. Add butter; blend gently but thoroughly. Spoon mixture into pie plate. Using the back of a spoon—and your fingers, if you wish—press mixture firmly over bottom and side of plate, but not over rim. Bake in preheated 350°F. oven 8 to 10 minutes. Cool before filling.

Hint

A meringue for a shell is beaten enough when you can no longer feel the grains of sugar when you rub a bit of the meringue between thumb and forefinger.

Crumb Crusts

Although precooked pie fillings of all kinds can be turned into baked pastry shells for serving, a crumb crust—cracker or cookie—will make such a pie all the better.

Crumb crusts can be cooked or not, but the very slight extra effort expended on the baked kind will repay with a crust of greater stability and better flavor.

Some cooks like to sprinkle the top of the pie filling with crumbs, rather than garnish with whipped cream or a topping; if extra crumbs are required, increase the ingredients by about a fourth. If you own a food processor, use the chopping blade to make fresh crumbs in a flash.

Meringue Pie Shell

Makes one 9-inch pie

- 1 cup sugar
- ¼ teaspoon cream of tartar
- 4 egg whites

Sift sugar, cream of tartar together. Beat egg whites stiff but not dry. Gradually add sugar mixture, continuing to beat until thoroughly blended and stiff. Pile into greased pie pan. Push out to sides, leaving a hollow in center; bottom should be about ¼-inch thick, sides should be 1-inch thick. Bake 1 hour at 275°F.; cool.

Individual Meringue Shells

On greased cookie sheet, divide mixture into 6 or 8 mounds. Make a hollow center in each mound with the back of a spoon. Bake 1 hour, or until creamy in color and firm to the touch. Cool on rack.

Perfect Meringue

Makes topping for 1 pie

- 3 egg whites, at room temperature
- ¼ teaspoon cream of tartar
- 6 tablespoons sugar

Preheat oven to 400°F. Place egg whites in small mixing bowl. Add cream of tartar. Beat at low speed of electric mixer until foamy. Add sugar, a little at a time, beating at medium-high speed until soft peaks form. Spoon mounds of meringue around outer edge of pie filling. Spread carefully around edge, being certain that meringue touches inner edge of crust. Spoon remaining meringue over center of filling; spread to border. Bake 8 to 10 minutes, or until peaks are golden brown. Cool pie in pan on wire rack.

Lemon Filling

    1 cup sugar
    3 tablespoons cornstarch
    ½ teaspoon salt
    1 cup water
    2 tablespoons grated lemon rind
    ½ cup lemon juice
    2 tablespoons butter or margarine
    4 egg yolks

Combine sugar, cornstarch, salt, water, rind, juice, and butter in saucepan. Bring to boil, stirring constantly; boil 1 minute, continuing to stir. Remove from heat; beat in egg yolks; cook 1 minute longer, stirring constantly. Chill before using.

Orange Filling

Make Lemon Filling, substituting orange juice for the water, grated orange rind for the lemon rind, and 1½ tablespoons lemon juice for the ½ cup lemon juice.

Boston Cream Pie

Makes 1 cake

    2 cups sifted Martha White Self-Rising Flour
    1½ cups sugar
    1 cup buttermilk
    ⅓ cup vegetable shortening
    ⅓ cup butter or margarine
    3 eggs
    1 teaspoon vanilla extract
       Cream Filling (recipe follows)
       Chocolate Glaze (see index)

Preheat oven to 350°F. Grease and flour two 9-inch baking pans; set aside. Combine all ingredients except Cream Filling and Chocolate Glaze in large mixing bowl. Beat at low speed of electric mixer 3 minutes. Pour into prepared pans. Bake 30 minutes, or until toothpick inserted in centers comes out clean. Cool in pans 10 minutes. Turn out of pans onto wire racks to cool completely. Place bottom layer on cake plate. Spread Cream Filling evenly over layer. Add top layer. Drizzle warm Chocolate Glaze over top of cake.

Cream Filling

    ½ cup sugar
    ⅓ cup sifted Martha White Self-Rising Flour
    2 eggs, lightly beaten
    2 cups hot milk
    1½ teaspoons vanilla extract

Combine sugar and flour in top of double boiler; gradually stir in eggs and hot milk. Cook over simmering water 20 mintes, stirring occasionally. Remove from heat; stir in vanilla. Cover with plastic wrap. Chill thoroughly before filling cake.

> ### Good to Know
> Chiffon, custard, and cream pies do not freeze well, but all other pies can be Alcoa Wrapped, frozen, and baked when you want them, without thawing; they'll taste fresh as new. Even when you don't wish to freeze a whole or leftover piece of pie, Alcoa Wrap it and it will keep several days in a state of maximum freshness.

Vanilla Cream Pie

Makes 4 to 6 servings

Select a different crumb crust each time (see index).

    ⅔ cup sugar
    ½ cup all-purpose flour
    ½ teaspoon salt
    2 cups milk
    3 egg yolks, lightly beaten
    2 tablespoons each butter or margarine and vanilla
       extract
    1 Crumb Crust (see index)
       Whipped Cream (optional)

You will need: Corning Ware 1-quart saucepan

Combine sugar, flour, and salt in saucepan. Stir in milk. Cook over low heat, stirring until mixture thickens, about 10 minutes. Remove from heat. Stirring constantly, add about half the hot milk mixture to egg yolks; then pour egg yolk mixture into hot mixture. Continue to cook until thickened. Do not let mixture boil. Remove from heat. Stir in butter and vanilla. Cool 10 minutes, then pour into crust. Chill in refrigerator. Garnish with whipped cream, if desired.

Butterscotch Cream Pie

Substitute 1 cup firmly packed light brown sugar for granulated sugar. If desired, stir in ½ cup finely chopped nuts; garnish with shaved chocolate.

Chocolate Cream Pie

Increase sugar to 1 cup and add 2 squares (2 ounces) unsweetened chocolate, cut up, to hot milk mixture.

Coffee-Rum Cream Pie

Add 3 tablespoons instant coffee to hot milk mixture and substitute 1 tablespoon rum for vanilla extract.

Banana Cream Pie

Makes one 9-inch pie

    1½ cups milk
    1 package (6 servings) instant vanilla pudding
    3 medium bananas
    1 9-inch baked Pastry Crust or Vanilla Crumb
       Crust (see index)
       Whipped cream and banana slices (optional)

Put milk and pudding mix into blender container. Cover; blend at medium speed until mixed. Slice bananas into pastry or crumb crust. Pour pudding over bananas. Chill until set. Garnish with whipped cream and banana slices, if desired.

Strawberry-Rhubarb Crisscross Pie (page 41). General Foods

Sour Cream Apple Pie

Makes 8 servings

- 1 unbaked 9-inch pie crust (see index)
- 5 large tart apples
- 1 tablespoon lemon juice
- ¾ cup C & H Granulated Sugar
- ⅓ cup all-purpose flour
- 1 teaspoon ground cinnamon
- ¼ teaspoon *each* ground nutmeg and salt
- ¼ cup butter or margarine, softened
- ½ cup sour cream

Prepare pie crust. Preheat oven to 350°F. Peel apples and cut into thick slices. Arrange slices in overlapping rows in pastry-lined pie pan; sprinkle with lemon juice. Blend sugar, flour, cinnamon, nutmeg, and salt. Cut in butter with pastry blender or fingertips until mixture resembles coarse meal; spoon over apples. Spread sour cream over top. Bake 45 to 50 minutes, until apples are tender.

All-American Apple Pie

Makes 8 servings

- 1 cup C & H Granulated Sugar
- 6 to 7 medium apples, peeled, cored, and sliced ⅛-inch thick
- 1 tablespoon lemon juice
- ¼ teaspoon ground cinnamon
- ⅛ teaspoon ground nutmeg
- 1 unbaked 9-inch Easy No-Fail Pie Crust (see index)
- 1 tablespoon butter or margarine
- 1 egg white (or 1 tablespoon cream or milk)
- 1 tablespoon C & H Granulated Sugar
  Vanilla ice cream or cheddar cheese slices (optional)

Combine 1 cup sugar, the apples, lemon juice, cinnamon, and nutmeg in bowl. Marinate 1 hour, stirring occasionally.

Preheat oven to 450°F. Prepare pastry and line pie pan with half. Drain apples, reserving juice, and arrange in pie pan. Dot with butter and add top crust. Brush top crust with egg white and sprinkle with 1 tablespoon sugar. Cut 4 slits in top crust. Bake pie 15 minutes. Reduce heat to 375°F. and bake 30 minutes longer, or until apples are tender when pierced with knife through slit.

Meanwhile, in small heavy saucepan, cook reserved apple juice over low heat until sugar dissolves. Raise heat and boil until reduced by about half. Remove from heat before juice caramelizes. Pour juice through slits in crust, tilting pie pan to distribute evenly. If filling appears dry, use all the juice; if not, adjust amount accordingly so pie doesn't become soggy. Serve warm or cold with ice cream or cheese, if desired.

Sour Cream Apple Pie. C&H Sugar Company

-Apple-Mince Pie

astry for 2-crust pie (see index)
2 cups mincemeat
1 cup chopped peeled apples
½ cup whole berry cranberry sauce
½ cup currants or raisins

Preheat oven to 425°F. Line 8-inch pie pan with bottom pastry; trim overhang to ½ inch. Combine mincemeat, apples, cranberry sauce, and currants in large bowl; blend well. Roll out dough for top crust; cut into strips with knife or pastry wheel; set aside. Pour filling into pie shell. Weave lattice pattern over filling. Seal and flute edge. Bake 30 minutes, or until golden brown. Cool in pan on wire rack.

Cranberry-Orange Pie

Makes 1 pie
1 can (16 ounces) whole berry cranberry sauce
½ cup firmly packed brown sugar
1 package (3 ounces) orange gelatin
1 cup heavy cream, whipped
½ cup chopped nuts
1 baked 9-inch pie shell (see index)

Combine cranberry and brown sugar in saucepan; cook over moderate heat, stirring frequently, until mixture begins to bubble. Remove from heat. Add gelatin; stir until dissolved. Let stand until as thick as an unbeaten egg white. Fold in whipped cream and nuts. Spoon into pie shell. Refrigerate 3 to 4 hours, or until firm.

Blue Ribbon Cherry Pie

Makes 1 pie
Pastry for 2-crust pie (see index)
1 cup sugar
3 tablespoons cornstarch
⅛ teaspoon salt
1 can (16 ounces) cherries, drained; reserve ½ cup juice
¼ teaspoon red food coloring
1 tablespoon butter or margarine
¼ teaspoon almond extract

Line 8-inch pie pan with bottom pastry; trim overhang to ½ inch. Combine sugar, cornstarch, and salt in 2-quart saucepan. Add cherries, reserved juice, and food coloring; cook over moderate heat until thick, stirring constantly. Remove from heat. Add butter and almond extract. Let stand until cool. Roll out dough for top crust; cut into strips with knife or pastry wheel; set aside. Preheat oven to 425°F. Pour filling into pie shell. Weave lattice pattern over filling. Seal and flute

edge. Bake 10 minutes. Reduce oven temperature to 350°F. Bake 35 minutes, or until golden brown and juices begin to bubble. Cool in pan on wire rack.

Fresh Peach Pie

Makes 1 pie
Pastry for 2-crust pie (see index)
3 cups sliced, peeled fresh peaches
¾ to 1 cup sugar
¼ cup Martha White All-Purpose Flour
½ teaspoon ground cinnamon
Dash salt
1 tablespoon butter

Line 8-inch pie pan with bottom pastry; trim overhang to ½ inch. Roll out dough for top crust; set aside. Preheat oven to 425°F. Place peaches in large bowl. Combine sugar, flour, cinnamon, and salt in small bowl. Sprinkle sugar mixture over peaches; toss lightly to mix. Arrange peaches in pie shell. Dot with butter. Cover with top crust. Cut slits in top to allow steam to escape. Seal and flute edge. Bake 35 to 40 minutes, or until golden brown and juices begin to bubble. Cool in pan on wire rack.

Fresh Blueberry Pie

Prepare pastry and filling as for Fresh Peach Pie, substituting 3 cups fresh blueberries and adding 2 teaspoons lemon juice.

Key Lime Pie

Makes one 9-inch pie
1 package (4 servings) lime-flavored gelatin
Rind of ¼ lime, cut up
½ cup boiling water
½ cup lime juice
2 eggs, separated
1 can (14 ounces) sweetened condensed milk
1 teaspoon aromatic bitters (optional)
1 9-inch baked Pastry Crust or Graham Cracker Crust (see index)

Put gelatin and lime rind into blender container. Add boiling water. Cover; blend at medium speed until gelatin is dissolved and rind is finely chopped. Add lime juice and egg yolks. Cover; blend at medium speed until thoroughly mixed. Add condensed milk and bitters. Cover; blend at medium speed until mixed. Beat egg whites with electric mixer until stiff but not dry. Fold gently into lime mixture. Turn into crust. Chill until set.

Key Lime Tarts

Substitute individual tarts for Pastry Crust or Graham Cracker Crust. Proceed as for Key Lime Pie.

Decorating Pies

Top Crusts

Jewel top: Using your fingers, moisten the top crust—after it is in place—with a little water. Sprinkle it evenly with sugar. If you're feeling festive, use colored sugar in a color compatible with the filling.

Egg-wash top: Beat together 1 whole egg and 1 tablespoon of milk, or 1 egg yolk and 2 teaspoons of milk or cream. Using a pastry brush, paint over the top crust. If anyone asks you, this is dorure, the easy egg-wash French chefs use to give their pastries a richly golden glaze.

Strip top I: Roll out as directed, and cut the pastry in ½-inch strips with a small, sharp knife or with a fluted pastry wheel. Lay one strip across the top of the pie, then a second at right angles to it, lightly moistening the point where they meet with cold water. Continue to add strips, moistening the center each time, until you have a pattern of wheel spokes.

Strip top II: Roll out and cut the pastry as above. Put the first two strips in place as above. Fold a strip into a wedge shape and position it on one quarter of the pie, leaving a ½-inch space on each side between it and the cross strips. Repeat with three more strips. Then form smaller wedges and place within the first four, again allowing about ½ inch of space on each side.

Spiral top: Roll out and cut the pastry as above. Piece the strips together at the ends to make one long, continuous strip. Moisten the joints with cold water so that they adhere. Work slowly and gently— if you've made a good crust, it's also a delicate one. Twist one end of the strip and put it in place in the center of the pie. Twisting as you go, work the strip out from the center, going round and round to form a spiral.

Lattice top I: Roll out the pastry and cut it into ½-inch strips with a knife or fluted pastry wheel. Lay half the strips over the filling, spaced about 1 inch apart. Lay the remaining strips at right angles to the first set of strips, forming a square or diamond lattice pattern. Result, an unwoven lattice top.

Lattice top II: As directed above, lay half the strips evenly over the filling. Fold every other strip halfway back on itself. Place a cross strip over the center of the pie at right angles to the original strips. Bring the folded strips back over it. Fold back the alternate strips, and place another cross strip on the pie. Continue until one side of the pie is complete, alternating folded-back strips each time a cross strip is added, then repeat, starting from the center, for the other side of the pie. Result, a woven lattice top.

Decorative Edges

Fluted rim: Fold the overhanging edge of the pastry under so that it stands up even with the edge of the pie plate. Put the forefinger of one hand on the inside rim of the crust, and the thumb and forefinger of the other hand on the outside at the same point. Pinch the pastry. Move on and repeat all around the pie. For sharper points, pinch each one a second time.

Scalloped rim: Fold the overhanging pastry under to make a stand-up edge. Gently press the bowl of a measuring teaspoon on the inside of the rim; with your thumb and forefinger on the outside at the same spot, shape the pastry around the end of the spoon. Repeat all around the pie.

Double-scallop rim: Trim the pastry even with the edge of the pie plate. Using a teaspoon or after-dinner coffee spoon and working from the outside toward the center, gently press a series of scallops into the pastry with the tip of the spoon. Go once around the pie, then go around a second time, pressing the second set of scallops between the first set and in the opposite direction so that they reach to the edge of the plate.

Braided rim: For this you'll need extra pastry—a double-crust for a single-crust pie, a recipe and a half for a double-crust pie. Trim the bottom pastry even with the edge of the pie plate. Roll out the extra pastry and cut it into ¼-inch-wide strips. Braid three of these strips; fasten additional strips to the ends of first three with cold water, and continue to braid. Repeat until you have a braided strip long enough to encircle the pie. Moisten the rim with water and put the braid in place; join the ends neatly and press the braid gently to fasten it in place.

Libby's Famous Pumpkin Pie

Makes one 9-inch pie

- 2 eggs, lightly beaten
- 1 can (16 ounces) Libby's Solid Pack Pumpkin
- ¾ cup sugar
- ½ teaspoon salt
- 1 teaspoon ground cinnamon
- ½ teaspoon ground ginger
- ¼ teaspoon ground cloves
- 1 can (12 to 13 ounces) evaporated milk or 1½ cups half and half
- 1 9-inch unbaked homemade pie shell with high fluted edge (see index)

Preheat oven to 425°F. Combine filling ingredients in order given; pour into pie shell. Bake 15 minutes. Reduce temperature to 350°F. Bake an additional 45 minutes, or until knife inserted near center comes out clean. Cool; garnish, if desired, with whipped topping.

Variation

If regular 9-inch frozen pie shells are substituted, recipe fills two. Slightly thaw pie shells while combining other ingredients. Pour filling into pie shells. Preheat oven and cookie sheet to 375°F. Bake on cookie sheet 45 minutes or until pies test done with a knife as noted above.

Libby's Famous Pumpkin Pie. Libby's The Great Pumpkin Cookbook

Pie Toppers

For a delightful change of pace, crown your next pumpkin pie, or other favorite, with one of these delectable toppings.

Peanut Crunch Topping

Crush enough peanut brittle with a rolling pin to make 1 cup; sprinkle over cooled pumpkin pie before serving.

Zesty Orange Glaze

In saucepan, combine ½ cup sugar and 2 tablespoons cornstarch; mix well. Gradually add ¾ cup orange juice. Cook until clear and thickened, stirring occasionally. Add 2 tablespoons thinly shredded orange peel. Cool slightly. Spoon over cooled pumpkin pie. Chill until serving time.

Golden Walnut Crunch Topping

Mix 1 cup coarsely chopped walnuts with ⅔ cup firmly packed brown sugar. Drizzle with 3 tablespoons melted butter or margarine; stir until mixture is uniformly moistened. Sprinkle over cooled pumpkin pie. Broil about 5 inches from heat for 1 or 2 minutes, or until topping is bubbly. Cool; garnish with whipped topping and extra walnut halves, if desired.

Crunchy Pecan Topping

In small bowl, combine 1 cup chopped pecans, ⅔ cup firmly packed brown sugar, and 3 tablespoons melted butter or margarine. Sprinkle mixture over baked, cooled pumpkin pie. Broil, about 5 inches from heat, 2 minutes, or until topping is bubbly. Cool. Garnish, if desired, with whipped topping or whipped cream and additional pecans.

Honey Blossom Topping

Drizzle a thin stream of orange blossom or clover honey over cooled pumpkin pie.

Coconut Cream Topping

In small bowl, beat 2 packages (3 ounces each) softened cream cheese with ¼ cup sugar and 1 egg yolk until smooth. Carefully spread over ·pumpkin pie which has been baked only half of total required baking time. Sprinkle with ⅓ cup flaked coconut. Continue baking remaining time, or until center is set. Cool. Garnish with toasted slivered almonds.

Sesame Cream Garnish

Spread 1 tablespoon sesame seeds in shallow pan. Toast at 400°F. about 3 minutes, or until nicely browned. Fold sesame seeds, 2 tablespoons powdered sugar, and 1 teaspoon rum flavoring into 2 cups whipped cream. Spoon over cooled pumpkin pie.

Almond Cream Topping

Combine 2 cups whipped topping with 1 tablespoon almond-flavored liqueur; mix well. Chill. Spoon over cooled pumpkin pie. Top with toasted, sliced natural almonds.

> **Q.** *My pies sometimes crack or pull away from the crust. How can I avoid this?*
>
> **A.** Positioning your oven rack too close to the top heating unit may cause your pie filling to crack as it bakes and to settle slightly on cooling. This may cause the filling to "pull away" from the crust. Another reason for "pulling away" from the crust is overbaking. If this is the case, try reducing your pie baking time by 5 to 10 minutes.

Pecan Pumpkin Pie

Makes one 9-inch pie

- 3 eggs, lightly beaten
- 1 cup sugar
- ½ cup dark corn syrup
- 1 cup Libby's Solid Pack Pumpkin
- 1 tablespoon vanilla extract
- 1 cup pecan halves
- 1 9-inch unbaked pie shell (see index)

Preheat oven to 375°F. Combine first five ingredients; mix well. Gently stir in pecan halves. Pour into pie shell. Bake 55 to 60 minutes, or until knife inserted near center comes out clean.

Northwest Pumpkin Apple Pie

Makes one 9-inch pie

- 3 medium apples, pared and cut into thin slices
- 1 teaspoon lemon juice
- ⅔ cup sugar, divided
- 2 teaspoons all-purpose flour
- 1 9-inch unbaked pie shell with high fluted edge (see index)
- 2 eggs, lightly beaten
- 1 cup Libby's Solid Pack Pumpkin
- 1 can (5⅓ ounces) evaporated milk
- 2 tablespoons butter or margarine, melted
- ½ teaspoon ground nutmeg
- 1 tablespoon cinnamon sugar

Preheat oven to 400°F. In bowl, toss apples with lemon juice, ½ cup sugar, and flour. In pie shell, arrange slices in overlapping circles; cover loosely with foil. Bake 20 minutes. Meanwhile, prepare custard mixture: in medium bowl, combine eggs, pumpkin, remaining ⅓ cup sugar, evaporated milk, butter, and nutmeg; mix well. Remove foil from pie shell. Carefully pour custard mixture over apples. Continue baking 10 minutes; sprinkle with cinnamon sugar (a mixture of 1 tablespoon sugar and ⅛ teaspoon ground cinnamon). Continue baking 10 minutes, or until custard is almost set. Cool on wire rack at least 2 hours before slicing. Serve warm or cool.

Note: Use any favorite baking apple, or, for sweeter flavor, use Red Delicious apples.

Pecan Pumpkin Pie; Northwest Pumpkin Apple Pie.
Libby's The Great Pumpkin Cookbook

Lemon Chiffon Pie

Makes one 9-inch pie

- 1 baked 9-inch pie shell (see index)
- 1 tablespoon plain gelatin
- ¼ cup cold water
- 4 egg yolks, beaten
- 1 cup sugar
- ½ cup lemon juice
- 1 teaspoon grated lemon rind
- 4 egg whites, unbeaten

Stir gelatin into cold water; set aside. Combine egg yolks, ½ cup of the sugar, and lemon juice and rind in top of double boiler. Cook over boiling water, stirring constantly until thickened. Add gelatin; stir until dissolved; remove from heat. Chill until slightly thickened. Beat egg whites until frothy; add remaining ½ cup sugar gradually, beating until stiff. Fold in chilled mixture. Pour into baked shell; chill until set. To serve, spread with whipped cream.

> To chill chiffon pies quickly, place saucepan containing filling in a large pan or bowl filled with ice cubes and water. Stir filling until mixture begins to thicken and mounds when spooned. Remove from chilled water immediately and quickly fold in any remaining ingredients.

Fruit Chiffon Pie

Makes one 9-inch pie

- 1 tablespoon (1 envelope) unflavored gelatin
- ¼ cup cold water
- 3 eggs, separated
- ½ cup sugar
- ¼ teaspoon salt
- ¼ cup orange juice
- 2 tablespoons lemon juice
- 1 tablespoon grated orange peel (optional)
- 1 can (12 ounces) Solo Apricot or Prune Filling
- 6 tablespoons sugar
- 1 baked 9-inch pie shell (see index)

Soften gelatin in cold water. Beat egg yolks in a saucepan. Add ½ cup sugar, salt, orange juice, and lemon juice and beat well. Cook over low heat, stirring constantly, until mixture is thick and smooth. Remove from heat; add gelatin and stir until gelatin is dissolved. When mixture is cool, stir in orange peel and filling. Beat egg whites until stiff. Beat in 6 tablespoons sugar, 1 tablespoon at a time, beating well after each addition. Fold egg whites into cooled fruit mixture. Blend lightly. Turn into baked pie shell. Refrigerate to chill thoroughly before serving.

Good Idea: Any Solo fruit filling can be used in this pie.

Think-Spring Chiffon Pie

Makes 8 servings

- 1 envelope Knox Unflavored Gelatine
- ½ cup sugar, divided
- 2 eggs, separated
- 1 cup milk
- ¼ cup cream sherry
- 1 cup pint) heavy cream, whipped
  Macaroon Crumb Crust (recipe follows)

In medium saucepan, mix unflavored gelatine with ¼ cup sugar. Beat egg yolks with milk and blend into gelatine mixture. Stir over low heat until gelatine is completely dissolved, about 5 to 8 minutes. Pour into large bowl; stir in sherry. Chill, stirring occasionally, until mixture mounds slightly when dropped from spoon.

In medium bowl, beat egg whites until soft peaks form; gradually add remaining ¼ cup sugar and beat until stiff. Fold egg whites, then whipped cream into gelatine mixture. Turn into prepared Macaroon Crumb Crust and chill until firm. Garnish with additional whipped cream and toasted coconut, if desired.

Macaroon Crumb Crust

- 1½ cups crisp macaroon cookie crumbs
- ¼ cup butter or margarine, softened

Preheat oven to 375°F. In small bowl, combine crumbs and butter; press into a 9-inch pie plate. Bake 8 minutes; cool, then chill.

Fried Fruit Pies

Makes 6 pies

- 1 cup cooked dried fruit (such as apricots, peaches, apples, pears, prunes, or raisins), drained
- 1 teaspoon lemon juice
- ½ cup sugar
- ½ teaspoon ground nutmeg
- ½ teaspoon ground cinnamon
  Pastry for 1-crust pie; use ¼ cup vegetable shortening (see index)
  Oil for deep-fat frying

Combine fruit, lemon juice, sugar, nutmeg, and cinnamon in small bowl; set aside. Roll out pastry on floured board or pastry cloth to ¼-inch thickness. Use sharp knife to cut into six 5½-inch rounds. (Use saucer as guide for size.) Place 2 to 3 tablespoons fruit mixture on one-half of each round. Fold pastry in half over filling; pinch edges to seal. Refrigerate 1 hour. Preheat oil in deep fryer or large skillet to 375°F. Cook 8 to 10 minutes, turning to brown evenly.

Strawberry-Rhubarb Crisscross Pie

Makes one 9-inch pie
  1¼ cups sugar
  ¼ cup Minute Tapioca
  ¼ teaspoon salt
  2 cups fresh strawberry halves
  2 cups sliced fresh rhubarb
    Pastry for 2-crust 9-inch pie (see index)
  1 tablespoon butter or margarine
  1 egg, lightly beaten (optional)

Combine sugar, tapioca, salt, and fruits. Let stand about 15 minutes. Meanwhile, roll out half the pastry very thin (less than ⅛ inch thick). Line a 9-inch pie pan. Trim pastry at edge. Roll out remaining pastry very thin and cut into ½-inch strips. Fill pie shell with fruit mixture. Dot with butter. Moisten edge of bottom crust. Adjust pastry strips in lattice pattern across top of filling; press ends of strips against edge of bottom crust. Flute edge. Brush top crust with egg, if desired. Bake at 425°F. for 45 minutes, or until syrup boils with heavy bubbles that do not burst.

Maggie's Lemon Pie

Makes one 9-inch pie
  1 9-inch baked pie shell
  2 cups sugar
  4 tablespoons cornstarch
  5 tablespoons all-purpose flour
  ½ teaspoon salt
  2 cups boiling water
  4 tablespoons butter or margarine
  4 egg yolks, beaten
  2 lemons, juice and grated rind

Combine sugar, cornstarch, flour, and salt in top of double boiler. Add boiling water slowly, stirring constantly; add butter. Cook over boiling water 30 minutes until clear and thickened; stir. Add egg yolks, lemon juice and rind; blend; cook 10 minutes longer, stirring twice; cool. Pour into baked shell. Cover with Meringue. Bake 8 to 10 minutes at 400°F. until delicately browned.

Sour Cream Pie

Makes 6 to 8 servings
  2 eggs
  1 cup sour cream
  1 cup seeded raisins
  ⅔ cup sugar
  1½ teaspoons ground cinnamon
  ¼ teaspoon salt
  ¾ cup pecans
  1 unbaked 9-inch pastry shell (see index)

Preheat oven to 450°F. Put first 6 ingredients into blender; cover and process at Chop. When well mixed, turn off blender and add pecans; chop briefly. Pour mixture into an unbaked pie shell. Bake 15 minutes; lower oven temperature to 350° F. and bake 30 minutes, or until set.

Lemon Mist Cheese Pie

Makes 6 to 8 servings
  3 eggs, separated
  1½ cups creamed cottage cheese
  ⅔ cup light cream
  3 tablespoons lemon juice
  1 teaspoon grated lemon rind
  ⅔ cup sugar
  1 tablespoon all-purpose flour
  ¼ teaspoon salt
  1 unbaked 9-inch pie shell (see index)

Preheat oven to 450°F. Put egg yolks in large bowl and egg whites in small bowl of Sunbeam Mixmaster Mixer. Turn Dial to high and beat egg whites until stiff but not dry. Set aside. With same beaters, beat egg yolks on high. Add cottage cheese, cream, lemon juice and lemon rind and beat at medium-low until thoroughly mixed. Add sugar, flour, and salt, and continue to beat until well mixed. With Dial set at lower speed, fold into egg whites gently. Pour mixture into pie shell. Bake 10 minutes; reduce heat to 325°F. and bake 35 to 40 minutes, or until a knife inserted in the center comes out clean.

Tips for Perfect Pies

- When making pastry dough, work quickly, handle the dough as little as possible, and avoid overmixing.
- Use a pastry blender or 2 knives to cut shortening into flour.
- A pastry cloth and stockinet-covered rolling pin are recommended for rolling out dough. Since less flour is used to roll the dough out, a more flaky and tender pastry is produced.
- Use the proper size pie pan for the recipe. If the size is not shown on the bottom, measure across from inside of rim.
- Use dull metal or glass pie pans for best results.
- To ensure a tender pastry, chill dough in refrigerator before rolling out, especially if room is warm.
- Preheat oven to temperature called for in recipe.
- To prevent pie juice from running over pie pan, place a small funnel or 4-inch piece of uncooked macaroni in center of pie before baking.

Tangy Lemon Pie

Makes 6 to 8 servings
   1 **partially baked 9-inch Butter Pie Crust (see index)**
1½ **cups C & H Granulated Sugar**
      Grated rind from 2 lemons
   ⅓ **cup lemon juice**
   ⅓ **cup water**
   6 **eggs**
   1 **large lemon**
      Sweetened whipped cream

Prepare Butter Pie Crust. Preheat oven to 375°F. In bowl, mix sugar, lemon rind and juice, water, and eggs. Pour into partially baked crust. Peel lemon, removing all white pith. Cut into thin slices with a serrated knife and remove seeds. Arrange lemon slices on top of filling. Bake 30 to 35 minutes until filling is puffed and browned and a knife inserted in center comes out clean. Serve hot or cold with whipped cream.

Grasshopper Pie

Makes one 9-inch pie

Choco-Nut Crust
   1 **6-ounce package (1 cup) Nestlé Toll House Semi-Sweet Chocolate Morsels**
   1 **tablespoon vegetable shortening**
1½ **cups finely chopped nuts**

Line a 9-inch pie pan with foil. Over hot (not boiling) water, melt Nestlé Toll House Semi-Sweet Chocolate Morsels and shortening. Add chopped nuts; mix well. Spread evenly on bottom and side (not over rim) of prepared pie pan. Chill in refrigerator until firm (about 1 hour). Lift shell out of pan; peel off foil. Replace shell in pan or place on serving plate; chill in refrigerator.

Filling
   ½ **pound marshmallows (about 40 large)**
   ⅓ **cup milk**
   ¼ **teaspoon salt**
   3 **tablespoons green crème de menthe**
   3 **tablespoons white crème de cacao**
1½ **cups heavy cream, whipped**

Over hot (not boiling) water, combine marshmallows, milk, and salt; heat until marshmallows melt. Remove from heat. Add liqueurs; stir until blended. Chill in refrigerator, stirring occasionally until slightly thickened (about 30 to 45 minutes). Gently fold in whipped cream. Pour half the filling into prepared Choco-Nut Crust; spoon on remaining filling, forming a design. Garnish with Chocolate Curls (see index), if desired. Chill until firm (about 1 hour).

Pink Peppermint Pie. The Nestlé Company, Inc.

Variation
Substitute the following for the crème de menthe and crème de cacao. Garnish as indicated.
   Substitute: 3 tablespoons almond liqueur. Garnish: Toasted slivered almonds.
   Substitute: ¼ cup coffee liqueur and ¼ cup vodka. Garnish: Chopped Nestlé Toll House Semi-Sweet Chocolate Morsels.
   Substitute: 3 tablespoons orange liqueur; 1 teaspoon grated orange rind. Garnish: Orange rind slivers.

Grasshopper Tarts

Makes 10 tarts
   1 **6-ounce package (1 cup) Nestlé Toll House Semi-Sweet Chocolate Morsels**
   1 **tablespoon vegetable shortening**
1½ **cups finely chopped nuts**
      Grasshopper Pie filling or flavor variation (see previous recipe)

Line 10 tart or muffin cups with foil. Over hot (not boiling) water, melt Nestlé Toll House Semi-Sweet Chocolate Morsels and shortening. Add chopped nuts; mix well. Spoon 2 tablespoons mixture into prepared cups; spread evenly on bottom and up sides, using a spatula or spoon. Chill in refrigerator until firm (about 1 hour). Peel foil liners from chocolate cups. Place on serving plate. Using a pastry bag fitted with a decorative tip, pipe Grasshopper Pie filling (or flavor variation) into each chocolate cup. Chill until firm (about 1 hour).

Pink Peppermint Pie

Makes one 9-inch pie
   1 **9-inch baked pie shell (see index)**
   1 **6-ounce package (1 cup) Nestlé Toll House Semi-Sweet Chocolate Morsels**
   ⅓ **cup milk**
2½ **cups miniature marshmallows**
   ½ **cup milk**
   ¼ **teaspoon salt**
   ¼ **teaspoon peppermint extract**
   ⅛ **teaspoon red food coloring**
   1 **cup heavy cream, whipped**

Over hot (not boiling) water, combine Nestlé Toll House Semi-Sweet Chocolate Morsels and ⅓ cup milk; heat until morsels melt and mixture is smooth. Remove from heat; set aside. Over hot (not boiling) water, combine marshmallows, ½ cup milk, the salt, peppermint extract, and food coloring; heat, stirring constantly, until marshmallows melt and mixture is smooth. Transfer to a large bowl; chill in refrigerator until slightly thickened (about 45 to 60 minutes). Stir until smooth. Gently fold in whipped cream. Spread half the peppermint mixture into pie shell. Dollop with half the chocolate mixture. With a knife, swirl chocolate mixture in a figure-eight pattern. Repeat procedure with remaining peppermint and chocolate mixtures. Chill until firm (about 2 hours).

Easy Brandy Alexander Pie

Makes 8 servings
   2 **envelopes Knox Unflavored Gelatine**
   ¾ **cup half and half or light cream, divided**
   ¼ **cup sugar**
   3 **tablespoons brandy**
   3 **tablespoons crème de cacao**
   1 **cup ice cubes (6 to 8)**
      Chocolate-Coconut Crust (recipe follows) or
      9-inch Graham Cracker Crust (see index)

In a 5-cup blender, sprinkle unflavored gelatine over cold half and half. Let stand 3 to 4 minutes. Add hot half and half and process at low speed until gelatine is completed dissolved, about 2 minutes. Add sugar, brandy, and crème de cacao. Add ice cubes, 1 at a time; process at high speed until ice is melted. Pour into prepared Chocolate-Coconut Crust and chill until firm.

Chocolate-Coconut Crust

   1 **square (1 ounce) melted unsweetened chocolate**
   2 **tablespoons milk**
   2 **cup flaked coconut**
   ½ **cup confectioners sugar**

In medium bowl, combine chocolate and milk; stir in coconut and sugar. Press into 9-inch pie pan; chill.

Christmas Eggnog Pie

Makes one 9-inch pie
   1 **baked 9-inch Graham Cracker Crust (see index)**
   1 **tablespoon plain gelatin**
   ¼ **cup cold water**
   3 **egg yolks, beaten**
   1½ **cups milk**
   ½ **cup sugar**
   ⅛ **teaspoon salt**
   4 **egg whites**
   ¼ **teaspoon ground nutmeg**
   1 **cup heavy cream**
   2 **tablespoons sugar**
   2 **teaspoons rum**
   ½ **square (½ ounce) unsweetened chocolate**

Stir gelatin into cold water; set aside. Combine egg yolks, milk, ¼ cup of the sugar, and salt in top of double boiler. Cook over hot (not boiling) water, stirring constantly until mixture coats spoon. Add gelatin; stir until dissolved; remove from heat. Chill until slightly thickened. Beat egg whites until frothy; add remaining ¼ cup sugar gradually, beating until stiff. Fold in chilled mixture. Pour into shell; sprinkle nutmeg over top; chill until set. To serve: whip cream; fold in sugar and rum; spread over filling; grate chocolate over top.

Ingredients for pies should be at room temperature unless otherwise specified. This is particularly true for butter, eggs and liquids. Eggs separate more easily when cold, but allow them to come to room temperature before using.

Apricot Trifle Pie

Makes 1 pie
   1 **envelope Knox Unflavored Gelatine**
   ¼ **cup sugar**
   2 **eggs, separated**
   ⅔ **cup milk**
   2 **tablespoons cream sherry**
   12 **ladyfingers, split, or 24 strips (1x3 inches) pound cake**
   ½ **cup apricot preserves**
   1½ **cups whipping or heavy cream, whipped**
   1 **can (17 ounces) apricot halves, drained and chopped (reserve 8 halves)**

In medium saucepan, mix unflavored gelatine with 2 tablespoons sugar; blend in egg yolks beaten with milk. Let stand 1 minute. Stir over low heat until gelatine is completely dissolved, about 5 minutes. Stir in sherry. Pour into large bowl and chill, stirring occasionally, until mixture mounds slightly when dropped from spoon.

Meanwhile, cut one end off enough ladyfingers to stand, rounded side out, around side of 9-inch pie plate. Arrange remaining ladyfingers and ends, rounded side down, on bottom of pie plate. In small saucepan, heat apricot preserves; strain and reserve half. Brush remainder over ladyfingers.

In medium bowl, beat egg whites until soft peaks form; gradually add remaining sugar and beat until stiff. Fold egg whites, then 2 cups whipped cream and chopped apricots into gelatine mixture. Turn into prepared pan. Chill until firm. Garnish with remaining whipped cream and reserved apricot halves brushed with reserved preserves.

Peanut Butter Pie

Makes one 9-inch pie

- ½ cup sifted confectioners sugar
- ¼ cup chunky peanut butter
- 1 baked 9-inch pie shell (see index)
- ⅔ cup sugar, divided
- 2 tablespoons cornstarch
- 1 tablespoon Martha White All-Purpose Flour
- ¼ teaspoon salt
- 2¼ cups milk, divided
- 3 egg yolks, lightly beaten
- 1 tablespoon butter or margarine
- 1 teaspoon vanilla extract
  Perfect Meringue (see index)

Combine confectioners sugar and peanut butter in small bowl; blend well. Sprinkle half of peanut butter mixture over bottom of pie shell. Combine ⅓ cup sugar, cornstarch, flour, and salt in small bowl; blend thoroughly. Add ¼ cup milk and egg yolks; blend well; set aside. Combine remaining ⅓ cup sugar and 2 cups milk in saucepan. Bring to a boil over medium-high heat, stirring constantly. Remove from heat. Slowly stir about 1 cup hot milk mixture into egg yolk mixture; return all to saucepan. Bring to a boil over medium-high heat, stirring constantly. Boil 4 minutes, or until thickened. Remove from heat. Stir in butter and vanilla. Let stand until cool. Preheat oven to 400°F. Pour filling into pie shell. Spoon mounds of Perfect Meringue around outer edge of filling. Spread carefully around edge, being certain that meringue touches inner edge of crust. Spoon remaining meringue over center of filling; spread to border. Sprinkle remaining peanut butter mixture over meringue. Bake 8 to 10 minutes, or until peaks are golden brown. Cool in pan on wire rack away from draft.

Almond Crown Pie

Makes one 9-inch pie

- 3 eggs
- 1 cup firmly packed brown sugar
- 1 cup light corn syrup
- 1 teaspoon vanilla extract
- ½ can (6¼ ounces) Solo Almond Filling
- ½ cup whole blanched almonds
- 1 unbaked 9-inch pie shell (see index)
- ½ cup slivered blanched almonds

Preheat oven to 350°F. Beat eggs and brown sugar together until thoroughly blended and foamy. Beat in corn syrup, vanilla, and almond filling. Form a crown inside pie shell by placing whole almonds on their sides around the edge. Carefully pour filling mixture into shell. Sprinkle with slivered almonds. Bake 1 hour, or until a knife inserted in center of pie comes out clean. Cool; refrigerate to chill thoroughly before cutting.

Jean Klever's Quick Pecan Pie

Makes 8 to 10 servings

- 1 9-inch frozen, unbaked pastry shell (see index)
- 3 eggs
- ¼ cup butter, melted
- 2 cups dark brown sugar
- ¼ cup milk
- 1 teaspoon vanilla extract
- ¾ to 1 cup pecans
  Sweetened whipped cream

Remove pastry shell from freezer. Break eggs into a bowl, add melted butter, sugar, milk, and vanilla. Beat with electric mixer or spoon until well combined. Add pecans. Pour into shell. Bake in 325°F. oven for 50 minutes. Cool and serve topped with a little slightly sweetened whipped cream.

Nuts

Pecans: When you buy pecans in the shell, look for unblemished shells and check to see that the nuts inside do not rattle freely—a sign of old age. Store in a cool, dry place up to 6 months, even longer in the refrigerator. Shelled nuts in vacuum cans or jars will keep almost indefinitely until opened, when they should be refrigerated; those in ordinary cans and bags should also be refrigerated after opening.

To blanch almonds: Cover shelled almonds with boiling water and let stand about 3 minutes. At this point, the brown skins should slip off easily between the fingers. Remove from the water one at a time, slip off skins, dry on absorbent paper.

To slice or sliver the nuts (blanched or not), use a very sharp knife and keep a sharp eye on your fingers. Or, more conveniently, buy the almonds already cut. To chop, use the blender or a nut chopper. To grate, use a small drum-type grater made especially for nuts and dry cheese.

To toast almonds: Spread the chopped or slivered nuts on a baking sheet, bake at 350°F. until they are a shade of brown that suits you, stirring frequently.

Delta Pecan Pie

Makes 1 pie

- 3 eggs, lightly beaten
- 1 cup sugar
- 1 cup dark corn syrup
- 2 tablespoons butter or margarine, melted
- ¼ teaspoon salt
- 1 teaspoon vanilla extract
- 1 cup pecans
- 1 unbaked 9-inch pie shell (see index), chilled

Preheat oven to 375°F. Combine eggs, sugar, corn syrup, butter, salt, and vanilla in bowl; blend until smooth. Stir in pecans. Pour into pie shell. Bake 40 to 45 minutes, or until filling is set. Cool in pan on wire rack.

Blue Ribbon Cherry Pie (page 36). Martha White Foods

Q. *Why do my pies sometimes bake unevenly?*
A. If your oven temperature is not accurate or the oven rack you place your pies on is not level, your pies may bake unevenly. Pies should be placed on the middle or lower racks in the oven to prevent over-browning of the top. The top of the oven is always the hottest area.

Toll House Walnut Pie

Makes one 9-inch pie

  2 eggs
  ½ cup all-purpose flour
  ½ cup sugar
  ½ cup firmly packed brown sugar
  1 cup butter, melted and cooled to room temperature
  1 6-ounce package (1 cup) Nestlé Toll House Semi-Sweet Chocolate Morsels
  1 cup chopped walnuts
  1 9-inch unbaked pie shell (see index)
    Whipped cream or ice cream (optional)

Preheat oven to 325°F. In a large bowl, beat eggs until foamy; beat in flour, sugar, and brown sugar until well blended. Blend in melted butter. Stir in Nestlé Toll House Semi-Sweet Chocolate Morsels and walnuts. Pour into pie shell. Bake 1 hour. Serve warm with whipped cream or ice cream, if desired.

Chocolate Velvet Pie

Makes one 9-inch pie

  4 cups miniature marshmallows
  ⅓ cup milk
  2 envelopes (2 ounces) Nestlé Choco-bake Unsweetened Baking Chocolate Flavor
  2 teaspoons grated orange rind
  1 cup heavy cream, whipped
  1 9-inch baked pie shell (see index)
    Whipped cream (optional)
    Chocolate Curls (see index) (optional)

In a medium saucepan, combine marshmallows and milk. Cook, stirring constantly, until marshmallows are melted. Remove from heat. Stir in Nestlé Choco-bake Unsweetened Baking Chocolate Flavor and orange rind; mix well. Transfer to a small bowl; chill until slightly thickened (about 30 minutes). Stir until well blended. Fold in whipped cream. Pour into baked pie shell. Chill until firm (about 1 hour). Garnish with whipped cream and Chocolate Curls, if desired.

Black Bottom Pie

Makes 1 pie

  1 cup sugar, divided
  1½ tablespoons cornstarch
  4 eggs, separated
  2 cups hot milk
  1½ squares (1 ½ ounces) semisweet chocolate, melted
  1 teaspoon vanilla extract
  1 baked 9-inch pie shell (see index)
  1 envelope unflavored gelatin
  ¼ cup cold water
  ¼ teaspoon cream of tartar
  1 tablespoon brandy extract
  1 cup heavy cream
  2 tablespoons shaved chocolate

Combine ½ cup sugar and cornstarch in small bowl; set aside. Place egg yolks in saucepan; beat with electric mixer until lemon colored. Gradually stir in milk. Add sugar mixture. Cook over moderate heat, stirring constantly, until custard coats back of spoon. Pour 1 cup custard into large measuring cup. Stir in chocolate and vanilla. Pour into pie shell. Refrigerate until cool. Dissolve gelatin in cold water. Stir into remaining custard in saucepan. Refrigerate until cool. Place egg whites in small mixing bowl. Add cream of tartar. Beat at low speed of electric mixer until foamy. Add 6 tablespoons sugar, a little at a time, beating until soft peaks form. Gently fold into custard-gelatin mixture. Stir in brandy extract. Pour over chocolate layer in pie shell. Refrigerate until set. Beat cream at high speed of electric mixer in small mixing bowl until stiff peaks form, gradually beating in remaining 2 tablespoons sugar. Garnish pie with sweetened whipped cream and shaved chocolate.

Toll House Walnut Pie (page 46). The Nestlé Company, Inc.

Sweet Cherry Tarts

Makes about 30 tarts

    2 cups all-purpose flour
    ¼ cup sugar
    ¾ cup butter or margarine
    1 egg, lightly beaten
    ½ teaspoon almond extract
    2 packages (3 ounces each) cream cheese, softened
    ¼ cup confectioners sugar
    2 teaspoons milk
    1 can or jar (17 ounces) dark sweet cherries
    1 tablespoon sugar
    5 teaspoons cornstarch
    ¼ teaspoon almond extract

Combine flour and sugar; cut in butter or margarine. Mix in egg and almond extract with fingers until mixture forms a ball. Using a scant tablespoon of dough for each, press into 2-inch round tart pans. Bake at 400° F. 12 to 14 minutes, or until golden brown. Cool.

Beat cream cheese with sugar and milk until light. Place in pastry bag. Pipe about 1 teaspoon mixture into each cooled tart shell. Drain cherries, reserving syrup. Combine sugar and cornstarch in saucepan. Gradually add cherry syrup. Cook over medium heat, stirring constantly, until mixture thickens and boils. Stir in almond extract and cherries. Spoon 1 cherry with a portion of sauce into each tart shell. Chill.

Tangerine Tarts

Makes 8 to 10 tarts

       Pastry for one 9-inch 2-crust pie (see index)
    1½ cups Florida tangerine juice
    1 cup sugar
    3 teaspoons grated tangerine peel
    ⅔ cup unsalted butter or margarine
    8 eggs, beaten
    4 Florida tangerines, peeled and sectioned

On a lightly floured surface, roll dough out ⅛ inch thick. Cut out eight to ten 5-inch circles with a cookie cutter. Press each circle into a 3½-inch fluted tart pan; prick with a fork. Place on a cookie sheet. Bake in a 400°F. oven 10 to 12 minutes, or until lightly browned. Cool on a wire rack. Carefully remove shells from pan, cool thoroughly. In the top of a double boiler over simmering, not boiling, water, combine tangerine juice, sugar, peel, and butter. Stir until sugar dissolves and butter melts. Gradually whisk about 2 cups of the tangerine mixture into beaten eggs, then return mixture to top of double boiler. Stir constantly until mixture thickens. Cover. Chill. Before serving, spoon mixture into tart shells. Top each tart with tangerine sections.

Creamy Raisin-Apple Tart

Makes 8 servings

Crust

    ½ cup butter or margarine, softened
    ¼ cup sugar
    1 teaspoon grated lemon peel
    ½ teaspoon almond extract
    1 cup all-purpose flour

Cream the butter with the sugar until smooth. Add the lemon peel, almond extract, and flour and mix well. Pat onto the bottom and 1 inch up the side of a greased 9-inch springform pan. Set aside.

Filling and Topping

    1 package (8 ounces) cream cheese, at room
          temperature
    ½ cup sugar, divided
    1 egg
    1 tablespoon lemon juice
    ½ teaspoon almond extract
    ¾ Sun-Maid® Seedless Raisins
    2 tart cooking apples, peeled and chopped
    ¼ cup slivered almonds
    ¼ teaspoon ground cinnamon
    ¼ teaspoon ground ginger

To make filling and topping: Preheat the oven to 375°F. Beat the cream cheese, ¼ cup of the sugar, and the egg, lemon juice, and almond extract until smooth. Stir in the raisins and spoon the mixture over the crust in the springform pan. Toss the ¼ cup remaining sugar with the apples and the remaining ingredients. Spread the mixture evenly over the cream cheese filling. Bake for 45 minutes, or until the apples are tender and the filling is set. Cool in the pan on a wire rack. Remove the side from the pan and serve the tart cut into wedges.

Solo Mini Tarts

Makes about 2½ dozen tarts

    1 package (3 ounces) cream cheese, softened
    ½ cup butter or margarine
    1 cup all-purpose flour
    1 can (12 or 12½ ounces) Solo filling, any desired
          flavor

Preheat oven to 400°F. Combine cream cheese and butter or margarine and blend well. Add flour and blend well. Shape dough into 1-inch balls and place in 1¾-inch muffin pan cups. Press dough with fingers to cover sides and bottom of each cup. Bake 15 minutes, or until lightly browned and done. Cool shells in pan. When cool, remove from pans and fill with desired flavor of filling. Top with a dollop of flavored whipped cream, if desired.

Chiffon Pumpkin Tarts

Makes 8 servings

- ¾ cup firmly packed brown sugar
- 1 envelope unflavored gelatin
- 1¼ teaspoon ground cinnamon
- ½ teaspoon ground nutmeg
- ¼ teaspoon ground ginger
  Dash salt
- 1 can (16 ounces) Libby's Solid Pack Pumpkin
- ½ cup milk
- ½ teaspoon vanilla extract
- 1 cup heavy cream, whipped
- 8 baked tart shells, cooled

In saucepan, combine sugar, gelatin, spices, and salt; mix well. Stir in pumpkin and milk. Cook over low heat, stirring constantly, until boiling and thickened, about 10 minutes. Remove from heat; stir in vanilla. Chill 1 hour. Fold in whipped cream. Spoon into tart shells. Chill until firm. Garnish with coconut, toasted pecans or slivered crystallized ginger, if desired.

Raisin Tartlets

Makes 2 dozen tartlets

- Cream Cheese Pastry (recipe follows)
- 1 egg, beaten
- ¾ cup firmly packed light brown sugar
- 1 tablespoon butter, softened
- ½ teaspoon grated orange peel
- ½ teaspoon vanilla extract
  Dash salt
- ⅓ cup chopped Sun-Maid® Puffed Seeded Muscat Raisins
- ⅓ cup semisweet chocolate pieces
- ⅓ cup chopped pecans

Divide the pastry into 24 pieces. Chill dough. Press into 1¾-inch muffin cups. Preheat the oven to 350°F. Beat the egg with the brown sugar, butter, orange peel, vanilla, and salt until smooth. Stir in the raisins, chocolate pieces, and pecans. Spoon the filling into the pastry-lined muffin cups. Bake for 25 minutes. Let stand 10 minutes on a wire rack before removing the tartlets from the cups to cool completely.

Cream Cheese Pastry

Makes one 9-inch pie shell or 2 dozen tartlet shells

- 1 package (3 ounces) cream cheese, at room temperature
- ½ cup margarine, softened
- 1 cup all-purpose flour

Cut the cream cheese and margarine into the flour with a pastry blender or the fingertips. Work until the mixture forms a smooth dough.

Tart Shells

Prepare Flaky Pastry or use packaged pie crust. Make tarts in desired shape; prick well; chill 30 minutes before baking. Bake 10 to 15 minutes at 450°F., or until golden brown. Fill as desired.

Little Pies

Make one- or two-crust pies using small individual pie pans.

Tulip Cups

Cut pastry into 5-inch squares with sharp knife or pastry wheel. Snugly fit 1 square into each muffin cup; let corners stand upright.

Petal Tarts

Cut 6 circles 2¼ inches in diameter. Place 1 in bottom of custard or muffin cup. Wet edges; place 5 circles around sides so they overlap each other and bottom circle.

Fluted Tarts

Measure fluted tart pan with piece of cord—up one side, across bottom, down other side; cut cord to this length. Make Alcoa Wrap circle with diameter the length of cord; for example, if cord is 4 inches long, cut 4-inch circle; use as a pattern. Using pattern, cut desired number of circles with pastry wheel. Fit circles over outside of fluted shells; a wooden skewer will help fit pastry into grooves.

Pleated Tarts

Measure inverted muffin pan cup and cut pattern as in Fluted Tarts. Fit pastry circle over outside of every other muffin cup. Pinch pastry into pleats to make it fit snugly.

Shortcake Tarts

Cut pastry circles with 3½-inch biscuit cutter. Remove centers from half the circles with 1½-inch biscuit cutter. Place on ungreased cookie sheet; bake. Spread full circle with filling; top with the circle with hole in center to make shortcake.

Turnovers

Any two-crust pie recipe can be used to make turnovers. Roll out the pastry, half at a time, and cut it into 4-inch squares or 5- or 6-inch rounds (use a giant cookie cutter or trace around a saucer). Place about a tablespoon of filling on one half, fold the other half over, seal the edges, and prick the tops in several places with a fork to allow steam to escape. Two cautions: Don't use too much filling and make certain the edges are well sealed or you'll have leakage problems.

A Jarful of Wonderful Cookies

*Scents of cookies wafting from the kitchen mean the cookie
jar will soon be full—and just as quickly empty again.*

Crisp Cutouts

Makes 5 dozen cookies

*Crisp Cutouts are fun to make at any time of the year but
add a particularly festive note to holidays.*

    1 cup C & H Granulated Sugar
    1 cup shortening (or ½ cup butter, softened, and ½
        cup shortening)
    2 eggs
    1 teaspoon vanilla extract
    ½ teaspoon almond extract
 3½ cups all-purpose flour
    1 teaspoon salt
    ½ teaspoon baking powder
      Candied fruits, sprinkles, and colored sugar
        (optional)
      Frosting (optional)

Gradually beat sugar into shortening, creaming well.
Mix in eggs, 1 at a time, beating well after each addition. Add vanilla and almond extract. Mix flour, salt,
and baking powder and stir into creamed mixture.
Chill dough at least 30 minutes for ease in handling.

Preheat oven to 375°F. Roll dough to ⅛-inch thickness on lightly floured board. Cut shapes with cookie
cutters or trace around pattern with knife. If cookies
are to be hung for decoration, pierce small hole in
dough ½ inch from top edge. Bake on ungreased
cookie sheet 8 to 10 minutes, until lightly browned.
Cool on rack.

To decorate cookies: Decorate with candied fruits,
sprinkles, or colored sugar before baking or bake without decorations and frost or decorate afterward.

Butter Cookies

Makes about 7 dozen cookies

    ½ cup sugar
    1 cup butter
    1 egg
    1 tablespoon vanilla extract
    3 cups sifted Martha White All-Purpose Flour
    ½ teaspoon baking powder
      Confectioners Icing (recipe follows)

Combine sugar, butter, and egg in mixing bowl;
beat with electric mixer until smooth. Add vanilla;
blend well. Sift in flour and baking powder; blend well.
Cover and refrigerate about 1 hour. Preheat oven to
425°F. Roll out dough on lightly floured board or
pastry cloth to ¼-inch thickness. Cut out with decorative cookie cutters. Place on ungreased baking sheets.
Bake 5 to 7 minutes, or until golden brown. Transfer
to wire racks to cool. Cooled cookies can be frosted
with Confectioners Icing and decorated as desired.

Confectioners Icing

Makes 1½ cups

    3 cups sifted confectioners sugar
    ¼ cup hot milk
    ¾ teaspoon vanilla extract

Combine all ingredients in mixing bowl. Beat until
smooth.

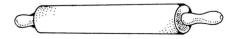

Golden Thumbprints

Makes 2½ dozen cookies

    ⅓ cup firmly packed C & H Golden Brown Sugar
    ½ cup butter or margarine, softened
    1 egg, separated
    ½ teaspoon vanilla extract
    1 cup all-purpose flour
    ¼ teaspoon salt
    ¾ cup minced walnuts
      Candied cherries, jelly, or melted semisweet
        chocolate

Preheat oven to 375°F. Cream sugar, egg yolk, and
vanilla. Stir in flour and salt. Roll dough into 1-inch
balls. Dip into lightly beaten egg white and roll in nuts.
Place on ungreased cookie sheet. Bake 5 minutes. Remove from oven. Quickly indent each cookie center
with thumb. Return to oven and bake 8 more minutes.
Cool on rack. Fill each thumbprint with half a candied
cherry, a bit of jelly, or melted chocolate.

*Counterclockwise, on table: Frosted Butterscotch Cookies with
Golden Butter Frosting (page 57); Anise Cookie Slices (page 61);
Fudge Strata Cookies (page 61); Glazed Brown Sugar Bars (page 63);
Jean's Molasses Cookies (page 53); Marzipan Bars (page 57).
On plate: Chewy Cocoa Bars (page 64); Golden Thumbprints.
C&H Sugar Company*

Peanut Butter Jack-O'-Lanterns

Makes about 18 large cookies

Filling
    1 cup Libby's Solid Pack Pumpkin
    ¾ cup sugar
    ½ teaspoon pumpkin pie spice
    ½ cup raisins

In small saucepan, combine pumpkin, sugar, spice, and raisins. Cook, over low heat, stirring occasionally, 10 minutes. Chill.

Cookie Dough
    2 cups all-purpose flour
    1 teaspoon baking powder
    ¼ teaspoon salt
    1 cup sugar
    1 cup smooth peanut butter
    2 eggs
    ¼ cup water
    1 teaspoon vanilla extract

Preheat oven to 350°F. In small bowl, combine flour, baking powder, and salt. In large bowl, cream sugar and peanut butter until light and fluffy. Add eggs, water, and vanilla; mix well. Add combined dry ingredients; mix until well blended. On lightly floured surface, roll out half the dough to ⅛-inch thickness. Cut with floured pumpkin-shaped cookie cutter. Place on ungreased cookie sheet. Top each with 1 rounded teaspoon filling. Roll out and cut remaining cookie dough. Top each filled cookie with a second cookie; press lightly at edges to seal. Bake 12 to 14 minutes, or until lightly browned.

Oatmeal Scotchies

Makes about 4 dozen 3-inch cookies
    1 cup all-purpose flour
    1 teaspoon baking soda
    ½ teaspoon salt
    ½ teaspoon ground cinnamon
    1 cup butter or margarine, softened
    ¾ cup sugar
    ¾ cup firmly packed brown sugar
    2 eggs
    1 teaspoon vanilla extract
    3 cups uncooked oats (quick or old-fashioned)
    1 12-ounce package (2 cups) Nestlé Butterscotch Flavored Morsels

Preheat oven to 375°F. In a small bowl, combine flour, baking soda, salt, and cinnamon; set aside. In a large bowl, combine butter, sugar, brown sugar, eggs, and vanilla extract; beat until light and fluffy. Gradually add flour mixture. Stir in oats and Nestlé Butter- scotch Flavored Morsels. Drop by level tablespoonfuls onto ungreased cookie sheets. Bake 7 to 8 minutes for chewier cookies or 9 to 10 minutes for crisper cookies.

Gingerbread Cookies

Makes about 2 dozen cookies
    2½ cups sifted all-purpose flour
    ½ teaspoon salt
    2 teaspoons ground ginger
    ½ cup butter
    ½ cup sugar
    ½ cup molasses
    ½ teaspoon baking soda
    ¼ cup hot water
      Cranberry Filling (recipe follows)
      Easy Icing (recipe follows)

Onto a sheet of wax paper, sift flour, salt, and ginger together. In a large saucepan, melt butter over low heat; remove from heat and add sugar and molasses. In small bowl, dissolve baking soda in hot water. Add dry ingredients to molasses mixture alternately with baking soda water, beginning and ending with dry ingredients. Chill dough 2 to 3 hours. Preheat oven to 350°F. Roll out dough, a small portion at a time, ⅛ inch thick. Cut with floured animal cutters. Place cookies on ungreased cookie sheets. Bake 10 to 12 minutes, or until lightly browned. Cool 2 to 3 minutes on the sheet. Remove to wire racks; cool thoroughly. While cookies cool, prepare Cranberry Filling and Easy Icing. Spread small amount of filling between two cookies. Decorate and outline animals with icing.

Cranberry Filling
    1 cup Fresh or Frozen Ocean Spray Cranberries, coarsely chopped
    2 tablespoons water
    2 tablespoons sugar

In medium saucepan, combine cranberries, water, and sugar; cook until thickened. Cool.

Easy Icing
    1 cup sifted confectioners sugar
    ¼ teaspoon salt
    ½ teaspoon vanilla extract
    1 tablespoon heavy cream

In medium bowl, combine sugar, salt, vanilla, and heavy cream; blend well.

Jean's Molasses Cookies

Makes 7 dozen cookies

- 1 cup firmly packed C & H Golden Brown Sugar
- 1 cup shortening
- 1 cup light molasses
- 1 cup boiling water
- 4 cups all-purpose flour
- 2 teaspoons *each* baking powder and ground cinnamon
- 1 teaspoon *each* salt and baking soda
- 1 cup chopped nuts
- ½ cup wheat germ (optional)

Preheat oven to 400°F. Grease cookie sheet. Stir sugar and shortening together until well blended. Add molasses, then stir in boiling water. Combine flour, baking powder, cinnamon, salt, and soda. Stir into sugar mixture along with nuts and wheat germ; mix well. Chill until firm. Drop by small teaspoonfuls onto cookie sheet and bake 8 to 10 minutes, until soft and puffy. Do not overbake. Cool on rack.

Praline Cookies

Makes 6 dozen cookies

- 1¼ cups sweetened condensed milk
- 2 tablespoons instant coffee
- ⅔ cup firmly packed dark brown sugar
- ⅓ cup water
- ¼ cup butter or margarine
- 2 eggs
- ½ teaspoon salt
- ½ teaspoon maple extract
- 1 teaspoon vanilla extract
- ½ cup sifted all-purpose flour
- 1 cup chopped pecans

Combine milk, coffee, and brown sugar; bring to boil; remove from heat. Add water and butter; stir until butter melts. Combine eggs, salt, maple extract, and vanilla; beat well; add coffee mixture slowly, stirring constantly. Add flour and pecans; mix well. Drop by half-teaspoonfuls, 2 inches apart, onto ungreased cookie sheet. Bake 10 minutes at 350°F.

Secrets to Successful Cookie Baking

Follow recipes carefully for order of adding ingredients and timing.

Bake only one sheet of cookies at a time in the oven and place it on a rack in the upper third of the oven. If you must bake 2 sheets at a time, place the second rack just above or below the first rack and stagger the cookie sheets so that one isn't directly above or under the other. Then reverse the position of the sheets halfway through the baking time for even browning.

Bake in a preheated oven at the temperature the recipe requires. Preheating—energy-savers to the contrary —is critical for the baking of cookies, cakes, and pies. (In any case, even where preheating isn't critical, baking time must generally be lengthened, so energy watchers are stealing time from one end and adding it to the other.) Most cookies bake in a relatively short time. Keep an eye on them.

Remove cookies—with a broad spatula—from the baking sheet as soon as it is removed from the oven, unless the recipe directs you to do otherwise. If you don't, you'll have a stick-to-the-pan problem. Besides, cookies continue to bake from the heat of the pan. If a ringing telephone or some emergency calls you away and the cookies do stick, return the sheet to the oven briefly, then remove the cookies from it at once. Cool them, not touching each other, on wire racks.

Cool the cookie sheet before placing another batch on it—hot cookie sheets can spoil the shape of cookies to be baked.

Lacy Cookie Rolls

Makes 4 dozen cookies

- ⅔ cup firmly packed C & H Golden Brown Sugar, packed
- ½ cup butter or margarine
- ½ cup corn syrup
- 1 cup all-purpose flour
- 1 cup minced nuts

Preheat oven to 325°F. Grease cookie sheet. Combine sugar, butter, and corn syrup in top of double boiler. Stir over direct medium heat until well blended. Remove from heat and mix in flour and nuts; place over boiling water to keep batter warm while working. Drop by teaspoonfuls onto cookie sheet, leaving 1 inch between cookies. (Stagger batches so they will not all finish baking at the same time.) Bake 10 to 12 minutes until golden brown. Remove cookie sheet from oven and cool 2 minutes. Loosen cookies with spatula 1 at a time and roll around any clean, round surface (such as the handle of a wooden spoon) until firm. If cookies become too firm to shape, return to oven for several seconds to soften.

To dust with confectioners sugar, place a piece of waxed paper under rack on which cookies are cooling. Place a small amount of confectioners sugar in a small strainer and rub through with a spoon. The sugar that drops through onto the waxed paper can be returned to the strainer and used until all the sugar is gone.

Graham Cracker Cookies

Makes about 3 dozen cookies
- 1 cup all-purpose flour
- ½ cup whole wheat flour
- 2 tablespoons sugar
- ½ teaspoon baking soda
- ¼ teaspoon salt
- ¼ teaspoon ground cinnamon
- ¼ cup vegetable shortening
- 1 tablespoon butter
- 2 tablespoons plus 1 teaspoon water
- 1 tablespoon honey
- 1 tablespoon molasses
- ½ teaspoon vanilla extract
- 1 jar Ocean Spray Cran-Orange Cranberry Orange Sauce

In medium bowl, combine flours, sugar, baking soda, salt, and cinnamon. Cut in shortening and butter until mixture is crumbly. In small bowl, combine water, honey, molasses, and vanilla. Sprinkle over dry ingredients, tossing with a fork until particles cling together and resemble small peas. Shape into a ball. Cover with plastic wrap. Chill in refrigerator for 1 hour. Preheat oven to 375°F. Divide dough in half. Between two sheets of wax paper, roll out half the dough to ⅛-inch thickness. Cut with floured animal cookie cutters. Prick with a fork. Place cookies on ungreased baking sheets. Bake in oven for 8 to 10 minutes, or until lightly browned. Remove to cooling rack. Sandwich cookies together with small amount of cranberry orange sauce.

Cranberry-Filled Sugar Cookies

Makes about 4 dozen cookies
- 3½ cups sifted all-purpose flour
- 2½ teaspoons baking powder
- ½ teaspoon salt
- 1 cup butter, softened
- 1½ cups sugar
- 2 eggs
- 1 tablespoon vanilla extract
- 1 can (16 ounces) Ocean Spray Whole Berry Cranberry Sauce

Preheat oven to 400°F. In large bowl, sift flour, baking powder, and salt together. In a separate bowl, beat butter, sugar, egg, and vanilla together until light and fluffy; add to sifted dry ingredients gradually; blend thoroughly. Chill for 2 hours. On a floured surface, roll out dough to ⅛-inch thickness. Cut with animal shape cookie cutters. Place dough on lightly greased cookie sheet. Bake in oven for 8 to 10 minutes, or until lightly brown. Remove from oven to cooling rack. Sandwich cookies together with a small amount of whole berry cranberry sauce.

Crisp Cutouts (page 51). C&H Sugar Company

Fudge Drops

Makes about 4 dozen cookies
- 1 11½-ounce package (2 cups) Nestlé Milk Chocolate Morsels
- 1¼ cups natural cereal
- 1 cup salted peanuts
  Whole walnuts, pecans, or cashews (optional)

Over hot (not boiling) water, melt Nestlé Milk Chocolate Morsels. Remove from heat; stir in natural cereal and peanuts. Drop by rounded teaspoonfuls onto waxed paper-lined cookie sheets. Garnish with whole nuts, if desired. Chill in refrigerator until firm (about 30 minutes).

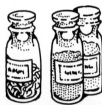

Lacy Cookie Rolls (page 53). C&H Sugar Company.

Q. *How should powdered sugar be stored?*
A. Like its brown cousins, powdered sugar should be stored in airtight containers, but for the opposite reason—to keep moisture out! If powdered sugar does become lumpy, shake the container gently or sift before using.

Peanut Butter Burst Cookies

Makes 6 dozen 2-inch cookies

  2 **cups all-purpose flour**
  1 **teaspoon baking powder**
  ¼ **teaspoon salt**
  1 **cup butter, softened**
  ¾ **cup firmly packed brown sugar**
  ½ **cup sugar**
  ½ **teaspoon vanilla extract**
  1 **egg**
  1 **12-ounce package (2 cups) Nestlé Peanut Butter Morsels**

Preheat oven to 375°F. In a small bowl, combine flour, baking powder, and salt; set aside. In a large bowl, combine butter, brown sugar, sugar, and vanilla extract; beat at medium speed until creamy (about 3 to 5 minutes). Add egg; beat well. Turn mixer to low. Gradually add flour mixture. Stir in Nestlé Peanut Butter Morsels. Drop by rounded teaspoonfuls onto ungreased cookie sheets. Bake 7 to 9 minutes. Let cool 2 minutes before removing from cookie sheets; cool completely. Cookies will be pale in color with a light brown edge.

Granola Cookies

Makes 3 dozen cookies

  ½ **cup butter or margarine, softened**
  ⅔ **cup firmly packed light brown sugar**
  1 **egg**
  1 **teaspoon grated orange peel**
  ¼ **teaspoon ground nutmeg**
  1 **cup all-purpose flour**
  ½ **teaspoon baking powder**
  ½ **teaspoon salt**
  2 **cups Sun-Maid® Raisin-Nut Granola (recipe follows)**

Preheat oven to 350°F. In a large mixer bowl, cream the butter and sugar until light and fluffy. Beat in the egg, orange peel, and nutmeg. Combine the flour with the baking powder and salt and add to the creamed mixture. Beat well. Stir in the granola. Drop rounded teaspoonfuls of the batter onto an ungreased baking sheet. Bake 10 minutes, or until browned.

Sun-Maid Raisin-Nut Granola

Makes about 5 cups

  ⅓ **cup firmly packed light brown sugar**
  ¼ **cup vegetable oil**
  ¼ **teaspoon salt**
  3½ **cups rolled oats**
  1 **cup Sun-Maid® Seedless Raisins**
  ½ **cup coarsely chopped walnuts**
  ½ **cup flaked coconut**

Preheat oven to 250°F. Combine the sugar, oil, and salt with ¼ cup water in a saucepan and heat, stirring until the sugar is melted. Pour the mixture over the oats, tossing well with a fork. Spread the oats in a 15x10x1-inch baking pan and bake for 30 minutes, stirring occasionally. Remove from the oven and cool. Add the raisins, nuts, and coconut. Store in a container with a tight lid.

Preparing Cookies for Mailing

Select cookies that travel well. Soft, moist bar cookies, brownies, and drop cookies are best; thin, crisp cookies crumble too easily. Avoid mailing cookies with fillings and frostings; they can become sticky during the trip. Select a sturdy packing container made of heavy cardboard or metal. Line it with plastic wrap, aluminum foil, or waxed paper. Have an ample supply of filler available. Suitable fillers include crumpled aluminum foil, waxed paper, tissue paper, newspaper, or paper towels. Place a layer of filler in the bottom of the container. Wrap cookies individually or back to back in aluminum foil or plastic wrap. If assorted cookies are used, place the heaviest ones on the bottom; arrange wrapped cookies neatly in rows, with filler between rows and layers. Place a filler layer on top. Tape container securely shut. Wrap in mailing paper and tie with string or use heavy-duty unbreakable wrapping tape. Mark box FRAGILE—HANDLE WITH CARE.

Fruitcake Cookies

Makes 4 to 5 dozen cookies

  1½ **cups sifted Martha White Self-Rising Flour**
  ½ **teaspoon baking soda**
  ½ **teaspoon allspice**
  ½ **cup firmly packed brown sugar**
  ½ **cup butter or margarine**
  2 **eggs**
  ¼ **cup milk**
  1 **cup chopped candied cherries**
  1 **cup chopped dates**
  1 **cup (3 slices) chopped candied pineapple**
  ⅓ **cup raisins**
  3 **cups chopped nuts**

Preheat oven to 350°F. Lightly grease 2 large baking sheets; set aside. Combine flour, baking soda, and allspice in bowl; set aside. Cream brown sugar and butter with electric mixer in mixing bowl until light and fluffy. Add eggs; blend well. Alternately beat in flour mixture and milk, blending well after each addition and scraping bowl with rubber spatula. Add fruit and nuts; blend well. Drop by teaspoonfuls onto prepared baking sheets. Bake 10 to 12 minutes, or until golden brown. Transfer to wire racks to cool.

Frosted Butterscotch Cookies

Makes 8 dozen cookies ,

1½ cups firmly packed C & H Brown Sugar
½ cup shortening
2 eggs
1 teaspoon vanilla extract
2½ cups all-purpose flour
1 teaspoon baking soda
½ teaspoon *each* baking powder and salt
½ pint (1 cup) sour cream
½ cup minced nuts
    Golden Butter Frosting (recipe follows)

Preheat oven to 400°F. Grease cookie sheet. Cream sugar and shortening. Add eggs and vanilla; mix well. Combine flour, baking soda, baking powder, and salt and add alternately with sour cream; mix well. Stir in nuts. Drop by teaspoonfuls onto cookie sheet. Bake 10 to 12 minutes, or until cookies are puffed and lightly browned. When cookies are cool, frost with Golden Butter Frosting.

Golden Butter Frosting

½ cup butter
2 cups C & H Powdered Sugar
1 teaspoon vanilla extract
    Coarsely chopped nuts

Heat butter until golden brown. Blend in sugar and vanilla. Spread on cookies. (If frosting becomes stiff, stir in a few drops of warm water.) Dip frosted top of cookies into nuts.

Storing Cookies Properly

To store soft cookies, allow them to cool thoroughly. Then place them in a container—cookie jar or tin—with a tight-fitting lid. A piece of apple, orange, or bread placed in the cookie jar will help to prevent cookies from drying out. Replace it often. Store bar cookies right in the baking pan, tightly covered. To store crisp cookies, allow them to cool and then place them in a container with a loose-fitting cover. If they soften, crisp them in a 300°F. oven for about 5 minutes before serving. Or freeze cookies; arrange on foil-covered cardboard in layers separated by foil and overwrap. Or pack in boxes and overwrap with foil. Frozen cookies should be placed on foil-covered cookie sheet in a 350°F. oven 10 minutes to crisp.

For fresh-baked cookies at a moment's notice, keep refrigerator cookie dough wrapped in foil in your refrigerator or freezer. Slice and bake as needed. Rewrap unused portion and return to refrigerator or freezer. Cookie dough keeps 2 weeks in the refrigerator, indefinitely in the freezer.

Marzipan Bars

Makes 3 dozen bars

2½ cups C & H Powdered Sugar
1½ cups ground blanched almonds
1 egg white
2 tablespoons water
2 cups all-purpose flour
2 teaspoons baking powder
1 cup butter or margarine, softened
1 egg
½ teaspoon vanilla extract

Preheat oven to 350°F. Grease 13x9x2-inch pan. Blend 2 cups sugar and the almonds. Stir in egg white and water; set aside.

Combine ½ cup sugar, the flour and baking powder. Cut butter into dry ingredients with pastry blender or fingertips until mixture resembles coarse meal. Stir in egg and vanilla. Set aside ¾ cup dough. Press remaining dough evenly into pan. Spread marzipan (almond mixture) over dough. Shape remaining dough into strips and arrange in open lattice pattern over filling. Bake 35 minutes. Cool completely before cutting into bars.

Meringue Mushrooms

Makes 15 to 20 mushrooms

2 egg whites, at room temperature
⅛ teaspoon salt
⅛ teaspoon cream of tartar
¼ teaspoon vanilla extract
½ cup sugar
    Nestlé Quik Chocolate Flavor
1 6-ounce package (1 cup) Nestlé Toll House Semi-Sweet Chocolate Morsels, melted (optional)

Preheat oven to 250°F. In a small bowl, beat egg whites until foamy. Add salt, cream of tartar, and vanilla extract; beat until soft peaks form. Gradually add sugar, 2 tablespoons at a time, beating at high speed until stiff peaks form. Fill a pastry bag fitted with large writing tip with meringue. Pipe 15 mounds resembling mushroom caps (1 to 1½ inches in diameter) onto foil-lined cookie sheet. On another foil-lined cookie sheet, pipe 15 "mushroom stems" (1 to 1½ inches long). Lightly sift Quik evenly over caps and stems. Bake 25 to 35 minutes. Cool completely. To remove, peel back foil or loosen with metal spatula. Make a small hole in bottom of each cap. Insert pointed end of stem into hole. Bottoms of caps may be decorated with melted Nestlé Toll House Semi-Sweet Chocolate Morsels, if desired. Store in tightly covered container.

Pumpkin Pops

Makes about 30 cookies

Nothing could be more fun than a cookie on a stick, unless it's a cookie on a stick frosted with a cheery, grinning jack-o'-lantern face.

- ½ **cup butter or margarine, softened**
- ¾ **cup maple syrup**
- ½ **cup sugar**
- 1 **egg, lightly beaten**
- 1 **teaspoon vanilla extract**
- 1 **cup Libby's Solid Pack Pumpkin**
- 2½ **cups all-purpose flour**
- 1 **teaspoon baking powder**
- 1 **teaspoon baking soda**
- 1 **teaspoon ground cinnamon**
- 1 **teaspoon ground nutmeg**
- 1 **cup chopped nuts**
  Wooden ice-cream sticks
  Candied green cherries, sliced
  Pumpkin Icing (recipe follows)
  Chocolate Glaze (recipe follows)

Preheat oven to 350°F. In large bowl, cream butter, syrup, and sugar until light and fluffy. Add egg, vanilla, and pumpkin; mix well. Combine flour, baking powder, baking soda, and spices; mix well. Add to pumpkin mixture; mix well. Stir in nuts. Drop round tablespoons of batter onto greased cookie sheets. Insert sticks into sides of unbaked cookies; insert cherry slice at opposite end of each, for stem. Bake 15 to 20 minutes. Remove from cookie sheets; cool on rack. Frost with Pumpkin Icing and Chocolate Glaze.

Pumpkin Icing

Combine 1¾ cups confectioners sugar with 2 tablespoons water, 2 drops of yellow food coloring, and 1 drop of red food coloring; mix until smooth. Frost cookies; allow to dry.

Chocolate Glaze

Melt ¼ cup semisweet real chocolate morsels with 1 tablespoon butter; mix well. Using small clean paintbrush or toothpick dipped in glaze, apply pumpkin features.

Make Your Own Confectioners Sugar

You can make your own confectioners sugar easily and quickly with granulated sugar and your blender. Put ½ to 1 cup granulated sugar into a Blender Plus jar and screw on the cutting assembly. Blend at high speed until pulverized.

Pumpkin Spice Cookies with Lemon Icing (page 60); Shortbread Pumpkin Bars (page 64); Peanut Butter Jack-O'-Lanterns (page 52); Pumpkin Pops; Pumpkin Pinwheels (page 61).
Libby's The Great Pumpkin Cookbook

Chocolate Pinwheels (page 61); Party Pecan Balls (page 60); Fruitcake Cookies (page 56); Iced Lemon Butter Bars (page 63).
Martha White Foods

Party Pecan Balls

Makes about 66 cookies

  1¼ **cups sifted confectioners sugar, divided**
  ½ **cup butter or margarine, softened**
  1 **teaspoon vanilla extract**
  1 **cup sifted Martha White All-Purpose Flour**
  ⅛ **teaspoon salt**
  1 **cup finely chopped pecans**

Cream ¼ cup confectioners sugar and butter with electric mixer in mixing bowl until smooth. Add vanilla; blend well. Add flour and salt; blend well. Stir in pecans. Cover with aluminum foil. Refrigerate about 1 hour. Preheat oven to 350°F. Lightly grease 2 baking sheets. Shape dough into ½-inch balls. Place on prepared baking sheets. Bake 15 minutes, or until lightly browned. Remove from baking sheets. Carefully roll each ball in remaining cup confectioners sugar to coat. Cool on wire racks. Roll again in confectioners sugar. Store in airtight container.

Cookie Press

A cookie press is something no dedicated cookie maker should be without. Traditional spritz cookies, and others less traditional but equally delightful, can be made with the press in a great many shapes, then further enhanced with a wide variety of decorations. The press is a metal cylinder with an open bottom. A pattern-making disk is dropped into the bottom, the cylinder is filled with dough, the top (a metal plunger) is screwed in place, and the cookies are pressed directly onto a baking sheet. To change the pattern a different disk is inserted. Be sure to use a recipe designed for spritz or cookie-press cookies and follow it to the letter, because the dough must have the proper consistency. If it's too soft, you'll get nothing but blobs; if it's too stiff, you won't be able to coax the cookies out.

Cookie-press cookies can be decorated with nuts, sprinkles, or colored sugars before baking. Or add chocolate sprinkles or finely grated chocolate to the dough. After baking, they can be frosted or glazed. Ribbon cookies made with the press take on elegance if one end—or both—is dipped in melted semisweet or sweet chocolate, then in chopped pistachios or blanched almonds, silver dragées, or flaked coconut. In whatever form, left plain in their pleasing shapes or decorated, all of these cookies have a buttery, melt-in-your-mouth richness.

Spritz Cookies

Makes 6 dozen cookies

  1 **cup butter or margarine**
  ⅔ **cup sugar**
  3 **egg yolks**
  1 **teaspoon almond or vanilla extract**
  2½ **cups sifted all-purpose flour**

Preheat oven to 400°F. Cream butter thoroughly in Sunbeam Mixmaster Mixer set at medium-high. Add sugar and continue creaming until mixture is light and fluffy. Beat in egg yolks and flavoring. Add 1 cup flour and beat until batter is smooth. Add remaining flour to dough and mix in by hand until mixture is well blended. Chill dough about 30 minutes. Place dough in a cookie press. Hold press upright and force dough onto an ungreased baking sheet into desired shapes. Bake about 8 minutes, or until cookies are set but not brown.

Pumpkin Spice Cookies with Lemon Icing

Makes 4 dozen cookies

  ½ **cup shortening**
  1 **cup sugar**
  2 **eggs, lightly beaten**
  1 **cup Libby's Solid Pack Pumpkin**
  2 **cups sifted all-purpose flour**
  2 **teaspoons baking powder**
  1 **teaspoon salt**
  2½ **teaspoons ground cinnamon**
  ½ **teaspoon ground nutmeg**
  ¼ **teaspoon ground ginger**
  1 **cup raisins**
  1 **cup chopped nuts**
    Lemon Icing (recipe follows)

Preheat oven to 350°F. Cream shortening; gradually beat in sugar. Add eggs and pumpkin; mix well. Sift flour, baking powder, salt, and spices together; add to pumpkin mixture; mix until blended. Add raisins and nuts. Drop in heaping teaspoons onto greased cookie sheets; bake for 15 minutes, or until cookies are firm to the touch. Remove cookies from cookie sheets and cool on rack; frost with Lemon Icing. Cookies may be frozen before frosting.

Lemon Icing

  2 **cups confectioners sugar**
  1 **tablespoon lemon juice**
  1 **tablespoon grated lemon peel**
  4 **to 5 teaspoons cream or milk**

Combine ingredients, mixing well; add just enough cream for spreading consistency.

Pumpkin Pinwheels

Makes 7 to 8 dozen cookies

Filling

    1 can (16 ounces) Libby's Solid Pack Pumpkin
    1 cup sugar
    ½ teaspoon pumpkin pie spice
    1 cup chopped nuts

In saucepan, combine pumpkin, sugar, and spice; mix well. Cook over low heat until thick, about 10 minutes. Add nuts; cool.

Cookie Dough

    1 cup shortening
    2 cups sugar
    3 eggs, well beaten
    4 cups all-purpose flour
    ½ teaspoon salt
    ½ teaspoon baking soda
       Yellow and red food coloring (optional)

Cream shortening and sugar until light and fluffy. Add eggs; continue mixing until well blended. Add flour, salt, and baking soda; mix well. If desired, add 8 drops of yellow and 4 drops of red food coloring, mixing until well blended. Divide dough into three parts. On lightly floured foil, roll each into an 8x12-inch rectangle; spread with one-third filling mixture. Starting from wide end, roll as for jelly roll. Wrap in foil. Repeat with remaining dough and filling. Place in freezer several hours or overnight. To bake, preheat oven to 400°F. Unwrap rolls, cut with a sharp knife into ¼-inch slices. Arrange on greased cookie sheets. Bake 10 to 12 minutes.

Chocolate Pinwheels

Makes about 5 dozen cookies

    ⅔ cup sugar
    ½ cup vegetable shortening
    1 egg
    1 tablespoon milk
    2 cups sifted Martha White Self-Rising Flour
    1 square (1 ounce) unsweetened chocolate, melted

Cream sugar and shortening with electric mixer in mixing bowl until light and fluffy. Add egg and milk; blend thoroughly. Gradually blend in flour. Divide dough in half. Add chocolate to 1 half; blend thoroughly. Refrigerate both halves 1 hour, or until firm enough to roll out. Roll out each half on floured waxed paper into 12x10-inch rectangle, ⅛ inch thick. Invert plain dough over chocolate dough; remove waxed paper. Roll up, jelly roll fashion, from long side. Wrap in plastic wrap. Refrigerate overnight. Preheat oven to 375°F. Carefully remove plastic wrap. Cut roll into ⅛-inch thick slices. Place slices on ungreased baking sheets. Bake 10 minutes. Transfer to wire racks to cool.

Fudge Strata Cookies

Makes 3 to 4 dozen cookies

    6 ounces semisweet chocolate
    1½ cups C & H Powdered Sugar
    ¾ cups chopped walnuts or pecans
    1 cup butter or margarine, softened
    2 teaspoons vanilla extract
    2¼ cups cake flour (or 2¼ cups all-purpose flour less
          2½ tablespoons)

Melt chocolate in double boiler over simmering water. Stir in ½ cup sugar and the nuts. Spread into a 4x12-inch rectangle on foil or waxed paper; chill.

Gradually beat 1 cup sugar into butter, creaming well. Add vanilla and flour and beat until smooth. Divide dough in half and shape each half into a 2x12-inch bar. Chill.

Cut chilled chocolate into 6 lengthwise strips. Cut each dough bar into 4 lengthwise strips. On foil or waxed paper make 2 striped bars, using 4 cookie strips and 3 chocolate strips in each bar. Press together; wrap and chill.

Preheat oven to 350°F. When ready to bake, remove wrap; cut chilled dough into ½-inch-wide sticks. Bake on ungreased cookie sheet 15 minutes, until lightly browned. Handle finished cookies gently.

Unsliced cookie rolls can be frozen wrapped in aluminum foil 3 to 4 weeks. Remove from freezer and thaw partially before slicing.

Anise Cookie Slices

Makes 4 dozen cookies

    1½ cups C & H Powdered Sugar
    ½ cup butter or margarine, softened
    1 package (3 ounces) cream cheese, softened
    4 eggs
    3¼ cups all-purpose flour
    1 tablespoon baking powder
    ½ teaspoon salt
    2 teaspoons anise seeds

Cream sugar, butter, and cream cheese. Add eggs, 1 at a time, beating well after each addition. (Mixture may look curdled.) Add remaining ingredients; mix well. Chill dough 3 hours.

Preheat oven to 350°F. Divide dough in half. On a 17x14-inch cookie sheet, shape each half into a log 1½ inches wide and 17 inches long (the length of the cookie sheet). Bake 30 to 35 minutes. Remove from oven and cut logs into ¾-inch-wide strips. Place on cookie sheet, cut side down, return to oven, and bake 10 minutes, or until toasted and crisp.

Glazed Brown Sugar Bars

Makes 2½ dozen bars

- 2 cups firmly packed C & H Golden Brown Sugar
- ½ cup butter or margarine, softened
- 2 teaspoons vanilla extract
- 2 eggs (1 separated)
- 2 cups all-purpose flour
- 1 teaspoon baking powder
- ¼ teaspoon salt
- 1 cup coarsely chopped nuts
  Pinch *each* salt and cream of tartar
- ½ cup finely chopped nuts

Preheat oven to 350°F. Grease 13x9x2-inch pan. Cream 1 cup sugar and the butter. Beat in 1 teaspoon vanilla, 1 egg, and 1 egg yolk (reserve egg white). Combine flour, baking powder, and salt. Stir into creamed mixture along with 1 cup coarse nuts. Spread evenly in pan. Beat reserved egg white with salt and cream of tartar until stiff. Beat in remaining 1 cup sugar and 1 teaspoon vanilla until completely mixed; stir in ½ cup fine nuts. Spread over top of dough. Bake 30 minutes. Cool in pan 10 minutes, then cut into bars and finish cooling on rack.

Butterscotch Thins

Makes 8 dozen cookies

- 1 6-ounce package (1 cup) Nestlé Butterscotch Flavored Morsels
- ½ cup butter
- ⅔ cup firmly packed brown sugar
- 1 egg
- 1⅓ cups all-purpose flour
- ¾ teaspoon baking soda
- ⅓ cup chopped nuts
- ¾ teaspoon vanilla extract

Over hot (not boiling) water, combine Nestlé Butterscotch Flavored Morsels and butter; stir until morsels melt and mixture is smooth. Transfer to a large bowl. Add brown sugar and egg; beat until light and fluffy. Add flour and baking soda. Stir in nuts and vanilla extract. Wrap in waxed paper; chill in refrigerator until firm enough to handle (about 1 hour). Shape into a log about 12 x 1½ inches; wrap and return to refrigerator.

To bake, preheat oven to 375°F. Cut log into slices ⅛ inch thick. Place on ungreased cookie sheets. Bake 5 to 6 minutes.

Graham Cracker Cookies (page 55); Cranberry-Filled Sugar Cookies (page 55); Gingerbread Cookies (page 52). Ocean Spray Cranberries

Oatmeal Marble Squares (page 64); Oatmeal Scotchies (page 52); Fudge Drops (page 55). The Nestlé Company, Inc.

Iced Lemon Butter Bars

Makes 16 bars

- 1⅓ cups sifted Martha White All-Purpose Flour
- 1 cup sugar, divided
- ½ cup butter, softened
- 2 eggs
- 2 tablespoons Martha White All-Purpose Flour
- 1 teaspoon grated lemon peel
- 2 tablespoons lemon juice
  Confectioners sugar

Preheat oven to 350°F. Combine 1⅓ cups sifted flour, ¼ cup sugar, and butter in bowl; blend until dough forms a ball. Pat into ungreased 9-inch square baking pan. Bake 15 minutes. Combine eggs, remaining ¾ cup sugar, 2 tablespoons flour, lemon peel, and lemon juice in bowl; blend well. Pour over partially baked crust. Bake 18 to 20 minutes, or until filling is set. Sift confectioners sugar over top. Cool in pan on wire rack. Cut into bars.

Chewy Cocoa Bars

Makes 2 dozen bars

- ¾ cup C & H Powdered Sugar
- 6 tablespoons butter or margarine, softened
- 1 cup all-purpose flour
- 1 tablespoon milk
- 1 cup C & H Granulated Sugar
- ½ cup cocoa powder
- 2 tablespoons all-purpose flour
- ½ teaspoon *each* baking powder and salt
- 2 eggs, lightly beaten
- 1 teaspoon vanilla extract
- ¼ teaspoon almond extract (optional)
- 1 cup chopped almonds or pecans

Preheat oven to 350°F. Cream powdered sugar and butter. Blend in 1 cup flour and the milk. Spread batter evenly on bottom of ungreased 9-inch square pan. Bake 10 minutes.

While crust is baking, combine granulated sugar, cocoa, 2 tablespoons flour, the baking powder, and salt in bowl. Beat in eggs, vanilla, and almond extract; fold in nuts. Spread topping on baked crust. Return to oven and continue baking about 15 minutes, or until top is no longer shiny. While warm, cut into bars.

Toll House Golden Brownies

Makes 35 squares

- 2 cups all-purpose flour
- 2 teaspoons baking powder
- 1 teaspoon salt
- ¾ cup butter, softened
- ¾ cup sugar
- ¾ cup firmly packed dark brown sugar
- 1 teaspoon vanilla extract
- 3 eggs
- 1 12-ounce package (2 cups) Nestlé Toll House Semi-Sweet Chocolate Morsels

Preheat oven to 350°F. In a small bowl, combine flour, baking powder, and salt; set aside. In a large bowl, combine butter, sugar, dark brown sugar, and vanilla extract; beat until creamy. Add eggs, 1 at a time, beating well after each addition. Gradually add flour mixture; mix well. Stir in Nestlé Toll House Semi-Sweet Chocolate Morsels. Spread evenly into well-greased 15x10x1-inch baking pan. Bake 30 to 35 minutes. Cool completely. Cut into 2-inch squares.

Storing chocolate: Keep chocolate in a cool, dry place. Storage temperature should be between 60° and 78° F., with relative humidity at less than 50 percent. Chocolate can be refrigerated, but wrap it tightly so it won't absorb odors. Airtight wrapping will also help prevent moisture from condensing on the chocolate when removed from the refrigerator. Chocolate becomes hard and very brittle when cold, so allow it to come to room temperature before using.

Shortbread Pumpkin Bars

Makes 2 dozen squares

- ¾ cup butter or margarine, softened, divided
- ⅔ cup sugar, divided
- ¾ teaspoon vanilla extract, divided
- 2⅓ cups all-purpose flour, divided
- ½ teaspoon baking powder
- ¼ teaspoon salt
- 2 eggs, lightly beaten
- 1 cup firmly packed brown sugar
- 1 cup Libby's Solid Pack Pumpkin
- ½ cup chopped pecans

Preheat oven to 400°F. In small bowl, cream ½ cup butter, ⅓ cup sugar, and ¼ teaspoon vanilla. Add 1 cup flour; mix well. Press dough into bottom of 13x9x2-inch baking pan. Bake 5 minutes. Reduce heat to 350°F. Combine ⅓ cup flour, baking powder, and salt; mix well. Combine eggs, brown sugar, pumpkin, and ½ teaspoon vanilla. Stir in dry ingredients and nuts. Spread over partially baked crust. Combine remaining 1 cup flour and ⅓ cup sugar. Cut in ¼ cup butter until mixture resembles coarse crumbs. Sprinkle over pumpkin layer. Continue baking 25 to 30 minutes. Cool. Cut into 1½-inch bars or squares.

Oatmeal Marble Squares

Makes 2 dozen squares

- ¾ cup all-purpose flour
- ½ teaspoon baking soda
- ½ teaspoon salt
- ½ cup butter, softened
- 6 tablespoons sugar
- 6 tablespoons firmly packed brown sugar
- ½ teaspoon vanilla extract
- 1 egg
- 1 cup uncooked quick oats
- ½ cup chopped nuts
- 1 6-ounce package (1 cup) Nestlé Toll House Semi-Sweet Chocolate Morsels

Preheat oven to 375°F. In a small bowl, combine flour, baking soda, and salt; set aside. In a large bowl, combine butter, sugar, brown sugar, and vanilla; beat until creamy. Beat in egg. Blend in flour mixture. Stir in oats and nuts. Spread into greased 13x9x2-inch baking pan. Sprinkle Nestlé Toll House Semi-Sweet Chocolate Morsels over top. Place in oven for 3 minutes. Run knife through to marbleize. Bake 10 to 12 minutes. Cool; cut into 2-inch squares.

Decorating Cookies

From little buttery melt-in-your-mouth one-bite cookies for a tea tray, through sturdy peanut butter crisscrossed cookies to greet the children with when they come home from school, to fat-and-sassy gingerbread families for the holidays, cookies are fun to make, a plesure to decorate, and a joy to serve to your family and friends. Most kinds are easy to make—there's nothing chancy in their baking—and decorating them doesn't tax the ingenuity or the skill of the average home cook.

When children want to help you cook, cookies are the place to begin. They love to roll and shape and cut them—and what does it matter if the finished products are a bit tough from too much flour, the designs a trifle lopsided, the kitchen a shambles? Cooking together is a learning experience, not only for the children but also for you. You may discover in a son or daughter some traits (persistence? latent artistic ability? a tendency to give in too easily to frustration?) that you didn't know existed, that you may want to develop or discourage.

The Easy Way Out

For the day-to-day job of keeping the cookie jar filled, nothing beats refrigerator cookies. (Icebox cookies, they used to be called, and still are sometimes.) They're easy to make, needing only to be quickly sliced and briefly baked—indeed, a roll can always be kept ready in the refrigerator. The dough can be vanilla, chocolate, lemon, spice, almond, or butterscotch flavored; it can be left plain or have nuts, raisins, currants, chocolate pieces, or candied fruit peel (all of these chopped fine) incorporated into it. The sliced cookies can be left as they are or sprinkled with plain or colored sugar or with nuts before being baked, or the finished cookies can be frosted or glazed or ornamented with piped-on decorations. A whole cookie repertoire from one recipe and variations!

Rolled cookies, in a wide variety of flavors, are old-fashioned favorites. If you make them often, invest in a few cutters of different shapes—there is an almost infinite variety on the market. The shapes of many of these are so attractive that they are decoration in themselves, or the shapes can guide such decoration as piped borders, glaze painting, or combinations of additions and frosting, such as pink-frosted ears and nose for a rabbit, a splash of white frosting for a cottony tail, raisins or small candies for the eyes.

Decorated animal-shaped cookies make a great hit with children. At a child's birthday party, you might make a giant-size animal cookie, appropriately decorated, for each guest. Pipe the child's name on in decorator's icing, and set the animals around the refreshment table to serve as place-cards.

Cookie Party

Decorating cookies of any shape can be a fun-project for children. Supply them with tubes of commercial decorator's frostings and gels, colored sugars, nuts, candies, and raisins and let their talents take over. In fact, a cookie-making party is a very satisfactory method of entertaining young guests and a fine way to pass a rainy Saturday when the picnic or beach trip has had to be postponed.

Cutout cookies, in fancy shapes, can be painted with a tinted egg yolk wash before they are baked. From the same batch of cookies, choose some to be deorated with "jewels" of colored sugar, using the white of the egg as a base.

Painted Cookies: Using a fork, blend 1 egg yolk with ¼ teaspoon of water. Divide it into small portions and tint each portion with food coloring, as desired. Using an artist's brush—a separate one for each color—paint the cookies in colors and designs appropriate to their shapes. You'll get a better effort if you use the paint as an accent, rather than covering the whole cookie.

Cookie Glaze: Blend ¾ cup sifted confectioners sugar with 3 to 4 teaspoons water and, if desired, a drip or two of food coloring.

Decorator's Frosting for Cookies: Sift 1 package (1 pound) confectioners sugar; then sift it again into a medium-size bowl with ½ teaspoon cream of tartar. Add 3 unbeaten egg whites and ½ teaspoon vanilla extract. Combine the ingredients with the mixer on low speed. Turn the mixer to medium speed and beat the frosting for about 6 to 8 minutes, until it is so stiff that a knife drawn through it leaves a clean-cut path. Tint the frosting, if desired, and use it with a bag or a cone and tube.

All Kinds of Savory Puddings

Any occasion becomes a celebration when a lavish pudding or an elegant hot soufflé graces your table.

Lemon Puff Pudding

Makes 6 servings

- 1 cup C & H Granulated Sugar
- ¼ cup all-purpose flour
- 3 tablespoons butter or margarine, softened
- 3 eggs, separated
- 2 teaspoons grated lemon rind
- ¼ cup lemon juice
- 1½ cups milk
- ¼ teaspoon salt
- ⅛ teaspoon cream of tartar
- Whipped cream (optional)

Preheat over to 325°F. Grease 1½-quart baking dish. Cream half the sugar, the flour, and butter. Stir in egg yolks, lemon rind, lemon juice, and milk. Beat egg whites with salt and cream of tartar until soft peaks form. Beat in remaining ½ cup sugar, 1 tablespoon at a time, and continue beating until egg whites are stiff but not dry. Fold in creamed mixture. Pour into dish; set dish into larger pan containing enough boiling water to reach halfway up its sides. Bake 1 hour. Cool. If desired, serve with whipped cream.

Old-Fashioned Lemon Soft Sauce

Makes about 2 cups

Use this flavorful finishing for plain cakes and puddings.

- 2 tablespoons cornstarch
- ½ cup sugar
- 2 tablespoons butter or margarine, softened
- 1 egg yolk
- 3 tablespoons lemon juice
- 1 teaspoon grated lemon peel
- ⅛ teaspoon ground nutmeg (optional)

You will need: Visions or Corning Ware 2-quart saucepan

Combine cornstarch and sugar in saucepan; stir in 2 cups cold water. Cook, stirring, over medium-low heat until thickened. Add butter; beat to blend. Beat egg yolk with 1 tablespoon cold water; add a small amount of hot sauce to egg, then add egg mixture to saucepan and cook, stirring, 1 minute. Do not boil. Remove from heat. Stir in lemon juice and peel, and, if desired, nutmeg. Serve hot.

Chocolate-Banana Milkshake Pudding

Makes 8 servings

Here's a great-tasting dessert that's also easy on the budget—children love it, and the grown-ups will make sure they also get their share.

- 2 envelopes Knox Unflavored Gelatine
- ½ cup cold water
- 1 cup boiling water
- ¼ cup sugar
- 2 tablespoons unsweetened cocoa
- ⅔ cup nonfat dry milk powder
- 2 ripe bananas, peeled and chunked
- 1 teaspoon vanilla extract
- 2 cups ice cubes or crushed ice (12 to 16 cubes)

In 5-cup blender, sprinkle unflavored gelatine over cold water; let stand 3 to 4 minutes. Add boiling water; process at low speed until gelatine is completely dissolved. Add sugar, cocoa, and dry milk; process until smooth. Add bananas and vanilla. Add ice cubes, 1 at a time, and process at high speed until ice is melted. Pour into individual dessert dishes or custard cups. Chill until set.

Note: Be sure to use ripe bananas for best flavor—sign of a ripe banana is little flecks of brown on the peel.

Lemon Puff Pudding. C&H Sugar Company

Pearl Tapioca With Rhubarb

Makes 4 servings

  ¼ **cup pearl tapioca**
  2 **cups milk**
  1 **cup sugar**
  ⅛ **teaspoon salt**
  ½ **teaspoon vanilla extract**
  2 **pounds fresh rhubarb, cut in 1-inch pieces**

You will need: Visions or Corning Ware 1½-quart covered saucepan; Visions or Corning Ware 2-quart covered saucepan

In a small bowl, soak tapioca in 1 cup cold water at least 3 hours—overnight, if desired. Transfer tapioca and the water to 1½-quart saucepan. Add milk, ⅓ cup of the sugar, and the salt. Simmer over low heat, stirring occasionally, 1 hour. Stir in vanilla. Cool, then cover and refrigerate. Combine rhubarb, ¼ cup water, and remaining sugar in 2-quart saucepan; bring to a boil. Cover; cook over low heat until rhubarb is tender—10 to 20 minutes, depending on age of the rhubarb. Taste; if desired, add more sugar. Cool, then cover and refrigerate. Serve tapioca topped with rhubarb.

Good to Know: Tapioca, from the roots of the cassava, is most familiar to us today in the finely granulated quick-cooking form. But the pearl variety—sometimes called fisheye—is still available, in both medium and large sizes. Use either size in this recipe.

Almond Rum Sauce

Makes about 1½ cups

  1 **tablespoon cornstarch**
1¼ **cups water**
  ⅓ **cup Solo Almond Paste**
  2 **tablespoons butter or margarine**
  2 **tablespoons dark rum**
  1 **tablespoon sugar**
  ½ **teaspoon salt**

In a saucepan, combine cornstarch and water. Bring mixture to a boil and cook until clear. Cut up almond paste and add to hot mixture; stir until well blended. Add remaining ingredients and heat until butter or margarine melts and mixture is well blended. Serve either hot or cold over steamed pudding, day-old cake, or ice cream.

Other Solo Sauces for Puddings or Ice Cream

Combine 1 can (12 ounces) Solo Date Filling, 2 tablespoons grated orange peel, and ¼ cup orange juice. Serve over ice cream and top with a few chopped pecans.

Combine 1 can (12 ounces) Solo Apricot Filling and ½ cup marshmallow creme. Serve over sherbet or ice cream and top with a few toasted salted almonds.

Combine 1 can (12 ounces) Solo Prune Filling, 1 tablespoon lemon juice, ¼ cup honey, and ¼ teaspoon ground cinnamon. Use to top ice cream or warm gingerbread.

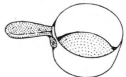

Blender Whipped Cream

Makes 1¼ cups

Pour 1 cup chilled heavy cream into blender container. Cover; blend at low speed just until cream thickens and begins to hold the shape of the blades. Remove cover during whipping so that you can watch carefully, as overblending will quickly turn cream to butter.

Note: To whip more than 1 cup of cream, repeat blender process after cleaning blender container.

Sweetened Whipped Cream

To each 1 cup heavy cream, add 1 to 2 tablespoons sugar and ½ teaspoon vanilla extract before blending.

Cocoa Whipped Cream

To each 1 cup heavy cream, add 2 tablespoons cocoa and 3 tablespoons confectioners sugar before blending.

Mocha Whipped Cream

To each 1 cup heavy cream, add 2 tablespoons cocoa, ¼ cup confectioners sugar, and 1 teaspoon instant coffee before blending.

Lemon Whipped Cream

To each 1 cup heavy cream, add ½ cup confectioners sugar, 1 tablespoon lemon juice, and a small piece of lemon rind before blending.

Navajo Pudding

Makes 8 servings

  4 **cups milk, divided**
  ¼ **cup butter or margarine**
  ⅔ **cup molasses**
  3 **tablespoons Sue Bee Honey**
  ⅔ **cup yellow cornmeal**
  1 **teaspoon salt**
  ¾ **teaspoon ground cinnamon**
  ¾ **teaspoon ground nutmeg**

Heat 3 cups milk. Stir in butter, molasses, and Sue Bee Honey. Combine cornmeal, salt, and spices and gradually stir into warm milk mixture, using a wire whisk. Cook over low heat, stirring constantly, approximately 10 minutes or until thick. Preheat oven to 300° F. Turn into oiled casserole, pour 1 cup milk over pudding (do not stir), and bake for 3 hours.

Raspberry Cream Parfait

Makes 4 servings

    3 tablespoons quick-cooking tapioca
    6 tablespoons sugar
    ¼ teaspoon salt
    1⅓ cups milk
    ½ cup heavy cream
    2 cups red raspberries

Mix tapioca, 4 tablespoons of the sugar, and salt in saucepan. Add milk gradually; stir. Cook, stirring constantly, until mixture boils. Remove from heat; cool. Whip cream; fold into tapioca mixture; chill. Crush raspberries slightly; add remaining sugar. Pile raspberries and tapioca mixture in alternate layers in parfait glasses. Serve plain or with whipped cream.

About Puddings

Baked puddings: These cook in the oven, generally in a considerably shorter time than a steamed pudding requires. They may be either firm or soft in texture, but few are firm enough to turn out as a mold. Examples are spoon bread, yorkshire pudding to serve with roast beef, blueberry cottage pudding, bread pudding, rice pudding.

Another baked sweet is the pudding cake. For this, a cakelike batter is spread in the baking pan and sprinkled with a dry mixture. Then hot water is poured over (but not stirred in) and the pudding is baked. Done, it forms into two layers—a cakelike, but very moist one, plus a sauce. Favorites are chocolate and lemon.

Stovetop puddings: These are cooked either in a heavy saucepan or a double boiler. They include those thickened with egg and cornstarch, and tapioca puddings. They may be chocolate, vanilla, or butterscotch flavored, and tapioca puddings are often made with fruit. All are soft, sweet, and must be spooned into individual dishes for serving.

Refrigerator puddings: These are made of layers of split ladyfingers or thin-sliced pound or sponge or angel food cake with a custard or whipped cream filling, sometimes gelatin-stiffened. They require 8 hours or more in the refrigerator to mellow and thicken. Some can be turned out, others must be dished. Chocolate and various fruit and berry flavors are favorites. Bavarians and spanish creams—without the cake—fall into this category, too.

Pudding Parfaits

Makes 6 servings

    1 package (3¾ ounces) pistachio-flavored instant
         pudding and pie filling
    2½ cups milk
    ¼ cup wheat germ
         Sun-Maid® Seedless Raisins

Prepare the pudding according to package directions, but increase the milk to 2½ cups. Spoon half of the pudding into 6 custard cups. Sprinkle each serving with 1 teaspoon wheat germ and some raisins, as many as you think right. Spoon the rest of the pudding into the cups and sprinkle each with 1 teaspoon wheat germ and some more raisins. Chill at least 30 minutes before serving.

Creamy Rice Pudding

Makes 4 to 5 servings

    ⅓ cup Uncle Ben's® Converted® Brand Rice
    1½ cups water
    ⅓ cup sugar
    1 teaspoon cornstarch
    ¼ teaspoon salt
    1⅓ cups milk
    1 tablespoon butter or margarine
    ½ teaspoon vanilla extract
    2 egg yolks, beaten

Combine rice and water in a medium saucepan. Bring to a boil. Reduce heat, cover, and simmer 25 minutes, or until rice is very tender and most of water is absorbed. Combine sugar, cornstarch, and salt. Add milk and sugar mixture to rice. Heat to boiling; boil 1 minute, stirring constantly. Remove from heat. Stir in butter and vanilla. Slowly stir about 1 cup of the hot rice mixture into beaten egg yolks in a bowl. Blend with remaining mixture in saucepan. Cook over medium heat, stirring frequently, just until mixture starts to bubble. Serve warm or chilled, plain or with favorite topping.

Brownie Rice Pudding

Makes 6 servings

    2 eggs, separated
    ½ cup sugar
    ¼ teaspoon salt
    1 teaspoon vanilla extract
    1 square (1 ounce) chocolate, melted
    1½ cups milk
    ½ cup chopped pecans or walnuts
    2 cups cooked Uncle Ben's® Converted® Brand Rice

Beat egg whites until they stand in soft peaks; beat in yolks. Blend in slowly the sugar, salt, vanilla, and melted chocolate (slightly cooled). Add milk and blend. Mix nuts and cooked rice in buttered 1½-quart baking dish. Pour chocolate mixture over. Place in pan of water and bake in 350°F. oven for approximately 50 minutes, or until a knife inserted in center comes out clean.

Elegant Raisin Rice Pudding

Makes 8 servings

- 6 tablespoons sugar, divided
- 2 envelopes unflavored gelatin
- ½ teaspoon ground nutmeg
- ½ teaspoon salt
- 2½ cups milk, divided
- ¼ cup long-grained rice
- ½ cup Sun-Maid® Seedless Golden Raisins
- 3 eggs, separated
- 1 cup heavy cream
  Raspberry Sauce (recipe follows) or Sherried Apricot Sauce (see index)

Mix 4 tablespoons of the sugar with the gelatin, nutmeg, and salt in a large saucepan. Slowly stir in 2 cups of the milk until smooth. Add the rice and raisins and bring to a boil. Reduce heat, cover, and simmer for 20 minutes, or until the rice is tender, stirring occasionally. Beat the egg yolks and the remaining ½ cup milk together. Slowly add some of the hot rice mixture to the egg-yolk mixture, beating constantly. Pour back into the saucepan and mix well. Refrigerate until the mixture is cool and will mound when dropped from a spoon, about 1½ hours.

Beat the egg whites until foamy; add the remaining 2 tablespoons sugar and beat until stiff peaks form. Fold into the rice mixture. Beat the heavy cream until soft peaks form; fold into the rice mixture. Spoon the pudding into a 6-cup mold or bowl. Refrigerate for 6 hours, or until firmly set. Loosen the pudding around the edge and invert on a dessert platter. Serve with Raspberry Sauce or Sherried Apricot Sauce.

Raspberry Sauce

Makes 1¼ cups

- 1 package (10 ounces) frozen raspberries
- ¼ cup ruby port
- 1 tablespoon cornstarch
- ⅛ teaspoon salt
- ⅛ teaspoon almond extract

Thaw the raspberries. Strain the juice into a small saucepan. Reserve raspberries. Stir in the port, cornstarch, and salt until smooth. Heat to boiling, stirring constantly; boil 1 minute. Cool to room temperature; stir in the almond extract, then fold in the reserved raspberries.

Elegant Raisin Rice Pudding with Raspberry Sauce. Sun-Maid Growers of California

Cherry Rice Dessert

Makes 6 servings

    ¾ cup Uncle Ben's® Converted Brand Rice
    2 cups water
    ¾ teaspoon salt
    ½ tablespoon butter or margarine
    1 can (20 ounces) sour cherries, well drained (reserve
        juice)
    ½ cup sugar
    ½ teaspoon vanilla (or almond) extract
    ½ cup whipping cream
        Cherry Sauce (recipe follows)

Combine rice, water, salt, and butter in a large saucepan. Bring to a boil, lower heat, and cover. Cook until all liquid is absorbed. Remove from heat and set in a pan of cold tap water to cool quickly, about 15 minutes. Prepare sauce. Combine cooled rice with cherries, sugar, and vanilla. Lightly fold in cream which has been beaten stiff. Serve immediately in sherbet glasses with cooled Cherry Sauce.

Cherry Sauce

    ½ cup sugar
    1 tablespoon cornstarch
        Dash salt
        Cherry juice and water to make 1 cup

Blending sugar, cornstarch, and salt, add liquid gradually. Cook over medium heat until clear, stirring constantly; cool.

Scotch Rice Pudding

Makes 6 servings

    2 cups water
    ½ teaspoon salt
    1 cup uncooked rice
    ⅔ cup firmly packed C & H Dark Brown Sugar
    1 teaspoon vanilla extract
    ½ cup heavy or light cream
    2 tablespoons butter or margarine
        Cream or vanilla ice cream

Bring water to boil. Add salt and slowly stir in rice. Cover pan and cook over low heat 25 to 30 minutes or until liquid is absorbed. Gently stir in sugar, vanilla, ½ cup cream, and butter. Serve immediately with cream.

Creamy Banana Pudding

Makes 8 to 10 servings

1 can (14 ounces) Eagle® Brand Sweetened
 Condensed Milk (not evaporated milk)
1½ cups cold water
1 package (3½ ounces) instant vanilla pudding
 and pie filling mix
2 cups (1 pint) whipping cream, whipped
36 vanilla wafers
3 medium bananas, sliced and dipped in lemon
 juice

In large bowl, combine sweetened condensed milk and water; mix well. Add pudding mix; beat until well blended. Chill 5 minutes. Fold in whipped cream. Spoon 1 cup pudding mixture into 2½-quart round glass serving bowl. Top with one-third the vanilla wafers, bananas, and pudding. Repeat layering twice, ending with pudding mixture. Chill at least 3 hours. Refrigerate leftovers.
Note: Mixture can be layered in individual serving dishes.

About Custards

Baked custards: Most of the savory ones are vegetable based, such as corn custard, the other ingredients being milk and eggs and appropriate seasonings. Sweet custards are combinations of milk, eggs, sugar, flavored with—usually—vanilla and/or nutmeg. Some of these are made with the yolks of the eggs only (freeze the whites for later use), which results in a somewhat firmer, more dense custard, and some with evaporated milk, which gives an excellent consistency. To tell when a baked custard is done, test it with the blade of a table knife halfway between the center and the edge—if the blade comes out clean, the custard can be removed from the oven even if the center looks a bit shaky; it will finish cooking as it cools.
Stovetop custards: These are flour (or cornstarch)-sugar-milk mixtures, cooked until thickened and bubbly. Then a portion of the mixture is stirred into beaten eggs, and the eggs added to the cooked mixture. The custard continues to cook until it is thickened once more, but must not be allowed to boil after the eggs are added. "Soft" or English custard, or custard sauce, is a much less thick version, which is cooked only until the mixture coats a metal spoon.

Cold Wine Custard

Makes 6 servings

6 egg yolks
6 tablespoons sugar
½ cup sweet Marsala wine
1 cup heavy cream
 Maraschino cherries

Put egg yolks into small Mixmaster Mixer bowl. With dial at low, beat yolks until blended. Continue beating and add the sugar, 1 tablespoon at a time. Continuing to beat, add wine gradually. Place mixture in top of a double boiler. Cook over boiling water, stirring constantly until thickened, 3 to 4 minutes. Cool. Place cream in large Mixmaster Mixer bowl. With dial set at high, whip cream stiff. With dial set at lowest, fold in cooled custard. Spoon into serving dishes; top each with a maraschino cherry and refrigerate.

Baked Apple Pudding

Makes 8 servings

1 cup C & H Granulated Sugar
¼ cup butter or margarine, softened
1 egg
2 cups unpeeled, finely shredded apples (2 or 3
 medium)
1 cup all-purpose flour
1 teaspoon *each* baking soda and ground cinnamon
¾ teaspoon ground nutmeg
¼ teaspoon salt
 Vanilla Sauce (recipe follows) or sweetened
 whipped cream

Preheat oven to 350°F. Grease 8-inch square pan. Cream sugar and butter until light and fluffy. Beat in egg. Stir in apples, flour, soda, cinnamon, nutmeg, and salt. Pour into pan. Bake 45 minutes. Serve warm with Vanilla Sauce or whipped cream.

Vanilla Sauce

1 cup C & H Granulated Sugar
½ cup milk
½ cup butter or margarine
1 teaspoon vanilla extract
⅛ teaspoon ground nutmeg

Stir sugar, milk, and butter together over low heat; do not boil! When slightly thickened, stir in vanilla and nutmeg. Serve warm.

Sicilian Cream with Cranberry Nut Sauce

Makes 6 servings

1 carton (15 ounces) ricotta cheese
1 package (8 ounces) cream cheese
2 tablespoons heavy cream
2 tablespoons Domino Liquid Brown Sugar
1½ cups fresh cranberries
1½ cups Domino Liquid Brown Sugar
1 cup water
⅔ cup coarsely broken pecans

Combine ricotta and cream cheese in small bowl of electric mixer. Beat until smooth. Gradually add heavy cream and 2 tablespoons Liquid Brown Sugar. Chill.

In saucepan, mix cranberries, Liquid Brown Sugar, water, and pecans. Bring to a simmer. Remove from heat and let stand 5 minutes. Repeat. Then simmer gently 5 minutes. Remove from heat and cool. Chill until serving time. (This method keeps most of the berries whole.) Serve sauce over Sicilian Cream.

Custards au Caramel

Makes 6 servings
  1¾ cups Domino Granulated Sugar
   4 eggs, lightly beaten
  ¼ teaspoon salt
  2⅔ cups milk, scalded
  1¼ teaspoons vanilla extract
  ⅛ teaspoon ground nutmeg

Place 1¼ cups sugar in thick skillet over medium heat. Stir continuously until sugar caramelizes into golden brown syrup. Divide syrup at once into 6 buttered ceramic custard cups. Rotate cups to coat sides. Blend remaining ½ cup sugar with beaten eggs and salt in mixing bowl. Stir scalded milk into mixture gradually. Add vanilla and nutmeg. Pour mixture carefully against spoon held over caramel into custard cups. Set cups in shallow pan of hot water. Bake in moderate oven (350°F.) about 35 minutes, or until knife blade comes out clean. Remove from heat; cool. Chill; unmold.

Baked Cranberry Pudding

Makes 8 servings
  1 cup C & H Granulated Sugar
  2 cups all-purpose flour
  2½ teaspoons baking powder
  ½ teaspoon salt
  ⅔ cup milk
  3 tablespoons butter or margarine, melted
  1 egg
  2 cups raw cranberries
     Butter Cream Sauce (recipe follows)

Preheat oven to 350°F. Grease 9-inch square pan. Combine sugar, flour, baking powder, and salt. Stir in milk, butter, and egg; beat 2 minutes. Stir in cranberries. Pour into pan. Bake 40 minutes. Serve hot with Butter Cream Sauce.

Butter Cream Sauce
  1½ cups C & H Granulated Sugar
  ¾ cup heavy cream
  ¼ cup butter
  2 egg yolks, lightly beaten
  1 teaspoon vanilla extract

Combine sugar, cream and butter in saucepan. Cook over medium heat, 5 minutes, stirring constantly. Gradually stir hot mixture into beaten egg yolks, then return to saucepan and stir over low heat until thickened and smooth. Stir in vanilla. Serve warm.

Biscayne Raspberry Soufflé with Raspberry Sauce

Makes 6 servings
     Raspberry Sauce (recipe follows)
  2 cups fresh or frozen raspberries, divided
  1 tablespoon lemon juice
  2 tablespoons sugar
  4 packets (1¼ teaspoons) Sweet 'N Low Granulated Sugar Substitute
  4 eggs, separated

Prepare Raspberry Sauce; set aside. Preheat oven to 350°F. Spray 1-quart soufflé dish with nonstick cooking spray. Purée 1½ cups raspberries and lemon juice. Press through fine sieve to remove seeds. In small saucepan, cook raspberry purée, sugar, and Sweet 'N Low over low heat until sugar dissolves, about 1 minute. Remove from heat. Beat egg yolks lightly. Add small amount of raspberry mixture to egg yolks, stirring constantly. Combine with all of raspberry mixture, stirring constantly. Stir in remaining ½ cup raspberries. In large bowl, beat egg whites until stiff. Fold into fruit mixture. Pour into prepared soufflé dish. Place soufflé dish into pan and fill with hot water to cover 2 inches of dish. bake about 20 minutes, or until golden brown. Serve immediately with Raspberry Sauce.

Raspberry Sauce
  1 cup fresh or frozen raspberries, thawed and drained
  ¼ cup orange juice
  1 teaspoon lime juice
  1 tablespoon raspberry liqueur
  1 tablespoon sugar
  2 packets (⅔ teaspoon) Sweet 'N Low Granulated Sugar Substitute

Purée raspberries. Press through a fine sieve to remove seeds. In small saucepan, cook raspberry purée, orange juice, lime juice, liqueur, sugar, and Sweet 'N Low over high heat until slightly thickened and reduced. Cover and chill until ready to serve.

Hard Sauce

Makes 1 cup
  2 tablespoons rum or brandy
  2 tablespoons heavy cream or milk
  2 cups confectioners sugar, divided
  ½ cup butter or margarine, softened

Put rum, cream and 1 cup confectioners sugar into blender container. Cover; blend at high speed until smooth. Add butter and remaining confectioners sugar. Cover; blend at high speed until smooth. If necessary, stop blender during processing and push ingredients toward blades with a rubber spatula.

Heritage Pumpkin Pudding with Fluffy Lemon Hard Sauce.
Libby's The Great Pumpkin Cookbook

Vanilla Soufflé

Makes 6 servings

    4 tablespoons butter or margarine
    5 tablespoons all-purpose flour
  ¼ teaspoon salt
    1 cup milk
    3 eggs, separated
  ⅓ cup sugar
    1 teaspoon vanilla extract
  ¼ teaspoon almond extract

Melt butter in top of double boiler over boiling water. Stir in flour and salt; blend; add milk. Cook, stirring constantly until thickened. Remove from heat; cool. Beat egg yolks until thick; stir in sugar; blend with milk mixture. Beat egg whites stiff; fold in milk-egg mixture, add flavoring. Grease bottom only of 8-inch square pan or 1½-quart casserole. Pour in mixture; set in pan of warm water. Bake 1 hour at 325°F., or until knife inserted in center comes out clean. Serve at once with whipped cream, or Vanilla Sauce (see index).

Stove-Top Chocolate Soufflé

Makes 4 servings

    2 squares (2 ounces) unsweetened chocolate
    1 cup milk
  ½ cup sugar
  ⅛ teaspoon salt
    1 teaspoon vanilla extract
    3 eggs
       Whipped cream

Combine chocolate, milk, sugar, and salt in top part of a double boiler. Place over boiling water and heat until chocolate is melted. Beat with a Sunbeam Mixmaster Hand Mixer until mixture is smooth. Add vanilla and eggs while continuing to beat. Beat mixture 1 minute. Cover and cook 20 minutes. Serve hot or cold, with whipped cream.

Blueberry 'n' Spice Bread Pudding

Makes 8 to 10 servings

   12 slices white bread, cut into cubes (about 6 cups)
    2 cups fresh or dry-pack frozen blueberries, rinsed and drained
    3 eggs
    1 can (14 ounces) Eagle® Brand Sweetened Condensed Milk (not evaporated milk)
  1½ cups warm water
  ¼ cup butter or margarine, melted
    1 teaspoon vanilla extract
  ½ teaspoon ground cinnamon
  ½ teaspoon ground nutmeg

Preheat oven to 350°F. In large bowl, toss together bread cubes and blueberries. Turn into a greased 9-inch square baking pan; set aside. In large bowl, beat eggs; add remaining ingredients. Mix well. Pour evenly over bread cubes and blueberries, completely moistening bread. Bake 45 to 50 minutes, or until knife inserted in center comes out clean. Cool. Serve warm or chilled. Garnish as desired. Refrigerate leftovers.

Barbara's Bread Pudding

Makes 6 to 8 servings
- **15 thin slices French or Italian bread**
- **2½ tablespoons butter or margarine, softened**
- **⅓ cup raisins**
- **2 cups milk**
- **1 cup grapefruit juice from Florida**
- **4 eggs, lightly beaten**
- **⅓ cup plus 2 tablespoons firmly packed light brown sugar, divided**
- **½ teaspoon grated grapefruit peel**
- **¼ teaspoon ground cinnamon**
- **2 grapefruits from Florida, sectioned**

Spread 1 side of each bread slice with butter. In a 1½-quart shallow baking dish, arrange bread, buttered side down, and sprinkle with raisins. In a medium bowl, beat together milk, grapefruit juice, eggs, ⅓ cup brown sugar, grapefruit peel, and cinnamon until combined. Pour over bread slices; let stand 30 minutes. Place baking dish in a pan of hot water. Bake in a 350°F. oven 45 minutes to 1 hour, or until tip of knife inserted in center comes out clean. Remove pan from oven; top with grapefruit slices and remaining 2 tablespoons brown sugar. Broil 2 to 3 minutes, or until sugar melts.

Heritage Pumpkin Pudding with Fluffy Lemon Hard Sauce

Makes 10 to 12 servings
- **1 package (18¼ ounces) spice cake mix**
- **1½ cups (½ of 30-ounce can) Libby's Pumpkin Pie Mix**
- **2 eggs**
- **1 cup chopped walnuts**
- **1 cup raisins**
- **1 cup chopped pitted dates**
- **Fluffy Lemon Hard Sauce (recipe follows)**

Preheat oven to 350°F. In large mixing bowl, combine cake mix, pumpkin pie mix, and eggs. Beat at medium speed 4 minutes. Stir in nuts, raisins, and dates. Carefully spoon batter into two greased 6-cup molds; cover tightly with foil and secure with string. Set in larger ovenproof glass bowl. Place on oven rack. Fill bowl with hot water almost to top of mold. Bake 1 hour and 50 minutes or until long wooden pick in-

Barbara's Bread Pudding. Florida Department of Citrus

serted in center comes out clean. Let pudding stand, uncovered, 15 minutes, before removing from mold. Serve hot with Fluffy Lemon Hard Sauce.

Fluffy Lemon Hard Sauce

Makes about 1¼ cups
- **½ cup butter or margarine, softened**
- **2 cups powdered sugar**
- **2 teaspoons lemon juice**
- **1 egg, separated**
- **1 teaspoon grated lemon peel**

Cream butter and sugar; beat in lemon juice, egg yolk, and lemon peel. Beat egg white until stiff; fold into sugar mixture.

Q. *My puddings develop a thick, gummy layer on top when refrigerated, even though I cover them tightly. What's wrong?*
A. We assume you mean egg-and-milk puddings, thickened with flour or cornstarch, and cooked on top of the stove. Covering this sort of pudding isn't enough. While the pudding is hot, press a layer of plastic wrap or a plastic storage bag on the top surface of the pudding, making sure it touches the entire surface, especially all around the sides.

Holiday Steamed Fig Pudding

Makes 8 servings

- ¼ **cup butter or margarine**
- ½ **cup light brown sugar**
- 1 **egg**
- 1 **cup sifted all-purpose flour**
- ½ **cup dry bread crumbs**
- 1 **teaspoon baking soda**
- ½ **teaspoon salt**
- ½ **teaspoon ground cinnamon**
- ½ **teaspoon ground nutmeg**
- ½ **teaspoon allspice**
- ¼ **cup milk**
- ½ **cup molasses**
- 1 **cup cut-up figs (about 6 ounces)**
- ½ **cup chopped walnuts**
  Velvet Sauce (recipe follows)

Cream butter with sugar; add egg and beat until fluffy. Sift dry ingredients together. Combine milk and molasses; add to butter mixture alternately with dry ingredients. Blend thoroughly; beat well. Add figs and nuts. Turn into a 1½-quart buttered mold or bowl, or eight 5-ounce cup molds. Cover with foil. Steam large pudding 2 hours, small puddings 1 hour. Serve hot with Velvet Sauce.

Velvet Sauce

- 2 **eggs**
- 1 **cup confectioners sugar**
- 2 **tablespoons lemon juice**
- 3 **tablespoons brandy or rum (or 1 teaspoon vanilla extract)**
- 1 **cup heavy cream, whipped**

Beat the eggs. Add sugar gradually, then the lemon juice and the flavoring, continuing to beat until mixture is very light and fluffy. Fold in whipped cream. Refrigerate until ready to serve. This is good on hot steamed puddings and on hot dessert soufflés.

Steamed Chocolate Pudding

Makes 8 servings

- 2 **cups sifted all-purpose flour**
- 2 **teaspoons baking powder**
- ¼ **teaspoon salt**
- 3 **tablespoons butter or margarine**
- ⅔ **cup sugar**
- 1 **egg**
- 1 **cup milk**
- 2 **squares (2 ounces) unsweetened chocolate, melted**
- 1 **teaspoon vanilla extract**
  Velvet Sauce (see index)

Sift dry ingredients together. Cream butter and sugar, then add the egg and beat until light. Add the dry ingredients alternately with the milk, mixing well. Fold in the chocolate and the vanilla. Fill buttered individual cups or small cans or a 1-quart bowl. Cover with foil and steam individual puddings 40 minutes, large puddings about 1½ hours. Serve hot with Velvet Sauce.

Steamed Puddings

Steamed puddings are wonderful old-fashioned desserts that deserve a revival of popularity. They may be made ahead and stored in the refrigerator for a few days—or for many months in the freezer. Use custard cups, small bowls, or aluminum cans for individual servings—a larger bowl for pudding to serve many. Fill each bowl only two-thirds full so pudding has plenty of room to rise.

The small aluminum cans used for potted meats, some brands of dehydrated soups, and tuna are seamless on the bottom and sides. These make fine individual molds. Puddings slip out easily. Heavy Duty Reynolds Wrap makes a good cover that will fit any container.

How to Steam Puddings: Use any pan large enough to accommodate the individual or large pudding. Put a wire rack in the bottom of the pan and place puddings on the rack. Pour in boiling water until it comes halfway up the sides of pudding containers. Cover pan and boil gently. Use towel to protect fingers when removing the finished pudding.

How to Freeze: If you don't need the containers for reuse, simply cool, seal foil cover, and freeze. Or cool and turn out puddings, package in heavy duty foil wrap, and freeze.

Pressure-cooked Puddings: Follow directions in instruction booklet that came with the cooker. It will reduce the cooking time. Secure foil cover on mold by tying with string.

To Serve Steamed Puddings: Reheat in the oven, still sealed in foil. If puddings are chilled, reheat individual puddings 30 minutes at 300°F., a large pudding 1½ hours at 300°F. If puddings are frozen, allow 10 minutes additional time.

To Serve Flaming Plum Pudding: Heat ½ cup brandy or rum in a small pan until lukewarm. Pour over large pudding or several small puddings arranged on warm serving plate. Light match and bring to table. Spoon flaming liquor quickly over puddings. Or moisten lumps of sugar in lemon or orange extract and arrange around pudding, or place one lump on top of each individual pudding. Light lumps with match.

Apple-Raisin Steamed Pudding

Makes 12 to 15 servings

- 6 slices dry bread
- 2 cups raisins
- 1 cup diced mixed candied fruits
- 1 medium apple, pared, quartered, and cored
- 1 medium carrot, pared and cut up
- 3 thin slices orange
- ⅓ cup brandy or rum
- 3 eggs
- 1 cup dark corn syrup
- ⅓ cup butter or margarine, softened
- 2 teaspoons baking powder
- 1 teaspoon ground cinnamon
- ½ teaspoon ground nutmeg
- ½ teaspoon salt
- ½ cup all-purpose flour
- 1 cup walnuts
  Hard Sauce (see index)

Break two slices bread into blender container. Cover; blend at medium speed until crumbed. Empty into measuring cup. Repeat process with remaining bread (you should have 2½ cups crumbs). Empty into large mixing bowl; stir in raisins and candied fruits; set aside. Put remaining ingredients except flour and walnuts into blender container in order listed. Cover; blend at high speed until smooth. Add flour and nuts. Cover; blend at medium speed until nuts are coarsely chopped and batter is blended. Add to bread crumbs and fruits; mix thoroughly. Turn into greased and sugared 2-quart mold or heatproof bowl. Cover tightly with aluminum foil; tie with string. Place on rack in large kettle. Add enough boiling water to kettle to come halfway up sides of mold. Cover kettle; steam 4 hours, adding more water as needed. Remove from kettle; let stand 15 minutes. Unmold. Serve with Hard Sauce.

Note: Pudding may be made ahead. After steaming, remove cover from mold; cool pudding. Cover and refrigerate. To reheat, steam 1½ hours.

Danish Pudding Cake

Makes 1 cake

- 2 cups sugar
- 1 cup butter or margarine
- 4 eggs
- 1 teaspoon vanilla extract
- 3 cups sifted Martha White All-Purpose Flour
- ½ teaspoon salt
- ½ teaspoon baking powder
- ½ cup milk
- 1 package (8 ounces) chopped dates
- 1 cup chopped pecans
  Orange Sauce (recipe follows)

Preheat oven to 325°F. Grease and flour 10-inch tube pan; set aside. Cream sugar and butter with electric mixer in large mixing bowl until light and fluffy. Add eggs, 1 at a time, beating well after each addition; stir in vanilla. Combine flour, salt, and baking powder in separate bowl. Alternately add flour mixture and milk to creamed mixture; blend well. Stir in dates and pecans. Pour into prepared pan. Bake 1 hour 15 minutes, or until toothpick inserted in center comes out clean. While cake is baking, prepare Orange Sauce. Remove cake from oven; immediately spoon sauce over top. Cool completely in pan.

Orange Sauce

- 1 cup sugar
- 1 cup orange juice
- 2 tablespoons grated orange peel

Combine all ingredients in small saucepan. Bring to a boil, stirring constantly. Remove from heat; cool slightly.

Mocha Pudding Cake

Makes 4 servings

This rich delight accommodatingly makes its own sauce as it cooks.

- 1 cup all-purpose flour
- 2 teaspoons baking powder
- 1 cup sugar
- ½ cup cocoa
- ½ cup milk
- 1 teaspoon instant coffee
- 3 tablespoons butter or margarine, melted
- 2 teaspoons vanilla extract
- ½ cup firmly packed light brown sugar
  Boiling water
  Whipped cream (optional)

You will need: Visions or Corning Ware 2-quart saucepan, buttered

Sift together flour, baking powder, and ¾ cup of the granulated sugar into a bowl. Stir in half the cocoa, the milk, coffee, butter, and half the vanilla. Pour into prepared saucepan. In a small bowl, combine remaining granulated sugar, cocoa, and vanilla, and the brown sugar. Sprinkle evenly over surface of batter in saucepan. Gently and evenly, pour 1 cup boiling water over top. Bake in preheated 350°F. oven 1 hour. Serve warm, for a fairly thin sauce, or cold for a thicker sauce. Either way, top each serving with whipped cream, if desired.

A Frosty Array of Chilled Desserts

Mealtime comes to a dazzling conclusion with make-ahead delights—gels, Bavarians, creams, mousses, cold soufflés, and no-bake cheesecakes—that come straight from your refrigerator.

Fresh Lemon Snow

Makes 10 servings

- 1 envelope Knox Unflavored Gelatine
- 1/3 cup sugar
- 1¼ cups boiling water
- ¼ cup lemon juice
- 1 teaspoon grated lemon peel
- 2 egg whites

In large bowl, mix unflavored gelatine with sugar; add boiling water and stir until gelatine is completely dissolved. Stir in lemon juice and peel. Chill, stirring occasionally, until mixture is consistency of unbeaten egg whites. With electric mixer, beat gelatine mixture with egg whites at high speed until mixture begins to hold its shape, about 7 minutes. Turn into dessert dishes or 5-cup bowl; chill until set.

Fresh Lime Snow

Substitute lime juice for lemon juice.

Zabaglione Snow

Makes 6 to 8 servings

- ¾ cup confectioners sugar
- 2 envelopes Knox Unflavored Gelatine
- 6 eggs, separated
- 1½ cups water
- ½ cup Marsala, sherry, or dry white wine

In medium saucepan, mix unflavored gelatine with ½ cup sugar; blend in egg yolks beaten with water. Let stand 1 minute. Stir over low heat, beating constantly with wire whip until gelatine is completely dissolved and mixture is thick and foamy, about 5 minutes. Stir in wine. Pour into large bowl and chill, stirring occasionally, until mixture mounds slightly when dropped from spoon.

In medium bowl, beat egg whites until soft peaks form; gradually add remaining sugar and beat until stiff. Fold in gelatine mixture. Turn into parfait glasses or dessert dishes and chill until set.

Fresh Lemon Snow. Knox Gelatine, Inc.

Berries 'n' Cream Bavarian

Makes about 12 servings

- 2 envelopes Knox Unflavored Gelatine
- ⅔ cup sugar
- 3 eggs, separated
- 1 cup milk
- 2 containers (8 ounces each) raspberry, strawberry, or boysenberry yogurt
- Red food coloring (optional)
- 1 cup whipping or heavy cream, whipped

In medium saucepan, mix unflavored gelatine with ⅓ cup sugar; blend in egg yolks beaten with milk. Let stand 1 minute. Stir over low heat until gelatin is completely dissolved, about 5 minutes. With wire whip or rotary beater, blend in yogurt and food coloring, if desired. Pour into large bowl and chill, stirring occasionally, until mixture mounds slightly when dropped from spoon.

In medium bowl, beat egg whites until soft peaks form; gradually add remaining sugar and beat until stiff. Fold egg whites, then whipped cream, into gelatine mixture. Turn into dessert dishes or 8-cup bowl and chill until set.

Snowy Coconut Cheese Dessert

Makes 12 servings

- 2 envelopes unflavored gelatin
- ½ cup cold water
- 1½ cups boiling water
- 2 containers (16 ounces each) cottage cheese
- 1 can (14 ounces) Eagle® Brand Sweetened Condensed Milk (not evaporated milk)
- 1 can (3½ ounces) flaked coconut
- Lettuce leaves
- Fresh or canned fruit

In large bowl, sprinkle gelatin over cold water; let stand 1 minute. Add boiling water and stir until gelatin is dissolved. Add cheese, Eagle Brand, and coconut; mix well. Turn into 2-quart mold or 10-cup fluted tube pan. Chill 4 hours, or until set. Unmold onto lettuce. Serve with fruit. Refrigerate leftovers.

Sunny Citrus Medley

Makes 8 servings
 2 envelopes Knox Unflavored Gelatine
 ⅓ cup sugar
 1 cup boiling water
1½ cup orange juice
 1 cup ginger ale
 ½ teaspoon grated orange peel
 1 package (3 ounces) cream cheese, softened
 2 oranges, peeled and cut into chunks, divided
 1 grapefruit, peeled and cut into chunks, divided

In a medium bowl, mix unflavored gelatine with sugar. Add boiling water and stir until gelatine is completely dissolved. Add orange juice, ginger ale, and orange peel.

In a small bowl, beat cream cheese until smooth; gradually beat in 1¼ cups gelatine mixture. Chill, stirring occasionally, until mixture is the consistency of unbeaten egg whites. Fold in a third of the fruit. Turn into a 5-cup mold; chill until almost set.

Meanwhile, chill remaining gelatine mixture, stirring occasionally, until mixture is the consistency of unbeaten egg whites. Fold in remaining fruit. Turn onto almost-set gelatine; chill until firm.

Oriental Floating Almond Dessert

Makes about 8 servings
 2 envelopes Knox Unflavored Gelatine, divided
 10 tablespoons sugar, divided
1¾ cups boiling water, divided
 1 can (5⅓ ounces) evaporated milk
 1 tablespoon almond extract
 1 can (11 ounces) mandarin oranges, drained, reserving syrup
   Orange juice
 1 cup sliced strawberries
 1 cup blueberries

Reserve 1½ teaspoons Knox Unflavored Gelatine. In medium bowl, mix remaining gelatine and 8 tablespoons sugar. Add 1¼ cups boiling water and stir until gelatine is completely dissolved. Stir in milk and almond extract; turn into 9-inch square baking pan and chill until firm, about 2 hours. Meanwhile, in medium bowl, combine reserved gelatine with remaining 2 tablespoons sugar. Add remaining ½ cup boiling water and stir until gelatine is completely dissolved. Combine reserved orange syrup with enough orange juice to equal 1½ cups; add to gelatine mixture. Chill until mixture is slightly syrupy.

To serve, cut almond gelatine into 1-inch diamond shapes. In dessert dishes, equally divide almond gelatine, mandarin oranges, strawberries, blueberries, and orange syrup.

Seven-Layer Blueberry Delight

Makes 9 servings
 2 cups crushed vanilla wafers
 ½ cup butter or margarine, softened
1½ cups confectioners sugar
 2 eggs
 1 can (12 ounces) Solo Blueberry Filling
 1 package (3¾ ounces) vanilla instant pudding
 2 cups milk
 1 cup heavy cream (or 2 cups whipped topping)

Sprinkle wafer crumbs on bottom of 9-inch square pan, reserving ¼ cup for topping. Beat butter or margarine, confectioners sugar, and eggs together with an electric mixer until smooth and well blended. Pour over crumbs in pan. Spread blueberry filling over creamed mixture. Prepare instant pudding according to package directions, using 2 cups milk. Pour over blueberry filling. Add layer of chopped nuts. Whip cream until stiff and spread on top of nuts. Sprinkle with reserved wafer crumbs. Refrigerate 8 hours before serving.

Spanish Cream

Makes one 1½-quart mold
 1 tablespoon plain gelatine
 3 cups milk
 ½ cup sugar
 ¼ teaspoon salt
 3 eggs, separated
 1 teaspoon vanilla extract
   Whipped cream, Chocolate Sauce, or Butterscotch Sauce (see index)

Stir gelatine into milk in top of double boiler; let stand 5 minutes. Add 2 tablespoons of the sugar and the salt. Cook over boiling water, stirring until gelatine is dissolved; remove from heat. Beat egg yolks with 2 tablespoons of the sugar. Add milk mixture gradually to egg yolks, stirring constantly. Return to double boiler; cook over hot (not boiling) water until slightly thickened; chill until thick and syrupy. Beat egg whites until stiff; beat in remaining ¼ cup sugar. Fold in vanilla, beaten egg white mixture. Rinse mold with cold water. Turn mixture into mold. Chill until set; unmold. Serve with whipped cream, Chocolate Sauce, or Butterscotch Sauce.

Chocolate Spanish Cream

Make Spanish Cream, adding 1½ squares unsweetened chocolate, melted, to the milk-gelatine mixture; beat until smooth. Serve with whipped cream.

Gelatin Terms

"Fold in": Gently is the key here. Using a rubber spatula or wooden spoon, cut down into the mixture in the center of the bowl, turn the spoon or spatula flat, sweep gently across the bottom, and bring the spatula to the surface of the mixture near the edge of bowl that is closest to you. Give the bowl a quarter turn and repeat, continuing until the gelatin mixture and the other ingredients are well blended. When folding in whipped cream or beaten egg whites, be particularly gentle—otherwise, you'll lose some of the air trapped in the whipped mixture, and the volume of the finished dish will not be as great, nor the texture as fluffy, as you'd like it to be.

"Chill until mixture mounds slightly when dropped from a spoon": This direction is most often given when beaten egg whites or whipped cream are to be incorporated into the gelatine mixture, in such dishes as chiffons or bavarians. To test, follow the directions—spoon up a little of the chilled mixture and let it slip off the spoon back into the bowl. It should mound or puddle slightly rather than stream off the spoon.

"Chill until firm": You know what firm is, but how long does it take? As with other steps in chilling, this varies, depending on the ingredients used and the temperature of your refrigerator. Individual molds and some pies will be firm in less than 3 hours. A large soufflé or other large gel may take 4 to 6 hours, or overnight. To be on the safe side, make a dish that will serve a large number the day before the party. Not only does this ensure a perfectly firmed product, but it also makes life easier on party day!

"Unmold to serve": To many cooks, this is the scary part. Take courage, it's easy when you know how. Dip the mold into warm (not hot) water to the depth of the gelatin contents for about 5 seconds. (Keep an eye on the clock, or count as kids do: one raccoon, two raccoons, and so on.) Remove it from the water. Carefully loosen the gel from the sides of the container with the tip of a sharp, thin-bladed knife. Tilt or shake the container gently to loosen the gel. Invert a serving dish on top of the container. Hold the container and the serving dish firmly together and turn both over. Shake them gently until the gelatin slips from the container onto the serving dish. If the gel doesn't come out easily, you've probably been too cautious—repeat the process.

To Make Whipped Cream Ahead of Time

When you beat the cream, add 1 teaspoon of white corn syrup for each cup of cream (measured before beating). It should hold up for at least three hours. To stabilize it for a longer period (and to use if you wish to pipe whipped cream decorations through a pastry bag), try this. Soften 1 teaspoon unflavored gelatin in 2 tablespoons of cold water. Measure 1 cup of heavy cream; remove 3 tablespoons of the measured cream and scald it. Add to the softened gelatin, stirring until the gelatin is completely dissolved; refrigerate until thickened but not set. Beat until frothy. Beat the remaining cream, adding a few grains of salt, 2 tablespoons confectioners sugar and ½ teaspoon vanilla extract. Fold in the gelatin mixture. If you'd like chocolate whipped cream, melt 1 (6-ounce) bag of semisweet chocolate bits; cool slightly, fold into the finished stabilized whipped cream.

Basic Dessert Gel

Makes about 4 servings

1 envelope Knox Unflavored Gelatine
2 to 4 tablespoons sugar
2 cups fruit juice,* heated to boiling

In a medium bowl, mix unflavored gelatine with sugar. Add boiling liquid; stir until gelatine is completely dissolved. Pour into a 2-cup bowl or individual dessert dishes; chill until firm.

*Do not use fresh or frozen pineapple juice. It contains an enzyme that prevents the mixture from gelling.

Fruited Dessert Gel

Decrease liquid by ¼ cup; chill mixture, stirring occasionally, until the consistency of unbeaten egg whites. Fold in up to 1½ cups chopped fresh, frozen (except pineapple), or canned fruit; turn into a 3-cup bowl or mold or into individual dessert dishes. Chill until firm.

What Goes with What?

Almost any fruit combines beautifully with unflavored gelatin: fresh, frozen, or canned fruit juice; fresh, frozen, or canned peaches, plums, pears, apricots, grapes, cherries, all varieties of berries and melons, canned pineapple, fruit cocktail.

Here are some anything-goes-with-anything combinations to try. Then use your inventiveness to go on from there: orange gel with peaches and strawberries; lemon gel with fruit cocktail; cranberry-juice gel with oranges and walnuts; fruit-punch gel with pears and grapes.

Creamy Peach Parfait (page 55); Topaz Parfait (page 85);
Banana Rum Parfait (page 84). General Foods

Orange and Rice Cream Mold

Makes 8 servings

  1 can (11 ounces) mandarin orange segments
    Milk
  3 cups cooked rice
  ½ teaspoon salt
  ⅓ cup sugar
    Grated peel and juice of 1 orange
  1 teaspoon vanilla extract
  1 package (2⅛ ounces) whipped topping mix,
     prepared
    Additional orange segments
    Banana slices
    Chocolate pieces

Drain orange segments; set segments aside. Add enough milk to juice to make 3 cups. Combine with rice, salt, and sugar. Cook over medium heat until thick and creamy, about 30 minutes, stirring occasionally. Stir in peel, juice, and vanilla. Spoon into a 6-cup ring mold. Chill. Unmold onto serving plate. Spoon whipped topping into center of ring. Circle mold with orange segments. Arrange additional orange segments, banana slices, and chocolate pieces on top of ring mold.

Bavarian Rice

Makes 6 servings

  1 tablespoon unflavored gelatin
  ¼ cup cold water
  ¼ cup milk, scalded
  ¼ cup sugar
  ¼ teaspoon salt
  1 teaspoon vanilla extract
  1 cup cooked Uncle Ben's® Converted® Brand
    Rice
  1 cup whipping cream, whipped
  1 cup apricot jam or preserves
    Maraschino cherries

Combine gelatin and cold water; let stand 5 minutes. Stir into hot milk. Stir sugar, salt, vanilla, and milk mixture into cooked rice. Cool. When partially thickened, fold in whipped cream. Turn into 1-quart mold or 6 individual molds that have been rinsed in cold water. Chill until firm. Unmold and cover with jam or preserves. Garnish with maraschino cherries.

Orange and Rice Cream Mold. Rice Council of America

Coffee Charlotte Russe

Makes 4 servings

½ **cup butter or margarine, softened**
1½ **cups confectioners sugar**
4 **egg yolks**
¼ **cup cold strong coffee (or ½ teaspoon instant coffee dissolved in ¼ cup water)**
12 **Ladyfingers (see index)**
Rum or sherry
Whipped cream
Toasted slivered almonds

Put butter, confectioners sugar, egg yolks, and coffee into blender container. Cover; blend at high speed until smooth. Arrange three ladyfingers in each of four dessert dishes or sherbet glasses; sprinkle with rum or sherry. Spoon coffee mixture into dishes. Chill several hours. Just before serving, top with whipped cream and toasted almonds.

Chocolate Charlotte Russe

Makes 8 to 10 servings

Ladyfingers (recipe follows)
6 **ounces semisweet chocolate**
½ **cup butter or margarine**
6 **egg yolks**
¾ **cup C & H Granulated Sugar**
⅓ **cup water**
2 **cups heavy cream**
2 **tablespoons rum, crème de cacao, or orange liqueur**
Additional liqueur
Sweetened whipped cream

Prepare ladyfingers. Melt chocolate and butter together in top of double boiler. Stir until smooth. Cool slightly at room temperature. Beat egg yolks 10 minutes or until thick, lemon colored, and tripled in volume. Combine sugar and water in small, heavy saucepan. Cook over low heat until sugar dissolves, swirling pan occasionally. Raise heat and cook until syrup reaches 236°F. on candy thermometer (soft ball stage). Gradually beat sugar syrup into egg yolks. Stir in melted chocolate mixture and continue beating until cool. Whip cream and rum together. Stir about one-quarter of cream into chocolate mixture to aerate, then fold in the rest.

Select a medium bowl or mold with narrow rounded bottom. Line with foil. Sprinkle ladyfingers lightly with additional liqueur. Using as many ladyfingers as necessary, arrange vertically around sides of bowl with flat sides toward center, overlapping slightly. Fill with half of chocolate mixture. Top with any remaining ladyfingers. Add remaining chocolate mixture. Cut off tops of ladyfingers extending above chocolate mixture and arrange pieces on top of chocolate filling. Cover bowl and chill overnight to set. Unmold and invert onto serving platter. Decorate with sweetened whipped cream.

Ladyfingers

Makes about 1½ dozen

½ **cup C & H Granulated Sugar**
4 **eggs, separated**
⅔ **cup all-purpose flour**
Pinch *each* salt and cream of tartar
C & H Powdered Sugar

Preheat oven to 300°F. Line 2 large cookie sheets with parchment or grease and flour sheets. Beat granulated sugar and egg yolks until thick and lemon colored. Fold in flour. With a clean beater in a different bowl, beat egg whites with salt and cream of tartar until stiff. Stir about one quarter of whites into yolk mixture; fold in the rest. Using a pastry bag with a ½-inch plain tube or a spoon, pipe out ¾-inch wide ladyfingers 4 inches long. Sprinkle with powdered sugar. Bake 15 to 20 minutes, until lightly browned. Cool on rack.

Mousses and bavarians—and chiffons, as well—can be served in a number of ways, dressed up for their final chilling. An orange chiffon, for example, turned into a chocolate cookie-crumb crust and decorated with chocolate curls, makes a delicious and beautiful pie you'll be proud to serve. Or turn any chiffon, mousse, or bavarian mixture into a serving dish or springform pan lined with ladyfingers. Presto—you've produced a superb charlotte.

Banana-Rum Parfait

Makes 5 servings

1 **package (3 ounces) Jell-O Brand Gelatin, Orange Flavor**
1 **cup boiling water**
1 **cup ice cubes**
1 **medium banana, sliced**
1 **cup (½ pint) vanilla ice cream**
1 **tablespoon light rum or ¼ teaspoon rum extract**
Whipped topping (optional)

Dissolve gelatin in boiling water. Measure ½ cup; add ice cubes and stir constantly until gelatin starts to thicken, about 3 to 5 minutes. Remove any unmelted ice. Add banana and spoon into 5 parfait glasses. Blend ice cream and rum into remaining gelatin. Spoon over clear gelatin in glasses. Chill until set, about 30 minutes. Garnish with whipped topping, if desired.

Topaz Parfait

Makes 4 to 6 servings

  1 cup brewed Maxwell House Coffee
  1 package (3 ounces) Jell-O Brand Gelatin,
       Lemon Flavor
  ⅓ cup granulated sugar
  ½ cup cold water★
  ¼ cup brandy or dark rum★
  2 tablespoons firmly packed brown sugar
  1 tablespoon brandy or dark rum or ½ teaspoon
       brandy extract
  1 container (4 ounces) Cool Whip Non-Dairy
       Whipped Topping, thawed

In medium saucepan, bring coffee to a boil. Add gelatin and granulated sugar and stir until dissolved. Add cold water and ¼ cup brandy. Pour into 8-inch square pan. Chill until firm, about 4 hours. Cut into cubes. Fold brown sugar and 1 tablespoon brandy into whipped topping. Layer coffee cubes and topping in parfait glasses.

★ Or increase cold water to ¾ cup and use 1 teaspoon brandy extract.

Creamy Peach Parfait

Makes 6 servings

  1 package (3 ounces) cream cheese, softened
  2 teaspoons sugar
  1 tablespoon milk
  1 package (3 ounces) Jell-O Brand Gelatin, Peach
       Flavor
  1 cup boiling water
  2 cups ice cubes
  1 cup diced peeled fresh peaches
  ¼ cup raspberry jam or preserves
       Whipped topping (optional)
       Fresh peach slices (optional)

Combine cream cheese, sugar, and milk in bowl, blending well; set aside. Dissolve gelatin in boiling water. Add ice cubes and stir gently until gelatin begins to thicken, 3 to 5 minutes. Remove any unmelted ice. Fold in peaches. Spoon half the fruited gelatin into 6 parfait glasses. Carefully spoon cheese mixture into glasses over gelatin. Add a layer of preserves. Top with remaining gelatin mixture. Chill until set, about 2 hours. Garnish with whipped topping and fresh peach slices, if desired.

Bavarian Cream

Makes 6 to 8 servings

  ¼ cup cold water
  2 envelopes unflavored gelatin
  ¾ cup milk, scalded
  ¼ cup sugar
  ¼ teaspoon salt
  1½ teaspoons vanilla extract
  ¼ teaspoon almond extract
  1¼ cups cracked or crushed ice
  1 cup heavy cream

Put cold water into blender container. Sprinkle on gelatin. Let stand 1 minute. Add milk, sugar, and salt. Cover; blend at low speed until gelatin is dissolved. Add vanilla, almond extract, and ice. Cover; blend at high speed. While blender is running, tip center cap and gradually add cream, blending until smooth. Pour into 1-quart mold. Chill until set. Unmold.

Serving Suggestion: Serve with Easy Zabaglione Sauce (recipe follows) or Melba Sauce (see index).

Coffee Bavarian Cream

Add 2 tablespoons instant coffee to blender container with gelatin; omit almond extract. Proceed as for Bavarian Cream.

Chocolate Bavarian Cream

Reduce sugar to 2 tablespoons. Add 1 cup semisweet chocolate pieces to blender container after gelatin has been dissolved. Cover; blend at high speed until chocolate is liquified. Omit almond extract. Proceed as for Bavarian Cream.

Easy Zabaglione Sauce

Makes about 2¾ cups

  1 cup cold milk
  1½ cups light cream
  1 package (4 servings) vanilla flavor instant pudding
       mix
  1 egg white
  2 tablespoons sugar
  ¼ cup sherry or Marsala wine

Put milk, cream, and pudding mix into blender container. Cover; blend at low speed until smooth. Beat egg white in medium mixing bowl with electric mixer until foamy; gradually beat in sugar; continue beating until stiff but not dry. Fold pudding mixture into egg white. Chill. Just before serving, gently stir in wine.

Serving Suggestion: Use to top Bavarian Cream, fruit, pound cake, etc.

Good Idea

When you remove a mixture from over the hot water in a double boiler and wish to cool it in a hurry, fill the bottom of the double boiler with ice water and place the top over it. Stir the mixture often so that it doesn't set faster than you want it to.

Blender Mousse

Makes eight 4-ounce servings

- 1 12-ounce package (2 cups) Nestlé Toll House Semi-Sweet Chocolate Morsels
- ½ cup sugar
- 3 eggs
- 1 cup hot milk
- 2 to 4 tablespoons brandy, rum, or almond or orange liqueur
-    Whipped cream (optional)

In blender container, combine Nestlé Toll House Semi-Sweet Chocolate Morsels, sugar, and eggs. Add hot milk and liqueur; blend at medium speed until mixture is smooth. Pour into pots de crème or demitasse cups and chill in refrigerator 1 hour. Garnish with whipped cream, if desired. Keep in refrigerator until ready to serve.

Mocha Mousse

Add 3 tablespoons instant coffee to blender along with eggs.

Blender Mousse; Butterscotch Thins (page 62). The Nestlé Company

Cold Pumpkin Soufflé

Makes 8 servings

- 2 packages plain gelatin
- 1 cup firmly packed C & H Golden Brown Sugar
-    Pinch of salt
- 4 eggs, separated
- ¾ cup milk
- 1 can (16 ounces) pumpkin puree
- 2 teaspoons pumpkin pie spice
- 1 cup heavy cream, whipped
-    Finely chopped walnuts

Prepare 1-quart soufflé dish: Fold a band of aluminum foil long enough to fit around dish (double thickness and 4 inches wide). Place around rim of dish to extend 2 inches above top. Fasten the ends securely with tape, string, or straight pin.

Combine gelatin, half the sugar, and the salt in top of double boiler. Set aside. Beat egg yolks and add to milk; stir into sugar mixture. Place over simmering water; stir until gelatin is dissolved. Remove from heat; stir in ¼ cup sugar, the pumpkin, and spice. Cool until slightly thickened.

Beat egg whites until foamy. Gradually add remaining ¼ cup sugar and continue beating until stiff. Fold into pumpkin mixture. Fold in whipped cream. Pour into prepared soufflé dish. Chill at least 4 hours. Remove band. Press chopped nuts around edge of soufflé.

Cold Pumpkin Soufflé. C&H Sugar Company

Lingonberry Mousse

Makes 6 to 8 servings

- 1½ cups water
- ¼ teaspoon salt
- ¼ cup quick-cooking farina
- 1 jar (14 ounces) lingonberry preserves
-    Whipped cream

Combine water and salt in saucepan; bring to boil. Add farina slowly to boiling water, stirring constantly. Cook 2½ minutes over medium heat, stirring constantly to prevent sticking; remove from heat; set aside. Press lingonberry preserves through fine sieve; add to cooked farina. Cook to lukewarm; beat with electric mixer or rotary beater until thick and fluffy. Pour into individual serving dishes; chill. Serve with whipped cream.

Good to Know: This mousse is delicious made with blackberry, black raspberry, or red raspberry preserves. Line the serving dish with crisp vanilla wafers for an added treat.

Raspberry Mousse

Makes about 8 servings

    1 cup milk
    4 eggs, separated
    3 tablespoons sugar
    1 tablespoon red maraschino cherry syrup (optional)
   ½ teaspoon vanilla extract
    2 cans (12 ounces) Solo Raspberry Filling
    2 cups heavy cream

In top part of double boiler, combine milk, lightly beaten egg yolks, and sugar. Cook over hot water, stirring, until the custard coats a spoon. Remove from heat. Blend in cherry syrup and vanilla. Refrigerate until thoroughly chilled. Rub raspberry filling though a wire strainer. Whip cream until stiff. Fold chilled custard and whipped cream into raspberry filling. Beat egg whites until stiff. Fold carefully into raspberry mixture. Turn into a serving bowl and refrigerate at least 4 hours. Garnish with additional whipped cream, if desired, before serving.

Apricot Mousse

Makes 6 to 8 servings

    1 envelope unflavored gelatin
    1 cup Sherried Apricot Sauce (recipe follows)
    3 egg whites
    2 tablespoons sugar
   ¾ cup heavy cream

Place ½ cup cold water in a small saucepan and sprinkle with the gelatin. Cook, stirring constantly, over low heat until the gelatin dissolves. Remove from the heat and stir in the apricot sauce. Pour the mixture into a large bowl, cover, and refrigerate until thickened.

Beat the egg whites in a large mixer bowl until fluffy. Gradually add the sugar, beating until the whites stand in stiff peaks. Set aside. With the same beater, whip cream until soft peaks form. Spoon 2 tablespoons each of whipped cream and beaten egg whites into the apricot mixture, stirring to mix well and lighten the mixture. Fold the remaining whipped cream and beaten egg whites alternately into the apricot mixture. Spoon into an attractive 6-cup mold or individual dishes. Refrigerate for 6 hours, or until firmly set. Spoon additional Sherried Apricot Sauce over mousse at serving time.

Sherried Apricot Sauce

Makes 1¾ cups

   ½ cup dried apricots (about 20)
   ½ cup firmly packed light brown sugar
   ¼ teaspoon salt
    2 to 3 tablespoons medium-dry sherry

Combine the apricots, sugar, and salt with 1½ cups water in a medium-size saucepan, and bring to a boil. Reduce heat and simmer, uncovered, for 15 to 20 minutes, or until the apricots are very tender. Stir in the sherry. Pour into a food processor (using chopping blade) or container of a blender. Cover and process until smooth.

Note: This sauce is good hot or cold and will keep for up to 2 weeks in the refrigerator.

Roundup of Sweet Sauces

Most common of the dessert sauces is **Crème Chantilly**—whipped cream. Another easy and simple—and very good—sweet sauce is made with fruit juice thickened with cornstarch, sweetened if desired, sometimes spiked with lemon juice to point up the flavor, sometimes with berries or cut-up fruit added. Another, even simpler, is cut-up or crushed fruit alone, sweetened if necessary.

Hard sauce is made by creaming together butter and confectioners sugar; it can be flavored with anything from rum or brandy to fruit juice or purée. Liqueurs in their infinite variety make excellent dessert sauces. Custard sauce—variously known also as English custard or Crème Anglaise or soft custard—sweetly and mildly sauces such desserts as plain cake or cake topped with sliced or crushed fruit or berries. And plain cream—heavy, but not whipped—is the best of sauces for such down-home desserts as apple betty, fruit dumplings, or cobblers.

Melba sauce designed for peach melba but most acceptable elsewhere, combines puréed raspberries with currant jelly for lovely color and piquant flavor. Try it on briefly baked bananas, or over baked custards turned out of their cups. Wine custard—Bavarian Weinschaum—or Italian Zabaglione are richly delicious variations on the custard theme. Spicy cider sauce dresses up a bland pudding or a plain cake.

Buttery brown sugar sauce, honey sauce, caramel sauce, butterscotch sauce, maple sugar sauce—these are all cousins, all delicious on ice cream, plain cake, dessert waffles, blancmange-type puddings.

And then, of course, there is **chocolate sauce** in many versions—thin and bittersweet, richly fudgy to be served hot, chocolate custard, chocolate-mint, the great mocha flavor of chocolate-coffee. Serve on ice cream, plain cake or pudding, and dress them further if you wish with such crisp sprinkle-on additions as chopped or slivered nuts or crushed candies, or top with brandied fruit.

Chocolate-Mint Soufflé

Makes 6 to 8 servings

- 1 6-ounce package (1 cup) Nestlé Toll House Semi-Sweet Chocolate Morsels
- 1 envelope unflavored gelatin
- 1 cup sugar, divided
- 6 eggs, separated
- ½ cup milk
- ¼ cup water
- 1 teaspoon peppermint extract
  Green food coloring
- ½ teaspoon salt
- 1 cup heavy cream, whipped

Prepare a 2-inch foil collar for a 1¼- to 1½-quart soufflé dish. Lightly oil collar and fasten to dish; set aside. In blender container, process Nestlé Toll House Semi-Sweet Chocolate Morsels at high speed about 15 seconds or until reduced to fine particles; set aside, reserving 1 tablespoon for garnish. In a large saucepan, combine gelatin and ½ cup sugar; set aside. In a small bowl, beat egg yolks with milk and water; blend into gelatin mixture. Cook over moderate heat, stirring constantly with a wire whisk, until gelatin is completely dissolved, and mixture thickens slightly and coats a spoon (about 8 to 10 minutes). Stir in peppermint extract and food coloring. Cool at room temperature 15 to 20 minutes, stirring occasionally (mixture will be lukewarm).

In a large bowl, beat egg whites and salt until soft peaks form. Gradually beat in remaining ½ cup sugar until stiff peaks form; set aside. Gently fold peppermint-egg yolk mixture, whipped cream, and ground chocolate into egg whites. Turn into prepared soufflé dish. Sprinkle top with reserved morsels. Chill in refrigerator until firm (about 4 to 5 hours). Remove collar before serving.

Strawberry Soufflé

Makes 6 servings

- 1 pint strawberries
- 1¼ cups sugar, divided
- 1 envelope unflavored gelatin
- 4 eggs, separated
- ⅛ teaspoon salt
- 1 cup heavy cream, whipped

Fold a long strip of wax paper or aluminum foil so that it is about 4 inches wide and long enough to extend around the outside of a 1½-quart soufflé dish. Lightly brush one side of the strip with oil. Fasten the strip, oiled side in, around top of soufflé dish. It can be tied with string or clipped together with paper clips. Clean berries. Put in blender and purée. Pour berries into a 2-cup measure. There should be about 1⅓ cups purée.

Stir ½ cup sugar into the berries. Remove ¼ cup of the purée. Sprinkle gelatin over top and let stand to soften. Combine egg yolks with ½ cup sugar in top of double boiler. Cook over boiling water, stirring until mixture is thickened. Add gelatin mixture and stir until gelatin is dissolved. Cool. Blend in remaining strawberry purée.

Place egg whites and salt in large bowl of Sunbeam Mixmaster Mixer. Beat at high until foamy. Gradually add remaining ¼ cup sugar and continue beating until mixture is shiny and forms stiff peaks. Fold in whipped cream. Gently fold in strawberry mixture. Turn mixture into prepared soufflé dish. Chill until firm. Remove collar and serve.

Almond Cream Bombe

Makes 10 to 12 servings

- 1 package (16 ounces) frozen pound cake, thawed
- 6 tablespoons almond-flavored liqueur, divided
- 3 cups whipping cream
- ¾ cup sifted powdered sugar
- 1 cup maraschino cherry halves
- 1 cup Libby's Pumpkin Pie Mix
- ½ cup slivered almonds, toasted
- ½ cup semisweet real chocolate morsels
- 1 tablespoon shortening

Cut pound cake into ½ inch slices; cut each slice diagonally in half. Drizzle cake slices with ¼ cup liqueur. Arrange slices against bottom and sides of 2-quart mixing bowl lined with plastic wrap. In large bowl, whip cream and sugar until stiff peaks form. Fold cherries into 2 cups whipped cream; spread in cake-lined bowl. Fold pumpkin pie mix into 2 cups whipped cream; spread over cherry layer. Fold 2 tablespoons liqueur and nuts into remaining whipped cream; spread over pumpkin layer. Top with remaining cake slices. Cover; chill several hours or overnight. Unmold on serving plate. In saucepan, melt chocolate and shortening over low heat. Drizzle over bombe.

Idea

Any mousse or parfait, if layered into a fancy mold, could become a bombe. Mousses can also be transformed into spectacular frozen soufflés by selecting a straight-sided dish with 2 to 2½ cups less volume than the mold specified and adding a soufflé collar.

To make a soufflé collar, fold an 8-inch wide band of aluminum foil in half lengthwise, grease it well and wrap it around the soufflé dish so that it extends 3 inches above the rim. Secure with a string or clip the ends together with a straight pin or paper clip. Gently remove collar before serving. Macaroon crumbs, ground nuts, or grated chocolate may be pressed into the side of the soufflé for decoration.

It's-A-Snap Cheesecake

Makes about 8 servings

- 1 **envelope Knox Unflavored Gelatine**
- ½ **cup sugar**
- 1 **cup boiling water**
- 2 **packages (8 ounces each) cream cheese, softened**
- 1 **teaspoon vanilla extract (optional)**
- 1 **9-inch Graham Cracker Crust (see index)**
  Fresh or canned fruit (optional)

In large bowl, mix unflavored gelatine with sugar; add boiling water and stir until gelatine is completely dissolved. With electric mixer, beat in cream cheese and vanilla until smooth. Pour into prepared crust; chill until firm. Garnish, if desired, with fresh or canned fruit.

Fruit 'n' Creamy Cheesecake

Chill cheesecake 10 minutes, then swirl in ⅓ cup strawberry or raspberry preserves.

Sunshine Cheesecake

Substitute ½ teaspoon orange extract for vanilla extract and add 1 teaspoon grated orange rind.

Butterscotch Swirl Cheesecake

Makes 10 to 12 servings

- **Graham Cracker-Walnut Crust (recipe follows)**
- 2 **envelopes Knox Unflavored Gelatine**
- 2⅓ **cups milk, divided**
- 4 **eggs, separated**
- 1 **teaspoon vanilla extract**
- 2 **packages (8 ounces each) cream cheese, softened**
- 1 **package (6 ounces) butterscotch-flavored pieces**
- ¼ **cup sugar**

Prepare Graham Cracker-Walnut Crust; chill.

In medium saucepan, sprinkle unflavored gelatine over 1 cup milk. Let stand 1 minute. Beat egg yolks with 1 cup milk and stir into gelatine mixture. Stir over low heat until gelatine is completely dissolved, about 5 minutes. Pour into large bowl. With electric mixer, beat in cream cheese and vanilla until smooth. Chill, stirring occasionally, until mixture mounds slightly when dropped from spoon. Meanwhile, in a small saucepan, melt butterscotch pieces with remaining ⅓ cup milk; cool. In medium bowl, beat egg whites until soft peaks form; gradually add sugar and beat until stiff. Fold into gelatine mixture. Combine butterscotch with 2 cups gelatine mixture and alternate spoonfuls with remaining gelatine mixture in prepared crust. Gently swirl with knife to marble. Chill until firm.

Graham Cracker-Walnut Crust

- 1 **cup graham cracker crumbs**
- 4 **tablespoons butter or margarine, melted**
- ½ **cup finely chopped walnuts**

Butterscotch Swirl Cheesecake. Knox Gelatine, Inc.

Q. *I usually don't have too much difficulty unmolding gelatin desserts and salads, but I do have trouble getting the food centered on the serving plate, and it resists being moved.*

A. Rinse the serving plate with cold water before unmolding the mixture. Then, if the food is off-center, you can give it a gently shove and it will slide into place. Rinsing the mold with cold water before you fill it helps gelatin dishes to unmold more easily. So does coating it with a *very thin* film of cooking oil before you fill it.

In small bowl, combine all ingredients. Press onto bottom of 9-inch springform pan; chill.

Dieter's Cheesecake

Makes 12 servings★

- 4 **graham crackers**
- ¼ **teaspoon ground cinnamon**
- 1½ **cups skim milk**
- 2 **envelopes unflavored gelatin**
- ¾ **cup sugar or equivalent amount of low-calorie sweetener**
- 2 **eggs, separated**
- 2 **tablespoons lemon juice**
- 1 **thin slice orange**
- 3 **cups creamed cottage cheese**
- 1 **teaspoon vanilla extract**
- ¼ **teaspoon salt**
- ¼ **cup sugar**

Break graham crackers into blender container. Cover; blend at medium speed until crumbed. Empty into bowl; stir in cinnamon. Sprinkle half the crumb mixture over bottom of 8-inch springform pan. Pour ½ cup milk into blender container. Sprinkle on gelatin; let stand 1 minute. Heat remaining 1 cup milk to boiling. Add to blender container. Cover; blend at low speed until gelatin is dissolved. Add ¾ cup sugar or equivalent amount of low-calorie sweetener and egg yolks. Cover; blend at high speed until smooth. Add remaining ingredients except egg whites to blender container in order listed. Cover; blend until smooth. If necessary, stop blender during processing and push ingredients toward blades with rubber spatula. Empty into large bowl. Beat egg whites in second bowl with electric mixer until foamy. Beat in ¼ cup sugar gradually. Continue beating until stiff but not dry. Fold into cheese mixture. Pour into prepared pan. Top with remaining crumbs. Chill until set.

★154 calories per serving with sugar, 109 with sweetener

Luscious Lemon Cheesecake

Makes 12 servings

Creamy no-bake cheesecake with only 150 calories a serving.

- **2 envelopes Knox Unflavored Gelatine**
- **¾ cup sugar, divided**
- **2 eggs, separated**
- **1½ cups skim milk, divided**
- **1½ tablespoons lemon juice**
- **1½ teaspoons grated lemon peel**
- **3 cups (24 ounces) low-fat creamed cottage cheese**
- **⅓ cup graham cracker crumbs (about five 2½-inch square crackers)**
- **¼ teaspoon ground cinnamon**
- **⅛ teaspoon ground nutmeg**

In medium saucepan, mix unflavored gelatine with ½ cup sugar. Beat egg yolks with milk and blend into gelatine mixture. Stir over low heat until gelatine is completely dissolved, about 5 minutes. Stir in remaining ½ cup milk, lemon juice, and peel. In large bowl, beat cottage cheese until smooth; gradually beat in gelatine mixture. Chill, stirring occasionally, until mixture mounds slightly when dropped from a spoon. In large bowl, beat egg whites until soft peaks form; gradually add remaining ¼ cup sugar and beat until stiff. Fold into cheese mixture. Turn into 8- or 9-inch springform pan. Combine graham cracker crumbs, cinnamon, and nutmeg and sprinkle over top. Chill until firm.

Variation

Mix gelatine with artificial sweetener equal to ½ cup sugar; cuts calories to 110 per serving.

Italian Cheesecake

Makes 12 to 16 servings

Crust

- **1 cup brown-edge wafer cookie crumbs**
- **¼ cup butter or margarine, melted**

Combine cookie crumbs and melted butter; press onto bottom of 9-inch springform pan; refrigerate.

Filling

- **2 envelopes Knox Unflavored Gelatine**
- **¾ cup sugar, divided**
- **4 eggs, separated**
- **1 cup milk**
- **4 cups (2 pounds) ricotta cheese**
- **⅓ cup finely chopped semisweet chocolate pieces**
- **¼ cup finely chopped mixed candied fruit**
- **¼ cup finely chopped blanched almonds**
- **¼ cup orange liqueur**
- **1 teaspoon grated lemon peel**
- **1 teaspoon vanilla extract**
  Grape clusters (optional)

In medium saucepan, mix unflavored gelatine with ¼ cup sugar. Beat egg yolks with milk; stir into gelatine mixture. Stir over low heat until gelatine is completely dissolved, about 5 minutes. Pour into a large bowl; add ricotta. With electric mixer, blend in ricotta until smooth. Stir in remaining ingredients.

In a large bowl, beat egg whites until soft peaks form; gradually add remaining ½ cup sugar and beat until stiff. Fold into gelatine mixture. Turn into prepared springform pan; chill until firm. To serve, loosen around edge of pan with sharp knife; release spring and remove sides of pan. Place on serving plate and garnish with small clusters of grapes, if desired.

Ambrosia Cheese Pie

Makes one 9-inch pie

- **1 package (8 ounces) cream cheese, softened**
- **1 can (14 ounces) Eagle® Brand Sweetened Condensed Milk (not evaporated milk)**
- **⅓ cup ReaLemon® Reconstituted Lemon Juice**
- **1 teaspoon vanilla extract**
- **1 9-inch Graham Cracker Crumb Crust (see index)**
- **½ cup peach or apricot preserves**
- **¼ cup flaked coconut**
- **2 tablespoons orange-flavored liqueur**
- **2 teaspoons cornstarch**
- **1 or 2 fresh oranges, sectioned**

In large mixer bowl, beat cheese until fluffy. Beat in Eagle Brand until smooth. Stir in ReaLemon and vanilla. Pour into crust. Chill 3 hours, or until set. Meanwhile, in small saucepan, combine preserves, coconut, liqueur, and cornstarch; cook and stir until thickened. Remove from heat. Chill thoroughly. When ready to serve, spread preserves topping over pie; arrange fresh orange sections over top. Refrigerate leftovers.

Cranberry Cheese Pie

Fill crust with cheese filling as in Ambrosia Cheese Pie. Prepare cranberry topping by combining, in a small bowl, 1 cup chilled cranberry-orange relish, ½ cup chopped walnuts, and 1 teaspoon grated orange rind. Spread over pie when set. Garnish with orange twists, if desired.

No-Bake Cherry Cheese Pie

Makes one 9-inch pie

- **1 package (8 ounces) cream cheese, softened**
- **1 can (15 ounces) sweetened condensed milk**
- **⅓ cup lemon juice**
- **1 can (12 ounces) Solo Cherry Filling**
- **1 baked 9-inch Graham Cracker Crust (see index)**

Beat cream cheese until soft and smooth. Add condensed milk slowly, beating thoroughly. Add lemon juice and continue beating until mixture is smooth and thick. Spoon filling into baked graham cracker crust. Top with cherry filling. Refrigerate several hours, or overnight, before serving.

Fantasy Rice Pie

Makes 6 servings

- 1½ cups cottage cheese
- ½ cup milk
- 1 package (3¾ ounces) lemon instant pudding and pie filling
- 1½ cups chilled, cooked Uncle Ben's® Converted® Brand Rice
- 1 8- or 9-inch Graham Cracker Crust (see index)
- ½ cup sour cream
  Fresh strawberry slices or other fruit for garnish

Beat cottage cheese using an electric mixer until fairly smooth. Add milk and pudding mix; beat until well blended. Stir in rice. Spoon into prepared crust. Chill. Spread sour cream over top before serving. Garnish with fruit.

Heavenly Cream Cheese Pie

Makes one 9-inch pie

Chocolate Nut Crust

- 1 6-ounce package (1 cup) Nestlé Toll House Semi-Sweet Chocolate Morsels
- 1 tablespoon vegetable shortening
- 1½ cups finely chopped nuts

Line a 9-inch pie pan with foil. Over hot (not boiling) water, melt Nestlé Toll House Semi-Sweet Chocolate Morsels and shortening; stir in nuts. Spread evenly on bottom and side (not over rim) of prepared pie pan. Chill in refrigerator until firm (about 1 hour). Lift out of pan; peel off foil. Replace crust in pan; chill until ready to fill.

Filling

- 1 6-ounce package (1 cup) Nestlé Toll House Semi-Sweet Chocolate Morsels
- 1 package (8 ounces) cream cheese, softened
- ¾ cup sugar, divided
- ⅛ teaspoon salt
- 2 eggs, separated
- 1 cup heavy cream
- 3 tablespoons brandy
  Whipped cream for garnish (optional)

Melt Nestlé Toll House Semi-Sweet Chocolate Morsels over hot (not boiling) water, cool 10 minutes. In a large bowl, combine cream cheese, ½ cup sugar, and the salt; beat until creamy. Beat in egg yolks, 1 at a time. Stir in cooled chocolate; set aside. In a small bowl, beat egg whites until foamy. Gradually add ¼ cup sugar and beat until stiff, glossy peaks form. Set aside. In a small bowl, beat heavy cream and brandy until stiff peaks form. Fold whipped cream and beaten egg whites into chocolate mixture. Pour into Chocolate Nut Crust. Chill in refrigerator until firm (about 3 hours). Garnish with whipped cream, if desired.

Spring Form or Cheesecake Pan

Spring form pans and soufflé dishes can be made from Heavy Duty Reynolds Wrap and will last through one or more uses.

Spring Form Pan: Trace a circle the desired size on lightweight cardboard. (Shirt cardboard is fine.) Spring form pans, usually come in 6, 8, and 10 inch diameters. Cover the circle with foil, securing it on the bottom with tape. Multiply the diameter by 4 and tear off a length of heavy duty foil to correspond. Fold this foil in thirds lengthwise and in half again to make a band 3 inches wide. Cut short ½-inch snips on one long side at 1-inch intervals. Place the foil-covered circle on a can or other object to elevate it. Fold the foil band around it, attaching it by bending the snipped ends flat against the bottom of the circle. Attach these with tape. Let the band overlap and secure it with tape. Stand upright and fill with food. Place on a shallow pan if the foil pan contains food which is to be baked.

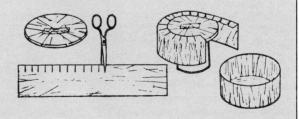

An Orchard of Fruit Desserts

Fresh, light desserts made from seasonal fruits are as sinfully delicious as they are wonderful to serve.

Chocolate-Dipped Fruit

Makes 1 cup

  1 12-ounce package (2 cups) Nestlé Toll House Semi-Sweet Chocolate Morsels★
  ½ cup vegetable shortening
    Fresh strawberries, washed and dried, or
    Mandarin orange slices, drained, or
    Pineapple chunks, drained, or
    Maraschino cherries, drained

Over hot (not boiling) water, combine Nestlé Toll House Semi-Sweet Chocolate Morsels and shortening; stir until morsels melt and mixture is smooth. Remove from heat but keep chocolate over hot water. (If chocolate begins to set, return to heat. Add 1 to 2 teaspoons shortening; stir until smooth.) Dip pieces of desired fruit into chocolate mixture, shaking off excess chocolate. Place on foil-lined cookie sheets. Chill in refrigerator 10 to 15 minutes until chocolate is set. Gently loosen fruit from foil with metal spatula. Choc-olate-Dipped Fruit may be kept at room temperature up to 1 hour. If chocolate becomes sticky, return to refrigerator.

★One 11½-ounce package (2 cups) Nestlé Milk Chocolate Morsels may be substituted for Nestlé Toll House Semi-Sweet Chocolate Morsels.

Figs and Strawberries Supreme

Makes 4 servings

  1 pint strawberries
  4 dried figs
  ¼ cup firmly packed light brown sugar
  ½ cup sour cream
  2 teaspoons grated lemon peel

Just before serving, rinse and hull the strawberries; slice. Stem the figs and thinly slice; combine with the berries. Spoon into a serving dish and sprinkle with the brown sugar. Top with sour cream and sprinkle with lemon peel.

Chocolate-Dipped Fruit. The Nestlé Company, Inc.

Ginger-Stuffed Figs

Makes 6 servings

  ½ cup finely chopped walnuts
  ⅓ cup finely chopped dried apricots
  2 tablespoons finely chopped crystallized ginger
  1¼ cups port, divided
  1 package (12 ounces) dried figs

Combine the walnuts, apricots, ginger, and ¼ cup of the port. Cut an opening in the blossom end of each fig and form a cavity with the handle of a small spoon. Stuff with the ginger mixture and pinch closed. Place the figs in a small container with the remaining 1 cup of port. Cover and marinate overnight. Serve with cheese and coffee.

Fresh Applesauce

Makes 6 servings

  ½ cup water
  2 tablespoons lemon juice
  3 large, tart, green-skinned apples
  ¼ cup sugar

Combine water and lemon juice in large bowl. Core apples; cut into 1-inch cubes, dropping them into lemon juice mixture as soon as they are cut. Put lemon juice mixture with half the apples and the sugar into blender container. Cover; blend at low speed until pu-reed. Turn blender to high speed; while blender is running, tip center cap and gradually add remaining apple pieces. Blend until smooth, adding a little more water if necessary. Serve at once.

Pink Applesauce

Reduce sugar to 3 tablespoons and add 2 tablespoons red cinnamon candies before processing. Proceed as for Fresh Applesauce.

Double Applesauce

Substitute apple juice or cider for water and reduce sugar to 3 tablespoons. Proceed as for Fresh Apple-sauce.

Spicy Baked Apples in Foil

For truly handsome and fine-tasting baked apples, good baking apples are a necessity. Rome Beauties are our preference. Remove the cores and peel halfway down from stem end. Place each apple on a large square of foil. Fill centers with sugar, ground cinnamon, ground nutmeg, a generous dot of butter. Or fill with raisins, nutmeats, and a small amount of sugar. Bring foil up over apples and crumple ends together, but not tightly. Some steam should escape. Place wrapped apples on a shallow pan and bake at 375°F. 45 minutes. Turn back foil about 10 minutes before apples are expected to be done. Test by piercing with fork. Spoon juices in foil over apples and continue baking. Serve warm or cold with cream.

Finnish Almond Apples

Makes 4 servings

- 4 medium baking apples, peeled and cored
- ½ cup Solo Almond Filling
- ½ cup all-purpose flour
- 1 cup corn flake crumbs
- 2 eggs, lightly beaten
- ¼ cup butter or margarine
  Heavy cream

Preheat oven to 350°F. Stuff apples with almond filling. Place flour and corn flake crumbs on separate pieces of waxed paper. Dip apples in flour, then in beaten eggs, and finally roll in corn flake crumbs, pressing crumbs in to cover apple smoothly. Place in a baking dish, with apples almost touching. Melt butter or margarine and pour over apples. Bake 45 minutes to 1 hour, or until apples are tender. Baste frequently during last 30 minutes of baking so that crusts will brown lightly. Serve warm or cool with heavy pouring cream.

Good Idea: For a different flavor, serve the apples topped with a custard sauce that is lightly flavored with almond extract.

Cherries Jubilee

Makes 4 to 6 servings

- 1 can (27 to 29 ounces) dark sweet cherries
- 3 thin slices lemon
- 1 teaspoon cornstarch
- ¼ cup sugar
- ½ cup brandy, warmed
  Vanilla ice cream

Put cherries, with juice, and lemon slices in Sunbeam Multi-Cooker Frypan. Set dial at Simmer. Combine cornstarch and 2 tablespoons cold water to make smooth paste. When cherry mixture is simmering, stir in cornstarch. Cook until mixture boils and thickens slightly. Sprinkle sugar over cherries. Carefully pour warmed brandy over cherries. Ignite with a wooden match. Carefully spoon over individual servings of ice cream.

Caution: Don't cook this—or any flamed dish—in a no-stick-surface pan; damage might result.

Ambrosia

Makes 4 servings

- ½ cup Sun-Maid® Seedless Golden Raisins
- ¼ cup Cointreau or other orange-flavored liqueur
- ½ cup shredded coconut
- 4 oranges

Combine the raisins and Cointreau and let stand for at least 10 minutes. Divide the coconut among 4 dessert plates. Peel oranges with a sharp knife, cutting off all the white pith; cut into sections and arrange on top of coconut. Spoon raisins and liqueur over orange sections.

Fruit 'n' Honey Celebration

Makes about 8 servings

- 2 envelopes Knox Unflavored Gelatine
- ½ cup cold orange juice
- 1 cup orange juice, heated to boiling
- 1 pint (16 ounces) vanilla or plain yogurt
- 2 tablespoons honey (optional)
- ¾ cup seedless raisins
- ¼ cup chopped walnuts
- 2 bananas, sliced

In large bowl, sprinkle unflavored gelatine over cold juice. Let stand 1 minute. Add hot juice and stir until gelatine is completely dissolved. With wire whip or rotary beater, blend in yogurt and honey. Chill, stirring occasionally, until mixture is consistency of unbeaten egg whites. Fold in remaining ingredients. Turn into 4-cup mold or bowl; chill until firm.

Golden Oranges

Makes 12 servings

    1 dozen medium navel oranges
    4 cups sugar
    ¼ cup light corn syrup
    ¼ cup coarsely shredded orange peel
       Golden Sauce (recipe follows)

Peel fruit, leaving fruit whole. Gently scrape off excess white membrane from oranges; carefully remove white center core. Separate sections very slightly at one end. If necessary, cut a thin slice from opposite end so that orange will stand up. In a heavy saucepan, combine sugar with 2 cups water; stir to dissolve. Bring to a boil; boil rapidly, 6 to 7 minutes, until syrup is pale amber color. Remove from heat. Carefully (it will spatter) add corn syrup and orange peel and 2 additional cups water. Boil rapidly until slightly thickened, 8 to 10 minutes. Place oranges in a large, shallow serving bowl. Pour syrup immediately over oranges. Refrigerate at least 6 hours, basting frequently. Just before serving, tuck sprigs of mint around edge of bowl. Serve Golden Sauce separately.

Golden Sauce

    2 cups sugar
    ½ cup light corn syrup
    ½ cup butter
    ⅔ cup light cream

In a heavy saucepan, cook sugar over medium heat, stirring frequently, until melted and golden brown. Remove from heat; blend in corn syrup, then butter. Add cream, a very little at a time, stirring until smooth. Serve at room temperature.

Watermelon Waikiki

Makes 6 to 8 servings

    ½ of 13-inch watermelon
    3 cups honeydew melon balls
    3 cups sweetened sliced fresh peaches
    1½ cups sweetened strawberry halves
    1 quart raspberry ice cream
       Mint leaves

Notch edges of watermelon, if desired. Remove seeds. Use large end of melon baller to make 4 cups watermelon balls. Scrape out melon to form bowl from watermelon shell. Combine melon balls, peaches, and strawberries. Mix gently. Spoon into watermelon shell. Chill until serving time. Just before serving, place scoops of ice cream on top of fruit. Garnish with mint leaves, and serve at once.

Cheese and Fruit Are Sure to Please

The easiest of desserts to prepare and warmly welcomed by everyone, fruit with cheese is an unbeatable combination and can be a very handsome one. Choose a good-looking tray or platter, large enough to accommodate several kinds of cheese and several varieties of fruit. If the container you choose is attractive, leave it as it is; if not, line it with flat leaves, such as grape leaves. Arrange the cheese in a pleasing pattern, keeping all of each kind together so that guests won't have to poke around on the tray to find what they want. Pile polished whole fruit or chunks or slices of prepared fruit at one end of the platter or, if you're pressed for space, in a pretty bowl. There should be crackers, too—plain, bland ones that won't fight for supremacy with the fruit and cheese flavors.

Be sure to provide tools—knives, cutters, and scoops for the cheese, butter knives to use as spreaders, and fruit knives if you've left the fruit whole. And, of course, dessert plates.

Bear in mind, in choosing cheese for such a dessert, that tastes differ. If you set out a combination of a whole soft cream cheese, a plump little edam or gouda, slices of swiss, fingers of cheddar, wedges of camembert, triangles of roquefort, and cubes of gjetost or mysost, you'll have something for everyone. Strident cheeses, such as bierkäse or limburger, don't belong here. Save them for a black bread, beer, and cheese party, which is an easy and inexpensive way to entertain.

Offer variety in the fruit, too. Pears and apples are ones that leap to mind, and they're available all year around. But peaches and nectarines, navel oranges and tangerines, grapes of all sorts, fingers of fresh pineapple, bing or royal anne cherries, cubes or wedges of papaya or mango or melon, big whole strawberries or loganberries or boysenberries—all these are good and unusual with cheese. At a time when many fresh fruits are out of season, offer dried fruits or dishes of excellent preserves, such as jam made of whole wild strawberries or jellies such as bar-le-duc or quince or guava.

Plantation Fritters

Makes 1½ to 2 dozen

  3 **ripe plantains or bananas**
3¼ **cups sifted cake flour**
  2 **tablespoons sugar**
  2 **teaspoons baking powder**
  ¼ **teaspoon salt**
  2 **eggs, beaten**
  ¼ **cup sweetened condensed milk**
  1 **teaspoon vanilla extract**
  ¼ **chopped salted peanuts**
  ½ **cup seedless raisins**
    Oil
    Confectioners sugar

Mash bananas with fork, leaving fairly small pieces. Sift together flour, sugar, baking powder, and salt. Combine eggs, milk, and vanilla; add to flour mixture; stir just to blend. Fold in banana pulp, nuts, and raisins. Batter should be the consistency of drop cookies. Pour oil into pan to depth of 2 inches; heat to 365°F., or until hot enough to brown 1-inch bread cube in 1 minute. Drop batter by teaspoonfuls into hot fat; fry 2 to 3 minutes until golden brown and cooked through. If desired, roll in sifted confectioners sugar while warm.

Nanas Goreng

Makes 6 servings

  2 **tablespoons flour**
  1 **egg, unbeaten**
  ¼ **teaspoon salt**
  6 **pineapple slices, cut in half**
  3 **tablespoons salad oil**

Mix flour, egg, and salt together to make batter. Dip pineapple into batter; fry in hot oil in fry pan; brown both sides; serve hot.

Frozen Pineapple

This is a delightful dessert for a Hawaiian luau or a party with a Caribbean theme. It can be prepared well ahead and brought from the freezer, as the handsome, perfect finishing touch at the end of an exotic dinner.

Select very small pineapples and let them ripen one or two days if necessary. Cut them in half lengthwise right through the green top, leaving the tops on. Cut out the cores, then loosen and remove the fruit, leaving a firm shell. Dice the fruit and combine with 2 tablespoons each of sugar and rum for each cup of diced pineapple. Refill the shells not quite full; cover with foil and place in the freezer for 1 hour or until very thoroughly chilled. Remove and top each filled pineapple half with vanilla or any fruit-flavored ice cream or sherbet. Sprinkle with coconut. Wrap completely with foil and store in the freezer. They may be kept for 24 hours. The pineapple should only partially freeze—the sugar and rum keep it from getting too hard.

Pineapple Boats with Strawberries

Makes 16 servings

  4 **small, ripe fresh pineapples**
  1 **cup kirsch or pear brandy**
 48 **whole fresh strawberries**

Cut a slice from bottom of each pineapple; cut each pineapple into quarters lengthwise, cutting through both fruit and foliage. Using a very sharp knife, cut the core from each quarter; run knife between fruit and skin, loosening fruit but leaving it in place. Cut each quarter into 8 to 10 slices, cutting through fruit but not through skin. Sprinkle with kirsch. Refrigerate. Wash and hull strawberries. Slice thin lengthwise. Arrange slices, overlapping, into flower shapes on top of each pineapple quarter.

Pineapple Banana Split Dessert

Makes 14 to 16 servings

  2 **cups graham cracker crumbs**
  ½ **cup butter or margarine, melted**
  ½ **cup butter or margarine, softened**
  2 **cups confectioners sugar**
  1 **egg**
  1 **teaspoon vanilla extract**
  3 **or 4 bananas, sliced**
  2 **cans (12 ounces each) Solo Pineapple Filling**
  1 **cup heavy cream (or 2 cups whipped topping)**
  ½ **cup chopped nuts**
    Maraschino cherries

Combine crumbs and melted butter or margarine. Press mixture firmly on bottom of 13x9x2-inch pan. Refrigerate to chill slightly. Combine softened butter or margarine, confectioners sugar, egg, and vanilla and beat until thick and creamy. Spread evenly over crumb mixture. Place banana slices on top of creamed mixture and top with pineapple filling. Whip cream until stiff and spread over filling. Refrigerate for several hours. To serve, slice into serving portions and top each with chopped nuts and a maraschino cherry.

Fruited Chocolate Trifle (page 104). General Foods

Flaming Bananas Martinique

Makes 4 to 6 servings

        Nougatine (recipe follows)
¼ cup firmly packed C & H Dark Brown Sugar
¼ cup butter
 4 medium bananas, sliced diagonally ¼ inch thick
⅓ cup *each* coffee and almond liqueurs
⅓ cup rum
        Vanilla or coffee ice cream

Prepare nougatine. Melt sugar and butter in heavy skillet or chafing dish. Add bananas and cook 3 minutes or until just tender. Stir in coffee and almond liqueurs. Pour rum into a corner of pan. Ignite and shake pan until flames subside. Spoon over vanilla ice cream. Top with chopped nougatine.

Nougatine

¼ cup C & H Granulated Sugar
 2 tablespoons water
⅓ cup coarsely chopped walnuts

Grease cookie sheet with sides. Combine sugar and water in small heavy saucepan. Cook over low heat until sugar dissolves, swirling pan occasionally. Raise heat and boil until sugar caramelizes, washing down any sugar crystals on sides of pan with brush dipped in cold water. Stir in walnuts and pour out onto greased cookie sheet. Chop coarsely when hard.

Sparkling Fruit Pyramid

Makes about 15 servings

 2 egg whites
        Sugar
 7 red eating apples
 5 medium navel oranges
 3 comice or d'anjou pears
 1 bunch red or purple grapes, separated into small clusters

In a medium bowl, beat egg whites with 1 teaspoon water just until mixed. Dip each piece of fruit into egg white and shake off excess; dip into sugar so that the fruit is lightly but evenly covered. Let stand on wire rack several hours, until coating is completely dry. Arrange apples in a circle on a serving dish. Make a smaller circle of oranges on top of apples; secure with small skewers or food picks. Top oranges with pears; fasten in the same manner. Tuck little clusters of grapes in the openings between fruit. Tuck fresh green leaves around the bottom of the pyramid.

Green Grapes with Cointreau

 1 pound seedless green grapes
 1 pint sour cream
¼ cup light brown sugar
¼ cup ground cinnamon
        Cointreau

Wash and remove stems from grapes. Drain thoroughly, then fold into the sour cream. Cover bowl with foil and refrigerate for 1 hour, or until thoroughly chilled. Serve in sherbet glasses. Pass attractive small dishes, 1 with brown sugar, 1 with cinnamon, and a small decanter of Cointreau. Each person seasons his own dessert, sprinkling on the brown sugar and cinnamon and pouring on a little of the liqueur. Pass the condiments a second time as, after the first taste, more of the condiments may make this dessert taste even better.

Hot Fruit Medley

Makes 6 to 8 servings

 1 9-inch square cake pan
 2 cups crisp macaroon crumbs (about 40 macaroons)(see index)
 1 can (16 ounces) sliced peaches, drained
 1 can (16 ounces) purple plums, pitted, drained
 1 can (20 ounces) pineapple chunks, drained
 1 can (16 ounces) bing cherries, pitted, drained
½ cup sherry

Sprinkle ½ cup macaroon crumbs in bottom of buttered pan. Combine peaches, plums, pineapple, and cherries; toss lightly. Place layer of fruit in pan; sprinkle with crumbs. Continue layering fruit and crumbs, ending with layer of crumbs. Pour sherry over top of crumbs. Bake 40 to 45 minutes at 350°F.

Wine-Poached Pears

Makes 4 servings

 4 fresh Western Bosc, Anjou, or Bartlett pears
1½ cups sugar
1½ cups rosé or burgundy wine
 1 cup water
 2 teaspoons grated lemon peel
        Few drops red food color (optional)

Pare pears, leaving whole with stems intact. Combine sugar, wine, water, lemon peel, and food color in large saucepan; bring to boil. Add pears to poaching liquid; return to boil. Reduce heat and simmer covered about 30 minutes, or until pears are translucent and syrup thickens; turn and baste pears occasionally. Serve warm or chilled.

Curried Tropical Fruit

Makes 6 servings

An exotic side dish for pork or duck, or an uncommon dessert to offer with cheese.

- ¾ cup chicken broth
- ¾ cup dry white wine
- 2 teaspoons curry powder (or to taste)
- 2 teaspoons quick-cooking tapioca
- ¾ cup flaked coconut
- ¾ cup toasted slivered almonds
- 3 tablespoons golden raisins
- 3 cups cubed fresh fruit (any combination of apples, bananas, mangoes, melons, papayas, pineapple)

You will need: Corning Ware 2-quart covered saucepan

Combine broth, wine, and curry powder in saucepan. Cover; simmer 30 minutes. Soak tapioca in 3 tablespoons water, 5 minutes; add to broth mixture. Stir until mixture thickens. Add coconut, almonds, and raisins; stir well. Gently stir in fruit. Simmer just until heated through. Serve warm.

Melon Balls or Baskets

Cut a cantaloupe or small honeydew in half for individual servings, or use larger melons to hold salads for several people. Remove the seeds and some of the pulp—in chunks or in balls, with a melon baller—to use in the salad, or for dessert on another occasion. Leave a shell sturdy enough to stand, however. You may serrate or scallop the edges or not, as you prefer. Fill the melon with ham, chicken, or seafood salad, or any kind of mixed-fruit salad. If you like, use a whole melon for each container, leaving a strip over the top for a handle, to make a melon basket. If you'd like a melon bowl or basket in which to serve fruit salad to a large number of people, use a watermelon, hollowing it in the same way and retaining part of the meat of the melon for the salad. Such a hollowed-out watermelon makes an excellent punch bowl for al fresco parties, too.

Dipped Fruit Balls

Makes about 3 dozen

- 2 packages (8 ounces each) pitted dates
- 2 cups dried apricots
- 1 11½-ounce package (2 cups) Nestlé Milk Chocolate Morsels
- 2 tablespoons vegetable shortening
   Paper candy liners

In a food processor or by hand, finely chop dates and apricots; mix well. Melt over hot (not boiling) water Nestlé Milk Chocolate Morsels and vegetable shortening. Remove from heat but keep chocolate over hot water. With greased hands, shape date-apricot mixture into 1-inch balls. Dip the balls into chocolate mixture, shaking off excess chocolate. Place on foil-lined cookie sheets. Refrigerate until ready to serve (about 15 to 20 minutes). Serve in paper candy liners.

Any-Fruit Rice Fluff

Makes 6 servings

- 2 cups coarsely chopped fresh or canned fruit or berries, well drained
- ¼ cup chopped pecans (optional)
- 1½ cups chilled, cooked Uncle Ben's® Converted® Brand Rice
- 2 tablespoons sugar
- ½ cup whipping cream, whipped, or 1 cup whipped topping

Add fruit and, if desired, nuts to chilled rice. Fold sugar gradually into whipped cream or topping. Fold into rice mixture before serving.

Fresh-Fruit Betty

Makes 4 to 6 servings

- 4 large apples, nectarines, peaches, or pears
- ¼ cup seedless raisins (optional)
- 1 tablespoon lemon juice
- ⅔ cup all-purpose flour
- 1 cup firmly packed light brown sugar
- 1 teaspoon ground cinnamon
- ½ teaspoon ground ginger
- ⅛ teaspoon ground mace
- ¼ cup butter or margarine, softened

You will need: Pyrex or Corning Ware 9-inch pie plate

Peel fruit; remove seeds or pits. Cut into thin slices. Arrange fruit in pie plate; sprinkle with raisins and lemon juice. Mix flour, sugar, and spices. Add butter; blend with pastry blender or 2 knives until well mixed and crumbly. Spread over fruit, patting firmly into place. Bake in preheated 350°F. oven about 45 minutes, or until fruit is tender and juices are bubbling. Serve warm.

Wine-Poached Pears (page 100). Oregon-Washington-California
Pear Bureau

Plum Cobbler

Makes 6 servings

    ¾ cup Karo Light Corn Syrup
    1 tablespoon cornstarch
    ½ teaspoon ground cinnamon
    2 pounds ripe fresh plums, pitted and quartered
    1¼ cups buttermilk baking mix
    ½ cup finely chopped nuts (optional)
    ⅓ cup milk
    ¼ cup sugar

Stir together first 3 ingredients; toss with plums. Spoon into 8-inch square baking dish. Bake in 400°F. oven 15 minutes. Meanwhile, mix remaining ingredients. Beat vigorously 20 strokes. Drop by spoonfuls onto hot plums. Bake 15 to 20 minutes longer.

Dixie Cobbler

Makes 6 to 8 servings

    2 cups sifted Martha White Self-Rising Flour
    ⅔ cup vegetable shortening
    3 to 4 tablespoons cold water
    1¼ to 2 cups sugar
    2 tablespoons cornstarch
    4 cups fresh or frozen sliced peaches or blackberries
    ½ teaspoon almond extract (or 1 teaspoon lemon
        juice)
    ½ cup butter or margarine
    2 tablespoons sugar

Place flour in bowl. Cut in half of the shortening with pastry blender or 2 knives until mixture is consistency of coarse crumbs. Cut in remaining shortening until mixture is consistency of small peas. Sprinkle water, 1 tablespoon at a time, over mixture; stir with fork until mixture leaves sides of bowl. Shape into ball. Wrap in waxed paper; set aside. Preheat oven to 375°F. Combine 1¼ to 2 cups sugar (according to tartness of fruit) and cornstarch in small bowl; blend well. Add fruit and flavoring (almond extract for peaches or lemon juice for blackberries); toss lightly to mix; set aside. Divide dough into thirds. Gather 2 thirds into ball. Roll out into circle to fit bottom and sides of 2-quart casserole; line casserole with dough. Arrange fruit mixture over dough in casserole. Dot with butter, reserving 2 tablespoons for top. Roll out remaining dough into circle ½ inch larger than top of casserole. Cover filling with pastry circle, pressing edge down side of casserole. Dot with remaining 2 tablespoons butter. Sprinkle with 2 tablespoons sugar. Bake 55 minutes, or until golden brown.

> Cobblers may bubble over toward end of baking time. For easy cleanup, place a pan or piece of aluminum foil under casserole in oven.

Mom's Apple Cobbler

Makes 8 servings

    ½ cup butter or margarine
    2 cups sugar
    2 cups water
    1½ cups sifted Martha White Self-Rising Flour
    ½ cup vegetable shortening
    ⅓ cup milk
    2 cups finely chopped peeled apples
    1 teaspoon ground cinnamon

Preheat oven to 350°F. Melt butter in 13x9x2-inch baking pan. Remove from oven; set aside. Combine sugar and water in saucepan; cook over moderate heat until sugar dissolves. Remove from heat; set aside. Place flour in bowl. Cut in shortening with pastry blender or 2 knives until mixture is consistency of coarse crumbs. Add milk; stir with fork just until dough leaves sides of bowl. Turn out onto lightly floured board or pastry cloth. Knead just until smooth. Roll out into ¼-inch-thick rectangle. Place apples in small bowl. Sprinkle cinnamon over apples; toss lightly to mix. Spread apples evenly over dough. Roll up, jelly roll fashion, from long side. Moisten edge with water; pinch to seal. Cut into ½-inch-thick slices. Place slices, cut sides down, over butter in baking pan. Pour sugar syrup over top. Bake 1 hour.

> **Q.** *How do professional cooks section oranges and grapefruit so neatly, without including any of the white membrane?*
> **A.** Cover the fruit with boiling water and let stand 5 minutes. Then peel—use a sharp knife, not your fingers. The outer membrane will come away with the peel. Hold the peeled fruit over a bowl. With the knife, cut down to the center along the edge of each membrane that separates the sections, turning the knife slightly at the end of each cut after the first to push out the section so it will drop into the bowl.

Superfast Blackberry Cobbler

Makes 6 to 8 servings

    ½ cup butter or margarine
    1 can (16 ounces) blackberries with juice (about 2
        cups)
    1 cup sifted Martha White Self-Rising Flour
    ¾ cup sugar
    ¾ cup milk
      Cream (optional)

Preheat oven to 350°F. Melt butter in 8-inch square baking pan in oven. Place blackberries and juice in small saucepan; place over low heat until heated through. Combine flour, sugar, and milk in bowl; blend well. Pour into baking pan with melted butter; do not stir. Spoon blackberries and juice evenly over batter; do not stir. Bake 40 to 45 minutes, or until golden brown. Serve warm with cream, if desired.

Individual Cherry Cobblers

Makes 6 servings

- 1 can (21 ounces) cherry pie filling
- 1 one-layer package (8¾ ounces) yellow cake mix
- ¼ cup butter or margarine

To make foil cups: Cut six 8-inch circles of Alcoa Wrap; mold each circle over 10-ounce custard cup; crimp edges of foil; place foil cups on baking sheet. Spoon pie filling into foil cups (about ⅓ cup per serving). Sprinkle dry cake mix over cherries (about ¼ cup). Top each with 4 very thin slices butter. Bake 20 to 25 minutes at 400°F., or until golden brown. Serve warm; may be topped with scoop of ice cream.

Blueberry Buckle

Makes 9 servings

- ¾ cup sugar
- ¼ cup shortening
- 1 egg, lightly beaten
- ½ cup milk
- 2 cups sifted all purpose flour
- 2 teaspoons baking powder
- ½ teaspoon salt
- 1 cup blueberries, well drained
  - Crumb Mixture (recipe follows)
  - Lemon Sauce (recipe follows)

Grease 9-inch square cake pan; dust lightly with flour. Mix together thoroughly sugar, shortening, and egg; stir in milk. Sift together flour, baking powder, and salt; stir into sugar mixture; carefully blend in blueberries. Pour into pan. Prepare Crumb Mixture; sprinkle over batter. Bake 45 to 50 minutes at 375°F. Top with Lemon Sauce.

Crumb Mixture

- ½ cup sugar
- ⅓ cup sifted all-purpose flour
- ½ teaspoon ground cinnamon
- ¼ cup butter or margarine, melted

Mix together sugar, flour, cinnamon, and butter.

Lemon Sauce

Makes about 1⅓ cups

- ½ cup butter or margarine
- 1 cup sugar
- ¼ cup water
- 1 egg, well beaten
- 3 tablespoons lemon juice
  - Grated rind of 1 lemon

Combine all ingredients in saucepan. Cook over medium heat, stirring constantly just until mixture comes to a boil. Serve warm over Blueberry Buckle.

Fruited Chocolate Trifle

Makes 8 to 10 servings

- ⅔ cup sugar
- 2 tablespoons cornstarch
- ⅛ teaspoon salt
- 2 eggs, lightly beaten
- 3 cups milk, scalded
- 3 squares Baker's Unsweetened Chocolate
- 3 tablespoons almond liqueur or ½ teaspoon almond extract
- 12 ladyfingers, split (see index)
- 1 pint fresh strawberries, hulled and halved
- 1 can (16 ounces) apricot halves, drained
  - Sweetened whipped cream (optional)
  - Chocolate Cut-Outs (recipe follows) (optional)
  - Strawberries (optional)

Combine sugar, cornstarch, and salt in bowl. Add eggs and mix well. Gradually pour in hot milk, stirring constantly. Return to saucepan. Cook and stir over very low heat until mixture is smooth and thickened. Remove from heat. Add chocolate and liqueur; stir until chocolate is melted. Cool slightly.

Arrange half of the ladyfingers, fruits, and chocolate custard in layers in a serving dish; repeat layers with remaining ingredients. Chill at least 2 hours. Before serving, garnish with sweetened whipped cream, Chocolate Cut-Outs, and additional strawberries, if desired.

Chocolate Cut-Outs

Makes about 20 cut-outs

Melt 4 squares Baker's Semi-Sweet Chocolate or 1 package (4 ounces) Baker's German's Sweet Chocolate in saucepan over very low heat, stirring constantly. Pour onto waxed paper-lined baking sheet; spread to ⅛-inch thickness with spatula. Chill until firm, about 15 minutes. Cut into desired shapes with cookie cutters or sharp knife and at once lift gently from paper with spatula. Set on desserts and frosted cakes.

Fresh Fruit Know-how

Apples

How to buy: Your eyes, nose and fingers—and common sense—are your best guides when you purchase fruit. Apples should be firm, crisp, well colored, should look bright and fresh. They should smell slightly winy but never musty. Watch for cuts, punctures, abrasions, bruises, or soft spots. All fresh fruit is perishable, and blemished fruit will spoil more rapidly than unblemished. Overripe apples yield to a slight pressure on the skin: the flesh will be soft and mealy.

You are your own best judge of quality, so take the time to buy carefully. If you can, buy by the piece or pound rather than the package, for a package could conceal spoiled fruit. Finally, buy apples of a variety suited to the use you are going to make of them—for eating out of hand, for sauce, for baking, or for other cooking purposes.

Blueberries

How to buy: Peak season is June, July, and August. When choosing all berries, look at the bottom of the container as well as the top, keeping an eye out for damp and/or stained spots that indicate spoilage. Smell them, too—fresh berries smell clean and earthy. Choose fresh-looking, dark blue, unwrinkled berries that are fairly uniform in size. The silvery powder on the berry is natural bloom, a protective coating. How to store: In the refrigerator, unwashed, in the original container if they will be used soon, or spread out on a flat surface—unwashed and covered—if you plan to keep the berries for two or three days. To prepare, pick over and wash just before using.

Lemons

How to buy: Quality lemons are heavy for their size. The skin is richly yellow; paler or green-tinged fruit is very young and will be slightly higher in acidity. Very coarse or rough texture means the skin is thick and will not yield as much juice as a thinner variety. Avoid dark color or dryness. Old lemons turn hard or their skins shrivel, but good lemons should be firm to the touch.

How to store: Lemons will keep up to 2 weeks at room temperature, but they will last up to 6 weeks—even longer if you put them in perforated plastic bags—in the refrigerator crisper. Close cut pieces of leftover lemon in a tightly sealed plastic bag; use within 1 week.

Oranges

How to buy: As with other citrus fruit, choose oranges that are heavy for their size and unblemished—any break in the skin, however small, allows molds to enter.

How to prepare: Wash oranges before eating, and from there go in any direction. Peel if you like—fingers work well, or there is a sturdy plastic orange-peeler that zips skins off in no time. Gently break into segments. Or slice with a sharp knife. Or section for fruit cups and salads by holding the peeled orange over a bowl (to catch juice) and cutting with a small, sharp knife between segments, from outside to center, once a segment is cut on each side, a flip of the knife will free it to drop, membraneless, into the bowl.

Strawberries

How to buy: Strawberries are most generally sold in pint baskets. Large size is not necessarily a sign of a top quality berry. Flavor depends on variety, not size. You'll get larger volume—often a better bargain—when you buy small or medium-size berries. Choose large ones if appearance matters—if they are to be used as a garnish, for example. Look for fully ripe berries, richly and brightly red; very dark color indicates that the berries are old and beginning to deteriorate. The berry should have a natural shine; the cap should be green and fresh looking. Pick up the basket and look at the bottom. Red stains and leaking juice indicate crushed or deteriorated berries under that inviting top layer. Plan on using strawberries the day, or at most the day after, you buy them. If for some reason strawberries are not used soon after purchase, cook them before they go to waste—make sauce to serve over ice cream or cake, or a combination of the two if you're feeling lavish, or over a simple pudding. Or bake a pie. Or make a jar of preserves.

Do not wash strawberries until just before you serve them or use them in a cooked dish. As soon as you get them home, remove the berries from their basket, leave the caps on, and spread the berries out on a baking sheet or other shallow container. Refrigerate immediately.

How to prepare: Leaving the caps in place, wash the berries quickly in a colander or strainer in cold water. Never soak them. Use the point of a sharp knife to remove the strawberry caps or, even better, the rounded point of your potato peeler. Leave the berries whole, slice or crush, depending on the use you are going to make of them; sweeten or not as you prefer.

A Crystal Palace of Frozen Desserts

No one can resist the icy goodness of ice cream, sherbets, or sorbets—especially in a dessert prepared by you.

Vanilla Ice Cream

Makes 3 cups
- 1 tablespoon cold water
- 1 teaspoon unflavored gelatin
- ⅛ teaspoon salt
- 2 egg yolks
- ½ cup scalded milk
- ½ cup sugar
- 1 teaspoon vanilla extract
- 1 cup heavy cream, whipped

Put water into blender container. Sprinkle on gelatin. Add salt, egg yolks, and milk. Cover; blend at low speed until smooth. Add sugar and vanilla. Cover; blend at medium speed until smooth. Fold gelatin mixture gently into whipped cream. Pour into freezer tray or shallow pan; freeze until firm. If ice cream is to be kept for later use, cover with foil or plastic wrap. If too solidly frozen to serve, let stand at room temperature until of desired consistency.

Chocolate Ice Cream
Add one square (1 ounce) unsweetened chocolate, cut up, to blender container with egg yolks; reduce vanilla to ½ teaspoon. Proceed as for Vanilla Ice Cream.

Chocolate Chip Ice Cream
Cut two squares (1 ounce each) semisweet chocolate into quarters. Put into blender container. Cover; blend at medium speed until grated. Empty onto wax paper. Proceed as for Vanilla Ice Cream, folding chocolate into gelatin mixture with whipped cream.

Strawberry Ice Cream
Reduce vanilla to ½ teaspoon; add 1½ cups strawberries, washed and hulled, to blender container with sugar and vanilla. Proceed as for Vanilla Ice Cream. Makes 1 quart.

Peach Ice Cream
Substitute ¼ teaspoon almond extract for vanilla; add 1½ cups peeled, sliced ripe peaches to blender container with sugar and almond extract. Proceed as for Vanilla Ice Cream. Makes 1 quart.

Coconut Rum-Raisin Ice Cream

Makes about 2 quarts ice cream
- 2 cups raisins
- ½ cup dark rum
- 2 cups half and half
- 1 cup sweetened flaked coconut
- 3 eggs
- ¾ cup sugar
- ¼ teaspoon salt
- 2 cups whipping cream

In covered jar, combine raisins and rum; let stand overnight to plump. In saucepan, scald half and half. Stir in coconut; set aside. In separate saucepan, whisk eggs, sugar, and salt. Gradually stir in half and half, reserving coconut in pan. Cook over medium-low heat, stirring constantly, 5 minutes. Remove from heat. Stir in reserved coconut. Cool; chill. Stir in whipping cream and raisins. Churn freeze in hand crank or electric ice-cream maker according to manufacturer's instructions. Transfer to covered container to store in freezer.

Old-Fashioned Caramel Sauce

Makes about 1½ cups sauce
- ¾ cup firmly packed brown sugar
- ⅓ cup light corn syrup
- ½ cup whipping cream
- 2 tablespoons butter or margarine
- ½ cup raisins

In saucepan, combine sugar, corn syrup, cream, and butter. Cook and stir over medium heat until sugar dissolves and mixture thickens, 4 to 5 minutes. Remove from heat; stir in raisins. Store in covered container in refrigerator. Warm over low heat before serving over ice cream.

Coconut Rum-Raisin Ice Cream; Raisin Rocky Road Hot Fudge Sauce (page 108); Golden Raisin Lemon Sauce (page 108); Old-Fashioned Caramel Sauce. California Raisin Advisory Board

Golden Raisin Lemon Sauce

Makes about 1½ cups sauce

¼ cup sugar
1 tablespoon cornstarch
1 cup hot water
¼ cup butter or margarine
1½ tablespoons grated lemon peel
¼ cup lemon juice
½ cup golden raisins

In saucepan, combine sugar and cornstarch. Gradually stir in water to blend. Cook and stir over medium heat until mixture boils and becomes thick and clear, 3 to 5 minutes. Remove from heat; add butter, stirring until melted. Stir in lemon peel, juice, and raisins. Cool. Store in covered container in refrigerator. Bring sauce to room temperature or warm over low heat before serving over ice cream or other desserts.

Raisin Rocky Road Hot Fudge Sauce

Makes about 1½ cups sauce

⅓ cup water
¼ cup butter or margarine
2 ounces semisweet chocolate
⅔ cup sugar
1 tablespoon light corn syrup
½ cup raisins
½ cup mini marshmallows
¼ cup chopped walnuts

In saucepan, combine water and butter. Bring to boil over medium heat, stirring. Add chocolate; cook and stir to melt. Stir in sugar and corn syrup; simmer gently 5 minutes. Remove from heat; stir in raisins. Store in covered container in refrigerator. Warm over low heat and stir in marshmallows and nuts just before serving over ice cream.

Black Forest Fudge Sauce

Plump raisins in 2 tablespoons kirsch before adding to sauce. Omit marshmallows and nuts.

About Rhubarb

Bright pink hothouse rhubarb is a harbinger of Spring that appears soon after the first of the year. It makes a delicately flavored and beautiful pie. Garden rhubarb has a somewhat more forthright flavor and is also delicious. Don't dream of peeling rhubarb—simply remove discolorations and trim off stem ends.

Orange Almond Sorbet

Makes 8 servings

4 large oranges, cut in half
1 can (16 ounces) Libby's Solid Pack Pumpkin
½ cup sugar
1 teaspoon lemon juice
Dash salt
1 cup almond-flavored liqueur

Squeeze juice from oranges; reserve juice. Remove pulp and fiber from oranges, leaving shells intact. Combine pumpkin, ¾ cup reserved orange juice, sugar, lemon juice, and salt; mix well. Freeze in ice cube trays until firm. Dip trays in warm water to release cubes. In blender container, place half of liqueur and half of frozen cubes. Cover; blend at high speed until smooth, using pulse button as needed. Repeat with remaining liqueur and frozen cubes. Fill orange shells with mixture; return to freezer until ready to serve. Garnish each serving with mint leaves, if desired.

Rhubarb Mousse

Makes 8 to 10 servings

1½ cups C & H Granulated Sugar
½ cup water
6 egg whites
Pinch *each* salt and cream of tartar
2 cups heavy cream
¼ teaspoon ground cinnamon
2 cups cooked rhubarb purée
2 pints strawberries
½ cup C & H Powdered Sugar
2 tablespoons kirsch, rum, or brandy

Combine granulated sugar and water in small heavy saucepan. Cook over low heat until sugar dissolves, swirling pan occasionally. Raise heat and cook without stirring until syrup reaches 236°F. on candy thermometer (soft ball stage). Meanwhile, beat egg whites with salt and cream of tartar until stiff peaks form. Gradually add syrup and continue beating about 10 minutes, until mixture is cool and thick. Whip cream until stiff and gently fold into beaten egg white mixture. Cover and freeze 2 hours.

Stir cinnamon into rhubarb purée and then mix purée into frozen cream. Pour into 8-cup ring mold or 8 individual molds. Freeze at least 2 more hours until firm. Marinate strawberries with powdered sugar and kirsch. To serve, unmold rhubarb mousse onto chilled serving plate(s). Fill center(s) with marinated strawberries.

Lemon Granita

Makes 6 to 8 servings

- ¼ cup C & H Superfine or Granulated Sugar
- 1½ cups water
- 1 teaspoon grated lemon rind (optional)
- ¼ cup freshly squeezed lemon juice
- 6 to 8 sprigs mint (optional)

Stir sugar, water, lemon rind, and lemon juice together in bowl until sugar dissolves. Freeze 6 hours, until solid, beating every 2 hours to break up ice crystals. Before serving, beat in food processor or blender to smooth texture or scrape with a fork and mound in goblets or frozen lemon shells. Garnish with mint.

Blackberry Mousse

Makes 4 to 6 servings

- ⅔ cup C & H Granulated Sugar
- 3 eggs, separated
- ½ pint blackberries, puréed and sieved to eliminate seeds
- 2 tablespoons cassis, brandy, or kirsch (optional)
- 1 tablespoon lemon juice
  Pinch *each* salt and cream of tartar
- 1 cup whipping cream
  Additional blackberries (optional)

Combine sugar, egg yolks, and blackberry purée in mixing bowl. Place in pan containing water and beat over medium heat until sugar is dissolved and mixture is thick and hot to the touch. Remove from heat and continue beating until cool. Stir in cassis and lemon juice. In separate bowl, beat egg whites with salt and cream of tartar until stiff. Stir about one-quarter of egg whites into blackberry mixture to aerate, then fold in the rest. Beat cream until softly whipped and fold into mixture. Turn into 1-quart mold and freeze 6 hours, or until firm. Unmold and transfer to refrigerator 30 minutes before serving. Garnish with additional fresh berries, if desired.

Creamy Orange Sherbet

Makes 4 servings

- 1 cup heavy cream
- 2 thin slices orange, halved
- ¾ cup orange juice
- 3 tablespoons sugar
  Dash salt

Put all ingredients into blender container in order listed. Cover; blend at high speed until smooth. Pour into freezer tray; freeze until firm.

Creamy Pineapple-Orange Sherbet

Substitute pineapple juice for orange juice. Proceed as for Orange Sherbet.

Fruited Yogurt Freeze

Makes 6 servings

With a supply of these in the freezer, you can invite the gang over as often as you like.

- ¼ cup sugar
- 1 envelope unflavored gelatin
- 1 can (12 ounces) peach nectar
- 1 container (8 ounces) peach-flavored yogurt
- 1 can (8 ounces) crushed pineapple
- ½ cup Sun-Maid® Seedless Raisins

Mix the sugar and gelatin in a 1-quart saucepan. Stir in the peach nectar and cook over medium heat, stirring constantly, until the sugar and gelatin dissolve. Cool slightly and place the saucepan in the refrigerator until the mixture begins to thicken. Fold the yogurt and undrained pineapple into the thickened mixture. Place saucepan in the freezer until the mixture is semifirm. Stir in the raisins and spoon the contents of the saucepan into 6 (4- to 5-ounce) plastic or paper drinking cups. Place in the freezer until mixture is very thick, about 30 minutes. Insert a Popsicle stick in each cup. Freeze until very firm, 3 to 4 hours.

Fruit ices such as sherbets (made with sweetened juice and milk, egg white, or gelatin) and granitas (made with sweetened juice and water alone) need to be beaten during the freezing process. Sherbets have a smoother texture, while granitas are enjoyed for the icy graininess of their texture.

Orange and lemon shells make attractive containers for serving frozen ices. Cut the required number of oranges or lemons in half, using a sawtooth cut to make fluted edges. Squeeze out the juice and scrape out the pulp. Freeze the shells and pack with sherbet or granita just before serving. Garnish each serving with a sprig of mint for a touch of color.

You can create the illusion of a vast repertoire of frozen desserts by merely varying the molded shape or container, by combining two or more in layers, or by switching sauces and toppings.

Orange Strawberry Bombe

Makes 8 servings

 1½ pints vanilla ice cream, softened
  1 cup sliced strawberries
  1 Sunkist orange, peeled, cut in pieces
  2 cups heavy cream
  ¼ cup sugar
  ½ cup finely chopped pecans
    Orange cartwheel slices (optional)
    Strawberries (optional)
    Fresh mint sprigs (optional)

Line a 1½-quart bowl or mold with heavy aluminum foil; smooth as evenly as possible. Line bowl with softened ice cream. Form a smooth shell using a wooden spoon. Freeze until firm. Whirl berries and orange pieces in an electric blender until smooth. Whip cream until soft peaks form; gradually add sugar and continue beating until stiff. Fold fruit and pecans into whipped cream. Spoon fruit mixture into ice cream shell. Cover with foil and freeze at least 4 hours, or overnight. Unmold onto serving platter. Garnish with orange cartwheels, whole or half strawberries, and mint sprigs, if desired.

Honey-of-a-Mousse

Makes 6 to 8 servings

  4 eggs, separated
  ¾ cup honey
  2 teaspoons grated lemon peel
  2 tablespoons lemon juice
  ⅛ teaspoon cream of tartar
 1½ cups heavy cream, whipped
    Whipped cream (optional)
    Grated lemon peel (optional)

You will need: Visions or Corning Ware 1½-quart saucepan; Pyrex 1-quart soufflée dish; 2-quart Culinaria Souffle Dish.

Beat egg yolks lightly in saucepan; stir in honey. Cook over medium heat, stirring often, until slightly thickened. Remove from heat; stir in lemon peel and juice. Cool, then chill; stir until mixture mounds slightly when dropped from a spoon. Meanwhile, beat egg whites with cream of tartar just until soft peaks

Honey-of-a-Mousse. Corning Glass Works

Orange Strawberry Bombe. Courtesy of Sunkist Growers, Inc.

form. Fold whipped cream, then egg whites into yolk mixture until no streaks of white remain. Turn into prepared soufflé dish. Cover; freeze overnight. To serve, gently free mousse from collar; remove collar. Garnish mousse with whipped cream; sprinkle with grated lemon peel. Serve at once.

Good to Know: You may fit a 1-quart Pyrex soufflée dish with a homemade collar. Use a sheet of waxed paper about 32 inches long. Fold in half lengthwise and wrap around the top of dish, leaving an extension of about 2 inches above the rim. Secure with tape.

Apricot Parfait

Makes 8 servings

　1　pound fresh apricots or 10 canned apricots, drained
1½　cups C & H Superfine or Powdered Sugar
　　Juice of 1 lemon
　1　tablespoon brandy
　1　cup heavy cream
　8　Crisp Cookie Cups (recipe follows)
　　Mint sprigs (optional)

Chop or sieve apricots to make 1¾ cups purée. Stir in sugar, lemon juice, and brandy. Whip cream until stiff; fold into purée. Freeze overnight. To serve, spoon parfait into Crisp Cookie Cups and garnish with mint sprigs.

Crisp Cookie Cups

Makes 8 cookie cups

½　cup C & H Granulated Sugar
¼　cup butter, softened
　　Grated rind of 1 lemon
　2　egg whites
⅓　cup all-purpose flour

Preheat oven to 425°F. Grease and flour 2 large cookie sheets. Using a saucer, trace 4 circles about 5½ inches in diameter on each cookie sheet. Lightly grease 8 coffee cups or bowls about 2 inches in diameter. Beat sugar, butter, and lemon rind together until fluffy. Mix in egg whites just until blended. Fold flour into batter. Place 1½ tablespoons batter in center of each circle on cookie sheet. With back of spoon, spread batter in thin even layer over circles. Bake about 5 minutes, or until cookies brown around edges. Wait 1 minute, then remove cookies with a spatula and press into prepared coffee cups. When firm, transfer to rack. If cookies become too stiff to form, return to oven for several seconds. If cookies are not to be served the day they are made, freeze until needed.

Variation

Create "saucers" by doubling the recipe and allowing half the circles to firm on cookie sheet after baking.

Surprise Baked Alaska

Makes 4 servings

　2　egg whites
　　Pinch *each* salt and cream of tartar
½　cup C & H Superfine or Granulated Sugar
　1　cup halved strawberries
　4　individual sponge cake shells
½　to 1 pint hard vanilla ice cream
　4　whole strawberries

Preheat broiler. Beat egg whites with salt and cream of tartar until soft peaks form. Gradually beat in half the sugar, 1 tablespoon at a time, and continue beating until meringue is stiff and glossy. Mix remaining ¼ cup sugar with strawberry halves. Arrange sponge cakes on large wooden board or heatproof serving platter. Working quickly, fill cakes with a spoonful of ice cream, top with sugared berries, then cover completely with meringue, making decorative swirls. Place under broiler 1 to 2 minutes, until lightly browned. Garnish with whole strawberries and serve immediately.

Lemon Parfait

Makes 4 to 6 servings

Serve this dessert in a glass that shows off to advantage its vivid color contrasts.

　1　cup C & H Powdered Sugar
　6　egg yolks
½　cup lemon juice
　2　teaspoons grated lemon rind
　1　cup heavy cream
　　Blueberry Sauce (recipe follows)

Beat sugar and egg yolks together until thick and lemon colored. Beat in lemon juice. Transfer to heavy saucepan or top of double boiler and stir over low heat 2 minutes, or until mixture is thick enough to see bottom of pan between strokes. Remove from heat and beat until cool. Stir in lemon rind. Whip cream until stiff and gently fold into yolk mixture. Cover and freeze at least 4 hours. To serve, spoon into dessert glasses or bowls and top with a spoonful of chilled Blueberry Sauce. Pass remaining sauce in a sauceboat.

Blueberry Sauce

½　cup C & H Granulated Sugar
　1　pint blueberries
　　Juice of 1 lemon
　1　teaspoon cornstarch dissolved in ¼ cup cold water

Place sugar, blueberries, and lemon juice in saucepan and stir over medium heat until sugar dissolves. Add cornstarch and cook until thickened. Cool, then chill.
Note: Try Blueberry Sauce over pancakes or waffles for a special treat.

Coffee Parfait

Makes 4 to 6 servings

½　cup C & H Powdered Sugar
　6　egg yolks
¾　cup strong liquid coffee
　1　cup heavy cream
　　Individual Meringue Shells (see index)
　　Chocolate Sauce (see index)

Beat sugar and egg yolks together until thick and lemon colored. Beat in liquid coffee. Transfer to heavy saucepan or top of double boiler and stir over low heat 2 minutes, or until mixture is thick enough so bottom of pan can be seen between strokes. Remove from heat and beat until cool. Whip cream until stiff and gently fold into coffee mixture. Cover and freeze at least 4 hours. To serve, spoon into Meringue Shells, top with Chocolate Sauce.

Note: Coffee Parfait may also be served in individual dessert glasses, topped with sweetened whipped cream, and sprinkled with freshly ground coffee powder.

Parfaits

A several-layered gooey delight, the parfait is a richly delicious dessert. It always contains ice cream of some sort—those desserts that substitute pudding for ice cream are not the real McCoy—sometimes of several sorts, layered with various sauces and other delights. Gild the dish by topping with whipped cream, a sprinkling of nuts, and, if you must, the ubiquitous maraschino cherry.

Anything goes, but here are some ideas to get you started. Layer so that the sauce or other non-ice cream ingredient comes out on top, and be generous with the sauce:

chocolate ice cream, marshmallow creme
chocolate-almond ice cream, crushed almond macaroons, white créme de cacao
orange ice, chocolate ice cream, green créme de menthe, slivered almonds
coffee ice cream, chocolate sauce, chopped peanuts
vanilla ice cream, crushed fresh papaya
vanilla ice cream, crushed fresh strawberries
strawberry ice cream, raspberry sauce
banana ice cream, pineapple-rum sauce, macadamia nuts
vanilla ice cream, highy spiced applesauce
butter pecan ice cream, caramella liqueur
vanilla ice cream, maple-blend syrup thick with slivered, toasted almonds
vanilla ice cream, pear slices, fudge sauce

Tangerine Sorbet

Makes about 1 quart sorbet

- ½ **cup sugar**
- 1 **envelope unflavored gelatin**
- 3 **cups Florida tangerine juice, divided**
- 1 **teaspoon grated tangerine peel**

In a medium bowl, combine sugar and gelatin. Heat 1 cup tangerine juice to boiling. Add to gelatin and stir until gelatin is completely dissolved. Stir in remaining 2 cups juice and grated peel. Cool. Pour into ice cube trays or a 9-inch square metal pan; cover and freeze. When almost frozen, scrape into a large mixing bowl. Beat until smooth, but still frozen. Return mixture to pan; cover and freeze until almost frozen. Beat again. Spoon into pan, cover, and freeze until firm.

Raspberry Parfait

Makes 4 to 6 servings

- ¾ **cup C & H Granulated Sugar**
- ¼ **cup water**
- 3 **egg whites**
  Pinch *each* **salt and cream of tartar**
- ½ **pint raspberries, puréed and sieved to remove seeds**
- 1 **cup heavy cream**
- 2 **tablespoons kirsch, rum, or Grand Marnier (optional)**
- 1 **additional pint raspberries**
- ¼ **cup C & H Powdered Sugar**
- 2 **additional tablespoons liqueur**

Combine granulated sugar and water in small heavy saucepan. Cook over low heat until sugar dissolves, swirling pan occasionally. Increase heat and cook until sugar syrup reaches 236°F. on candy thermometer (soft ball stage). Meanwhile, beat egg whites with salt and cream of tartar until stiff peaks firm. Gradually beat in sugar syrup and continue beating until mixture is thick and cool. Stir in raspberry purée. Beat cream and kirsch together until softly whipped. Stir about one-quarter of whipped cream into raspberry mixture to aerate, then fold in the rest. Freeze 4 to 6 hours until firm. Marinate additional raspberries with powdered sugar and kirsch. Transfer frozen raspberry parfait to refrigerator 30 minutes before serving. Spoon into goblets, layering with marinated raspberries.

Note: Raspberry parfait can also be frozen in a ring mold and served with marinated raspberries in the center.

Valentine Ice Cream Torte. The Nestlé Company, Inc.

Valentine Ice Cream Torte

Makes 16 servings

1   12-ounce package (2 cups) Nestlé Toll House Semi-Sweet Chocolate Morsels, divided
2   3½-ounce cans (2⅔ cups) flaked coconut, divided
2   cups chopped pecans, divided
½   cup plus 2 tablespoons vegetable shortening, melted, divided
2   quarts strawberry ice cream, softened
1   quart chocolate ice cream, softened

In blender container, process ½ cup Nestlé Toll House Semi-Sweet Chocolate Morsels at high speed about 10 seconds, or until reduced to fine particles. In a small bowl, combine ground chocolate, ¼ cup of the coconut, ¼ cup of the pecans, and 2 tablespoons melted shortening; mix well. Reserve for garnish. Over hot (not boiling) water, combine remaining 1½ cups Nestlé Toll House Semi-Sweet Chocolate Morsels and remaining melted shortening; stir until morsels melt and mixture is smooth. Remove from heat but keep mixture over hot water. Stir in remaining coconut and pecans.

Sprinkle about a third of the melted mixture evenly over bottom of 9x3-inch springform pan; press firmly. Chill in freezer until firm, about 5 minutes. Spread 1 quart strawberry ice cream evenly over chocolate mixture; chill in freezer about 10 minutes. Repeat chocolate-nut layer on top of strawberry ice cream; chill in freezer 5 minutes. Spread 1 quart chocolate ice cream evenly over second chocolate-nut layer. Form third and final chocolate-nut layer over chocolate ice cream. Top with remaining quart of strawberry ice cream. Chill in freezer about 10 minutes.

On top of strawberry layer, place a large heart-shaped cookie cutter (open type, without handle); press in about ¼ cup reserved grated chocolate mixture. Remove cookie cutter. Press remaining mixture around top edge of torte to form a decorative edge. Cover pan with plastic wrap or foil and return to freezer until firm, at least 3 hours.

To serve, dip a knife or metal spatula in hot water, run around edge of pan to loosen ice cream. Remove sides of pan. Let torte stand at room temperature 15 to 20 minutes before cutting.

Note: When warm chocolate mixture is spread between layers, ice cream will melt somewhat and seep through.

Q. *How long should ice cream store well in a home freezer —ice cream from the market, that is? Ours seems to get grainy after as little as a week or ten days.*
A. In a separate freezer, one that maintains a constant temperature of 0°F or lower, you can store ice cream about four weeks.

Back to front: Coffee Parfait (page 112) with Chocolate Sauce; Apricot Parfait in Crisp Cookie Cups (page 112); Rhubarb Mousse (page 108). C&H Sugar Company

Melba Refrigerator Cake

Makes 6 to 8 servings
  1 **package ladyfingers**
  1 **quart peach ice cream, slightly softened**
     Melba Sauce (recipe follows)

You will need: Pyrex 1½-quart round cake dish

Lightly oil cake dish. Pull apart packaged ladyfingers; line bottom and sides of dish with ladyfingers, flat side up. Spoon in ice cream. Freeze until 15 minutes before serving time; mellow in refrigerator 15 minutes. Cut in wedges; spoon warm Melba Sauce over each serving.

Melba Sauce

Makes about 1 ¼ cups
  2 **packages (10 ounces each) quick-thaw frozen raspberries**
  2 **tablespoons cornstarch**
  1 **teaspoon rum (or ½ teaspoon rum extract)**
  1 **teaspoon lemon juice**

You will need: Visions or Corning Ware 1½-quart saucepan

Thaw raspberries according to package directions, draining juice into saucepan. Blend cornstarch into juice. Cook, stirring, over medium heat until thickened. Reduce heat; simmer 5 minutes. Stir in rum and lemon juice. Gently stir in raspberries. Heat just to boiling point, or cool and reheat at serving time. Serve over plain cake or ice cream.

Pineapple Ice Cream Angel Cake

Makes 12 to 14 servings
  1 **10-inch angel food cake (see index)**
  1 **quart vanilla ice cream, slightly softened**
  1 **can (12-ounces) Solo Pineapple Filling**
  1 **cup heavy cream**
  2 **tablespoons sugar**
  1 **teaspoon vanilla extract**

Turn cake upside down and carefully slice 1 inch from bottom of cake. Using a fork, carefully dig out center of cake, leaving a 1-inch wall around outer edge, inner ring, and top of cake. (You can later fill the tube hole with the cake pieces or reserve them for use in another dessert.) Place cake upside down on a serving plate. Blend ice cream and pineapple filling together and spoon into scooped-out portion of cake. Replace bottom of cake. Beat cream until stiff. Beat in sugar and vanilla. Spread quickly over top and sides of cake. Place cake in freezer and freeze about 4 hours, or until very firm. Remove from freezer. Let stand about 10 minutes before serving.

Good Idea: If this cake proves difficult to serve, use a serrated knife, dipping it into hot water after every few slices.

Frozen Lime Pie

Makes one 9-inch pie
  6 **egg yolks**
  1 **cup sugar**
     Grated rind of 2 limes
     Juice of 3 limes
  6 **egg whites**
  2 **cups heavy cream, whipped**
1½ **cups chocolate wafer crumbs**
     Green food coloring

Combine egg yolks, sugar, grated lime rind, and lime juice in top of double boiler; cook over hot water, stirring until slightly thickened; cool. Beat egg whites stiff; fold into cooled lime mixture. Fold whipped cream into mixture. Cover bottom of ungreased pan with half of crumbs. Pour in lime mixture; sprinkle remaining crumbs on top. Cover with Alcoa Wrap; freeze firm. Place in refrigerator 30 minutes before ready to serve.

Frozen Strawberry Pie

Makes 8 servings
     Vanilla wafers
     Walnuts or pecans
  ½ **cup butter or margarine, melted**
  1 **package (10 ounces) frozen sliced strawberries, thawed**
  ½ **cup sugar**
  1 **egg white**
  1 **cup sour cream**

Preheat oven to 350°F. Break a few vanilla wafers into blender. Grate until of desired consistency. Pour crumbs into a measuring cup and continue process until 1½ cups crumbs are made. Blender-chop nuts to make ½ cup finely chopped nuts. Combine crumbs, nuts, and butter and blend thoroughly. Press mixture firmly on bottom and sides of a 10-inch pie plate. Bake 10 minutes; cool. In large bowl of Sunbeam Mixmaster Mixer combine strawberries, sugar, and egg white. Turn to high and beat until soft peaks form, about 10 minutes. Remove and fold in sour cream with a rubber spatula. Spoon into crust and place pie in freezer. When chilled, make swirls on top. Freeze until firm.

Hint

To fully savor desserts frozen for more than 6 hours, always refrigerate about 30 minutes before serving. Not only will texture and flavor be improved, but serving will be easier.

Chocolate Ice Cream Pie

Makes 6 to 8 servings
- ¼ cup C & H Granulated Sugar
- 1½ cups blanched almonds, toasted and ground
- ⅓ cup butter
- 1 ounce semisweet chocolate
- 1 quart chocolate ice cream, slightly softened
  Creamy Chocolate Sauce (recipe follows)
  Sweetened heavy cream (optional)
- ½ cup sliced almonds, toasted

Combine sugar and ground almonds in bowl. Melt butter and chocolate together and stir into nut mixture. Pat mixture into lightly greased 9-inch pie pan. Chill 1 hour or until set. Spread chocolate ice cream in crust. Freeze until serving time. Top with Creamy Chocolate Sauce, sweetened whipped cream, and sliced almonds.

Creamy Chocolate Sauce

- ⅓ cup C & H Powdered Sugar
- 2 ounces semisweet chocolate
- ⅓ cup whipping cream
- 1 tablespoon rum

Combine sugar, chocolate, cream, and rum in top of double boiler. Heat, stirring occasionally, until smooth. Serve warm.

Blueberry Syrup

Makes about 2 cups
- 1 can (1 pound) blueberries with syrup
- ½ cup light corn syrup
- ⅛ teaspoon salt

Put all ingredients into blender container in order listed. Cover; blend at high speed until smooth. Pour into saucepan. Bring to a boil. Cook over moderate heat, stirring constantly, for 5 minutes. Use warm or chilled.

Butterscotch Sauce

Makes about 1 cup
- ½ cup evaporated milk
- ¾ cup firmly packed brown sugar
- ¼ cup sugar
- 1 tablespoon light corn syrup
- 1 teaspoon vanilla extract
- ¼ teaspoon rum extract

Put all ingredients into blender container in order listed. Cover; blend at high speed until smooth.

Pineapple Sauce

Makes 1 cup
- 1 can (8 ounces) sweetened crushed pineapple
- 1 tablespoon cornstarch
- 2 tablespoons lemon or lime juice

Drain pineapple and reserve syrup. Add syrup gradually to cornstarch in heavy saucepan, making a smooth mixture. Cook, stirring constantly, until thickened and clear. Remove from heat. Add pineapple. Add lemon or lime juice. Cool.

Chocolate Skillet Sauce

Makes 1¼ cups
- ¼ cup butter
- 1 cup coarsely chopped nuts
- 1 6-ounce package (1 cup) Nestlé Toll House Semi-Sweet Chocolate Morsels

Melt butter in a large skillet.★ Add nuts and cook until browned, stirring constantly to prevent scorching. Remove from heat. Add Nestlé Toll House Semi-Sweet Chocolate Morsels and stir until morsels melt and mixture is blended. Serve warm over ice cream.

★This recipe may be made in an electric skillet set at 350°F.

Super Sundaes

ice cream:	topping:	add if you like:
chocolate	marshmallow cream	sprinkle of instant coffee powder
lemon	boysenberry syrup	fresh berries
coffee	chocolate fudge	chopped almonds
vanilla	crushed pineapple	melon balls
vanilla	raspberry syrup	fresh peach slices
butter pecan	butterscotch syrup	broken pretzel sticks
strawberry	almost-melted vanilla ice cream	sliced fresh strawberries
chocolate	whipped cream	crushed peppermint candy
vanilla	maple syrup	chopped walnuts
butterscotch	shaved semisweet chocolate	chopped peanuts
vanilla	applesauce	sprinkle of cinnamon
peach	raspberry syrup	crushed vanilla wafers
mint	orange liqueur	mint leaves
toffee	caramel liqueur	shaved chocolate

An Assortment of Unusual Desserts

When something special is called for, surprise your guests and yourself—try a pizza, waffles or doughnuts, dumplings or cream puffs for a sweet change.

Dessert Fruit Pizza

Makes 12 to 16 servings

- 1 **package (6½ ounces) Martha White Pizza Crust Mix**
- 2 **tablespoons sugar**
- 1 **package (8 ounces) cream cheese, at room temperature**
- 1 **can (29 ounces) sliced peaches, drained; reserve syrup**
- 1 **can (4 ounces) sliced pineapple, drained; reserve syrup**
- 1 **firm banana, peeled and cut into ¼-inch thick slices**
- 12 **hulled strawberries, cut in half**
- ½ **cup seedless green grapes**
- 1 **jar (10 ounces) apple jelly**

Preheat oven to 425°F. Lightly grease 12-inch pizza pan; set aside. Prepare pizza dough according to package directions, adding sugar along with ½ cup water called for on package. Roll out dough on lightly floured board or pastry cloth into 12-inch circle. Place on prepared pan. Bake 15 to 20 minutes, or until golden brown. Cool in pan on wire rack. Combine cream cheese and 2 tablespoons peach syrup in mixing bowl; beat with electric mixer until smooth. Spread evenly over crust. Combine pineapple syrup and remaining peach syrup in bowl. Add bananas; set aside.

Cut pineapple slices in half; set aside. Arrange strawberries in circle in center of crust. Arrange ring of grapes around strawberries. Drain bananas. Arrange pineapple, banana, and peach slices in rows to outside edge. Finish with strawberries and grapes. Melt jelly in small saucepan over low heat, stirring frequently, until smooth. Remove from heat; let stand until slightly thickened. Spoon evenly over fruit; use pastry brush to spread glaze evenly. Refrigerate until serving time. Cut into wedges or squares.

Dessert Fruit Pizza. Martha White Foods

Golden Clouds

Makes 6 servings, 3 clouds per serving

- 12 **egg yolks**
- 1 **egg white**
- 2 **cups sugar**
- 1 **teaspoon vanilla extract**

Preheat oven to 325°F. With Mixmaster Mixer set at medium-high, beat egg yolks and egg white together until thick and lemon colored, about 20 minutes. Lightly butter small custard cups. Pour 2 tablespoons of egg mixture into each custard cup. Set cups in a pan of hot water. Bake 30 minutes. While Clouds are baking, combine sugar and 3½ cups water in a saucepan. Bring to a boil and simmer 5 minutes. Add vanilla; remove from heat. When Clouds are baked, drop each into this warm syrup and turn to coat; place on a shallow dish and chill. Chill remaining syrup. Serve Clouds with a little syrup over each serving.

Chocolate Eclairs

Makes 14 eclairs

- 1 **recipe Cream Puffs (see index)**
  French Custard (see index)
  Chocolate Glaze (see index)

Preheat oven to 375°F. Grease 2 baking sheets; set aside. Prepare Cream Puff dough. Press dough through pastry bag with no tip, or use spoon to shape 4x1-inch logs on prepared baking sheets. Bake 30 to 35 minutes, or until golden brown and eclairs sound hollow when lightly tapped with fingertips. Immediately pierce each with tip of fork to allow steam to escape. Return to oven 5 to 7 minutes to dry out. Transfer to wire racks to cool completely. Slice off tops. Fill with French Custard. Replace tops. Place eclairs on wire rack. Pour warm Chocolate Glaze over tops.

Cream Puffs

Makes 10 regular-size puffs

    1 cup water
    ½ cup butter or margarine
    1 cup sifted Martha White Self-Rising Flour
    4 eggs, at room temperature
       French Custard (recipe follows)

Grease large baking sheet, set aside. Combine water and butter in saucepan; bring to a full boil over moderate heat. Reduce heat to low. While stirring vigorously, add flour all at once. Stir constantly over low heat until mixture pulls away from pan and forms a ball. Remove from heat. Add eggs, 1 at a time, beating well after each addition. (Electric mixer can be used.) Beat until shiny and smooth. Preheat oven to 375°F.

For miniature cream puffs, drop batter by teaspoonfuls, 2 inches apart, onto prepared baking sheet. For regular cream puffs, drop batter by tablespoonfuls, 3 inches apart, onto prepared baking sheet. Bake miniature puffs 25 to 30 minutes, regular puffs 35 to 40 minutes, or until golden brown and puffs sound hollow when lightly tapped with fingertips. Remove from oven. Immediately pierce each with tip of knife to allow steam to escape. Return to oven 5 to 7 minutes to dry out. Transfer to wire rack to cool completely. Slice off tops. Fill with French Custard or desired filling. Replace tops.

French Custard

    ⅓ cup sugar
    1 tablespoon Martha White All-Purpose Flour
    1 tablespoon cornstarch
    ¼ teaspoon salt
    1½ cups milk
    1 egg yolk, lightly beaten
    1 teaspoon vanilla extract
    ½ cup heavy cream, whipped

Combine sugar, flour, cornstarch, and salt in saucepan. Gradually stir in milk. Bring to a boil over moderate heat, stirring until thick. Reduce heat to low. Cook, stirring constantly, 2 to 3 minutes. Stir small amount of custard into egg yolk. Return all to saucepan. Cool and stir until custard just comes to a boil. Remove from heat. Stir in vanilla; let stand until cool. Beat with electric mixer until smooth. Fold in whipped cream until well blended.

Profiteroles

These are simply tiny cream puffs. Drop cream puff dough by rounded teaspoonfuls onto foil-covered cookie sheet and bake at 400°F. about 30 minutes. Fill with ice cream or custard filling. These tiny puffs look dainty and delicious served 3 or more on a pretty dessert plate with a sauce poured over. The above recipe makes about 40 tiny puffs.

Paris Brest

Place foil on a cookie sheet and mark an 8-inch circle on it. With a pastry bag or spoon form dough into a wreath, making it about 1½ inches wide and as high as possible. Sprinkle top with slivered blanched almonds, pressing them in. Bake at 400°F. 15 minutes, reduce heat to 350°F., and continue baking about 40 minutes longer. Cool on cake rack. Split the ring and fill with whipped cream or custard filling; garnish with whipped cream, grated chocolate, and toasted slivered almonds. To serve, cut in slices.

Cream puffs are a most versatile and delightful dessert. They may be made large or small; the dough may be shaped into eclairs and other forms, and they all may be filled in a variety of ways. Excellent cream puff mixes are available in markets, but making the dough from scratch is easy and fun. Baked cream puffs freeze beautifully and may be kept for 6 to 8 weeks.

Freezing Cream Puffs: Cream puffs, particularly the little ones, are a wonderful dessert to have on hand in the freezer. Split them, fill with ice cream, and put them in the freezer until firm. Arrange on foil-covered cardboard, completely wrap in foil, label, and return to the freezer. Large cream puffs and eclairs may be handled in the same way. Ice cream is the best filling if you wish the dessert ready. Serve the frozen puffs with a hot chocolate or other hot sauce. The puffs without filling may be frozen in the same way. To serve, place them in a 325°F. oven 10 minutes to regain crispness, then fill. The large Paris Brest may be frozen if an ice cream filling is used. Garnish it with whipped cream and almonds.

Strawberry Cream Puffs

Makes 12 to 16 large cream puffs

    1 can (6 ounces) Continental Strawberry Glaze
    ¾ pint fresh strawberries sliced
    1 package (8½ ounces) cream puff mix
    1 quart vanilla ice cream
       Whipped Cream (optional)
       Maraschino cherries (optional)

Mix strawberry glaze and sliced strawberries together. Chill. Prepare cream puff mix according to package directions for large cream puffs. Cool. Cut tops from puffs. Fill with ice cream. Top with chilled glazed strawberries. Garnish, if desired with whipped cream and maraschino cherry before serving.

Strawberry-Kiwi Trifle

Makes 8 servings
- **2 pints strawberries, hulled, halved, or sliced (about 4 cups)**
- **6 large kiwis, peeled and sliced (about 2 cups)**
- **2 tablespoons Karo Light Corn Syrup**
- **2 tablespoons orange-flavored liqueur**
- **1 8-inch Sponge Cake layer (recipe follows)**
- **1 recipe Custard (recipe follows)**
- **1 cup heavy cream, whipped**

In large bowl, toss together strawberries and kiwis. In small bowl, stir together corn syrup and liqueur. Split cake layer in half. Brush each half with corn syrup mixture. Place one-half cake layer crust side down in deep serving bowl. Arrange half of the fruit mixture (about 3 cups) on cake layer. Top with ½ cup of the Custard. Cover with the remaining half of cake layer. Arrange remaining fruit on cake. Top with remaining Custard. Cover; refrigerate at least 3 hours. Just before serving, garnish with whipped cream. If desired, garnish with additional fruit.
Note: Six cups assorted sliced fresh fruit may be substituted for the strawberries and kiwis.

Sponge Cake

Makes one 8-inch layer
- **2 eggs**
- **⅓ cup sugar**
- **¼ teaspoon salt**
- **⅓ cup all-purpose flour**
- **¼ cup Argo or Kingsford's Corn Starch**

Grease an 8-inch round cake pan. In small bowl, with mixer at high speed, beat eggs until foamy. Gradually add sugar and salt, beating until mixture is double in volume and mounds slightly when dropped from spoon. Sift flour and ¼ cup cornstarch over egg mixture. Fold in until batter is formed. Pour into prepared pan. Bake in 350°F. oven 25 minutes, or until cake springs back when lightly touched. Cool 5 minutes in pan. Remove and cool completely on rack.

Custard

Makes about 2½ cups custard
- **½ cup sugar**
- **2 tablespoons Argo or Kingsford's Corn Starch**
- **2 cups milk**
- **2 egg yolks, lightly beaten**
- **1½ teaspoons vanilla extract**

In 2-quart saucepan, stir together sugar and cornstarch. Gradually stir in milk until smooth. Stir in egg yolks. Stirring constantly, bring to boil over medium-low heat and boil 1 minute. Remove from heat. Stir in vanilla. Turn into bowl; cover surface with waxed paper or plastic wrap. Refrigerate 1 hour, or until cool.

Forgotten Torte

Makes 8 to 10 servings
- **6 egg whites, room temperature**
- **¼ teaspoon salt**
- **½ teaspoon cream of tartar**
- **1½ cups C & H Superfine or Granulated Sugar**
- **1 teaspoon vanilla extract**
- **½ cup heavy cream, whipped with 1 tablespoon C & H Powdered Sugar**
- **Berries, pineapple, or other fruit**

Preheat oven to 450°F. Grease bottom of 10-inch tube pan. Beat egg whites with salt and cream of tartar until soft peaks form. Beat in sugar, 1 tablespoon at a time, until stiff, glossy peaks form. Beat in vanilla. Spread evenly in pan. Put in oven and turn off heat immediately. "Forget" torte several hours, until oven is completely cold, or overnight. Loosen edges and turn out onto serving plate. Chill. Meringue will keep at least 1 week in airtight container. No more than 6 hours before serving, frost with whipped cream. Chill. Before serving, decorate with fruit.

Lazy Day English Trifle

Makes 6 servings
- **1 package (3¾ ounces) vanilla pudding and pie filling mix**
- **6 thick slices pound cake (about ½ pound)**
- **1 cup sweet sherry**
- **1 can (12 ounces) Solo Raspberry Filling**
- **½ cup heavy cream**

Prepare pudding and pie filling mix according to package directions. Cover and cool. Cut pound cake slices into thick fingers. Place half the fingers in bottom of a glass serving dish. Carefully spoon half the sherry over the fingers. Let stand until sherry is absorbed. Spread half the raspberry filling over the fingers. Pour custard over top of filling. Dip remaining fingers of pound cake in remaining sherry and place on top of custard. Spread top of custard with remaining raspberry filling. Refrigerate until thoroughly chilled. Whip cream until stiff and spread on top of trifle. Refrigerate 30 minutes before serving.

Lazy Day English Trifle (page 121). Solo Food Products

Apple Crêpe Cake

Makes 8 servings

- ½ **cup butter or margarine**
- 8 **large apples, peeled and sliced**
- 1 **cup firmly packed C & H Golden Brown Sugar**
- ½ **teaspoon ground cinnamon**
- ¼ **teaspoon ground nutmeg**
     Juice of 1 lemon
- 16 **8-inch crêpes (recipe follows)**
- 1 **cup sliced almonds, toasted**
     Hot Caramel Sauce (see index)

Melt butter in large, heavy skillet. Add apples and toss carefully to coat with butter. Add sugar and sauté apples until just tender, keeping their shape as much as possible. Add cinnamon, nutmeg, and lemon juice. Pour off any excess liquid. Reserve about 8 good slices for garnish.

On a heatproof serving platter, place a single crêpe, brown side up. Spread about 2 tablespoons of apple mixture over crêpe. Sprinkle a few almonds over apples. Repeat until all crêpes are used. Top with the reserved apple slices, making a pin wheel on top of the last crêpe. Cover with aluminum foil and heat in a low oven (225°F. to 250°F.) until warm. Serve with Hot Caramel Sauce.

Note: To make larger crêpes needed for this cake, use an 8-inch skillet.

Crêpes

Makes about 1½ dozen

- 2 **tablespoons C & H Granulated Sugar**
- ½ **cup all-purpose flour**
     Pinch of salt
- 1 **cup milk**
- 4 **eggs**
- 5 **tablespoons butter or margarine, melted**

Combine sugar, flour, and salt in bowl. Mix milk and eggs and gradually beat into sugar mixture, mixing until smooth. Chill at least 1 hour. Stir in 3 tablespoons of the butter. Heat heavy 6½-inch skillet or crêpe pan. Brush with melted butter. Heat over medium-high heat until almost smoking. Remove pan from heat, ladle about 3 tablespoons batter into one corner of pan, then tilt pan in all directions until bottom is covered with a thin layer. Pour out any excess. Cook until bottom is lightly browned. Flip crêpe over and cook for about 1 minute until brown. Slide crêpe out onto plate. Repeat with remaining batter.

Q. *Why does chocolate turn a nasty gray when stored over a long period—or even, sometimes, a short period? Can it still be used?*

A. That's the fat content (cocoa butter) rising to the surface, which it does when the chocolate is stored in too warm a place, or in summer when every place is warm. The flavor will not be affected unless the chocolate is old as well as having "bloom."

Crêpes, rolled with fresh fruit, Hot Caramel Sauce (page 125); Apple Crêpe Cake. C&H Sugar Company

Butterscotch-Nut Crêpes

Makes 8 filled crêpes

- 1¼ **cups milk**
- 1 **cup buttermilk pancake mix**
- 1 **egg**
- 1 **tablespoon vegetable oil**
- 2 **tablespoons butter, melted**
  Butterscotch-Nut Filling (recipe follows)
  Whipped cream

In a small bowl, combine milk, pancake mix, egg, and oil; heat until mixture is smooth. Heat an 8-inch crêpe pan or skillet; brush with butter. For each crêpe, pour about 3 tablespoons batter into pan; turn and tip pan immediately to coat bottom. Cook 10 to 15 seconds until lightly browned and set on top; turn and cook other side. Remove crêpe to a heated platter. Repeat with remaining batter. Spread 1 rounded tablespoonful Butterscotch-Nut Filling over each crêpe. Fold into triangles or roll up jelly roll fashion; place on a serving platter. Spoon remaining filling over crêpes and serve with whipped cream.

Butterscotch-Nut Filling

- 1 **6-ounce package (1 cup) Nestlé Butterscotch Flavored Morsels**
- 2 **tablespoons corn syrup**
- 2 **tablespoons butter**
- 2 **teaspoons water**
- 1¼ **teaspoons grated orange rind**
- ¼ **teaspoon salt**
- 1 **cup finely ground nuts**

Over hot (not boiling) water, combine Nestlé Butterscotch Flavored Morsels, corn syrup, butter, water, orange rind, and salt; stir until morsels melt and mixture is smooth.

Lemon Crêpes with Blueberry Sauce

Makes 6 servings

- 12 **6-inch prepared dessert Crêpes (see index)**
- 1 **package (8 ounces) cream cheese, softened**
- 1 **can (14 ounces) Eagle® Brand Sweetened Condensed Milk (not evaporated milk)**
- ⅓ **cup lemon juice**
- 1 **teaspoon vanilla extract**
- 2 **teaspoons grated lemon rind, divided**
- ½ **cup sugar**
- 1½ **tablespoons cornstarch**
- ½ **teaspoon ground nutmeg**
- ⅓ **cup hot water**
- 2 **cups fresh or dry-pack frozen blueberries, thawed, rinsed, and drained**
- 2 **tablespoons brandy or water**

In large mixer bowl, beat cheese until fluffy; beat in Eagle Brand Sweetened Condensed Milk until smooth. · Stir in lemon juice, vanilla, and 1 teaspoon lemon rind. Cover and chill at least 3 hours. Meanwhile, in small saucepan, combine sugar, cornstarch, remaining lemon rind, and nutmeg; gradually stir in water. Over low heat, cook, stirring constantly, until mixture thickens and comes to a boil. Stir in blueberries; cook and stir until mixture returns to a boil. Simmer 5 minutes. Stir in brandy. Fill crêpes with equal portions of cheese mixture; roll up. Serve with warm or chilled blueberry sauce. Refrigerate leftovers.

> Crêpes may be stored frozen up to 6 months. To freeze, place double layer of wax or plastic wrap between each cold crêpe. Place in plastic bag and seal.

Marmalade Dessert Omelets

Makes 8 servings

- 4 **eggs, separated**
- 3 **tablespoons sour cream**
- ½ **teaspoon salt**
- ¼ **cup all-purpose flour**
- 2 **teaspoons sugar**
- 4 **tablespoons butter or margarine**
  Orange or lime marmalade, heated

Place egg whites in large Mixmaster Mixer bowl, yolks in small bowl. With Mixmaster Mixer at highest speed, beat whites until stiff but not dry. Reserve. With dial set at medium, beat egg yolks until well blended. Beat in sour cream. Mix salt, flour, and sugar. Blend into yolk-cream mixture with dial set at lowest. Fold in stiffly beaten whites. At table: Melt butter in Multi-Cooker Frypan set at 340°F. Cook spoonfuls of egg mixture like pancakes, making thin individual omelets. Have heated marmalade ready in nearby warmer. Place omelets on serving plate, spoon marmalade over.

Cherry Waffle Sundaes

Makes 8 servings

- 1 **can (1 pound) pitted dark sweet cherries**
- 1 **can (1 pound) light sweet cherries**
- 1 **cup sugar**
- 2 **tablespoons grated orange rind**
  Few drops red food coloring
- 3 **tablespoons cornstarch**
- ¼ **cup cherry liqueur**
- 8 **Waffles (recipe follows)**
  Vanilla ice cream

Drain cherries, reserving syrup. Pit cherries, if necessary. Place cherry syrup, sugar, orange rind, and coloring in Sunbeam Multi-Cooker Frypan. Combine cornstarch with a little water and stir into remaining syrup in Frypan. Turn dial to 300°F. and bring to a boil, stirring until mixture is thick and clear. Add cherries and heat thoroughly. Lower heat to Simmer and stir in cherry liqueur. Make waffles in waffle baker. Spoon ice cream on top of Waffles and cover with hot cherry sauce.

Waffles

Makes 16 servings
    3   cups sifted all-purpose flour
    5   teaspoons baking powder
    1   teaspoon salt
    2   tablespoons sugar
    4   large eggs
  2¼   cups milk
  1½   teaspoons vanilla extract, if desired
    ⅔   cup butter or margarine, melted, cooled

Sift together in large bowl of Mixmaster Mixer flour, baking powder, salt, and sugar. Put eggs into small Mixmaster Mixer bowl and beat at highest speed 1 minute. Add milk and vanilla to beaten eggs, then add mixture to dry ingredients. Beat at medium-low about 1½ minutes until blended. Add butter; beat at low only until blended. Use measuring pitcher for easy pouring, or pour from 8-ounce measuring cup. Bake on preheated waffle bake at medium.

Blueberry Waffles

Sprinkle drained fresh or frozen blueberries over unbaked batter in waffle baker. Bake as directed.

Caramel Nut Waffles

Makes 6 waffles

Waffles served with a sauce that would be equally good on pancakes, French toast, or ice cream.
    3   tablespoons C & H Brown Sugar
    2   cups all-purpose flour
    1   tablespoon baking powder
    3   eggs, separated
  1½   cups milk
    ⅓   cup butter or margarine, melted, cooled
    ¾   cup coarsely chopped pecans
    ½   teaspoon salt
    ⅛   teaspoon cream of tartar
         Hot Caramel Sauce (recipe follows)

Preheat waffle iron. Combine sugar, flour, and baking powder in bowl. Mix egg yolks, milk, and butter. Stir into dry ingredients, mixing just until moistened. Stir in pecans. Beat egg whites with salt and cream of tartar until stiff, then fold into flour mixture. Bake in waffle iron following manufacturer's instructions. Serve with Hot Caramel Sauce.

Hot Caramel Sauce

Makes about 2 cups
  1¼   cups C & H Granulated Sugar
    ½   cup water
    1   cup heavy cream, heated
    ½   teaspoon vanilla extract

Combine sugar and water in heavy skillet and cook, stirring occasionally, over low heat until sugar melts. Raise heat and cook until sugar caramelizes and turns a deep mahogany brown. Stand back (in case mixture splatters) and slowly pour in cream. Stir over low heat until smooth, then mix in vanilla. Keep warm in double boiler.

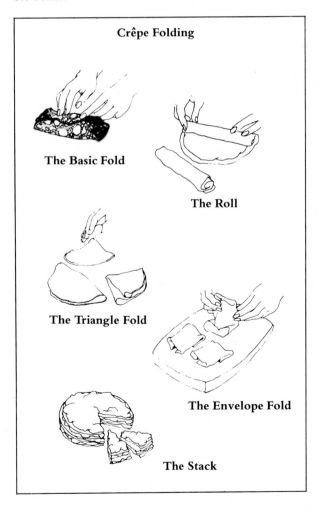

Crêpe Folding

The Basic Fold

The Roll

The Triangle Fold

The Envelope Fold

The Stack

Chocolate Floating Islands

Makes five ½-cup servings

- ½ cup sugar
- 3 tablespoons cornstarch
- ½ teaspoon salt
- 2 cups milk
- 1 egg
- 1 egg, separated
- 1 6-ounce package (1 cup) Nestlé Toll House Semi-Sweet Chocolate Morsels
- 1 teaspoon vanilla extract
- 2 tablespoons sugar

In a small saucepan, combine ½ cup sugar, cornstarch, and salt; stir to blend. Gradually add milk, stirring constantly, until smooth. Cook over high heat, stirring constantly, until mixture thickens (about 3 to 5 minutes). In a small bowl, beat whole egg and egg yolk lightly. Stir in some of the hot milk mixture; mix well, then quickly transfer to remaining hot milk mixture. Remove from heat. Add Nestlé Toll House Semi-Sweet Chocolate Morsels and vanilla; stir until melted and smooth. Cool at room temperature about 5 minutes, then spoon into dessert dishes. Chill in refrigerator at least 1½ hours, or until ready to serve.

In a small bowl, beat egg white until soft peaks form. Gradually add 2 tablespoons sugar and beat until stiff but not dry. In a shallow pan, bring water (¼-inch deep) to a simmer. Drop meringue by heaping tablespoonfuls into simmering water. Simmer uncovered over medium heat about 5 minutes. Lift meringues from water with a slotted spoon; drain on paper towels. Place on top of chilled chocolate custard.

Baklava

Makes 16 to 20 servings

- ½ pound filo dough
- 1 can (12½ ounces) Solo Nut Filling
- ½ cup finely chopped walnuts
- ½ teaspoon ground cinnamon
- ¼ teaspoon ground nutmeg
- ½ cup butter, clarified★
- ¼ cup margarine, clarified★
- 1 cup sugar
- 1 cup water
- 3 slices lemon
- 3 tablespoons honey

Be sure filo dough has defrosted well in advance of using. (Let frozen or chilled dough stand at room temperature about 15 minutes.) Preheat oven to 350°F. Combine nut filling, walnuts, cinnamon, and nutmeg. Set aside. Brush the bottom of an 8-inch square baking dish with part of the clarified butter and margarine. Cut filo dough into 8-inch square sections. Brush dough with butter-margarine mixture. Layer one-third of the dough in bottom of pan. Top with one-half of the nut mixture. Cover with another third of the dough. Top with remaining nut mixture. Arrange remaining buttered layers of filo dough over top of nut filling. Using a sharp knife, cut, almost all the way through, into diamond shapes. Pour remaining butter-margarine mixture over top. Bake 1 hour. About 10 minutes before baklava is baked, combine sugar, 1 cup water, and lemon slices in a small saucepan. Bring to a boil and simmer about 5 minutes. Remove from heat, remove lemon slices, and stir in honey. Remove baklava from oven to pour hot honey syrup over top. Let stand at room temperature at least 2 hours—preferably more—before serving.

Note: Filo dough, which is extremely thin and used in the baking of Greek delicacies, can be purchased in any gourmet shop or Near Eastern food store.

★To clarify butter and margarine, combine them in a small saucepan. Melt over low heat. Using a teaspoon, skim the bubbles from the top of the mixture and discard. Carefully pour the melted butter into a small bowl, leaving the white sediment on the bottom of the pan. Discard sediment, using just the clear butter mixure in the bowl. Use a pastry brush to brush the butter mixture on the filo dough.

Floating Islands with Orange Gelatin

Makes 6 servings

- 2 envelopes unflavored gelatin
- 3½ cups fresh orange juice, divided
- ¾ teaspoons grated orange rind
- 5 packets (1¼ teaspoons) Sweet 'N Low Granulated Sugar Substitute, divided
- 6 large egg whites
- 2 tablespoons sugar
- ½ teaspoon vanilla extract
- 2 oranges, sectioned
- 6 strawberries, fanned

In saucepan, sprinkle gelatin over 1 cup orange juice; set aside 5 minutes. Heat to dissolve gelatin. Add remaining orange juice, rind, and 3 packets Sweet 'N Low. Pour into 8-inch square pan; chill until set. Cut into 1-inch cubes.

Preheat broiler. Beat egg whites until stiff, gradually adding 2 packets Sweet 'N Low, sugar, and vanilla. Drop 18 spoonfuls onto ungreased baking sheets. Place 4 inches beneath broiler 1 to 2 minutes, or until lightly browned.

On 6 chilled dessert plates, arrange gelatin cubes; top with 3 meringues each and garnish with orange segments and fanned strawberries.

Index